.

THE RNAS

AND THE BIRTH OF
THE AIRCRAFT CARRIER
1914-1918

THE RNAS

AND THE BIRTH OF
THE AIRCRAFT CARRIER
1914-1918

IAN M. BURNS

FONTHILL

Fonthill Media Language Policy

Fonthill Media publishes in the international English language market. One language edition is published worldwide. As there are minor differences in spelling and presentation, especially with regard to American English and British English, a policy is necessary to define which form of English to use. The Fonthill Policy is to use the form of English native to the author. Ian M. Burns was born and educated in England and now lives at Toronto, Canada, therefore Canadian English has been adopted in this publication.

Fonthill Media Limited
Fonthill Media LLC
www.fonthillmedia.com
office@fonthillmedia.com

First published in the United Kingdom
and the United States of America 2014

British Library Cataloguing in Publication Data:
A catalogue record for this book is available from the British Library

Copyright © Ian M. Burns 2014

ISBN 978-1-78155-365-7

Typeset in 10pt on 13pt Sabon
Printed and bound by CPI Group (UK) Ltd, Croydon, CR0 4YY

Contents

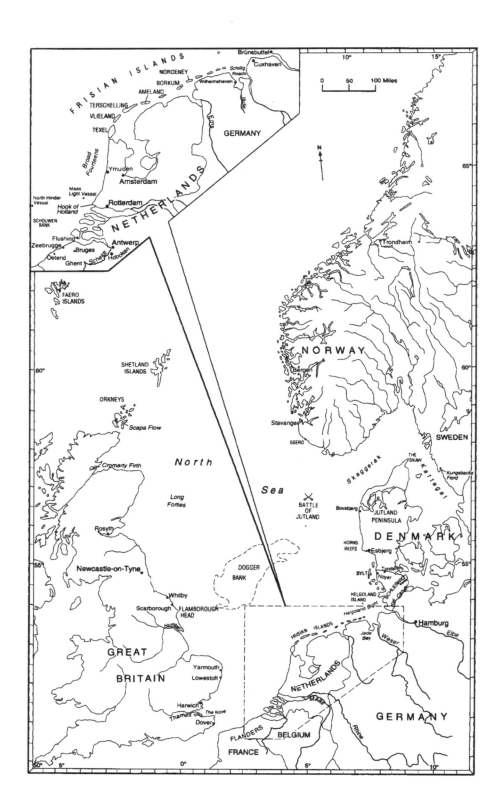

Introduction

For a number of years I have been researching and writing about Royal Naval Air Service operations in the Eastern Mediterranean. I was always scanning new book lists hoping 'someone' would write about the Royal Naval Air Service (RNAS) in Home Waters. Well, this is that book.

Parts of this story have been told and retold in various publications over the years. However, this book attempts to gather the whole together into a coherent story—a story of slow but steady progress toward a distant but definable goal—the aircraft carrier.

This is not the story of the British aircraft carrier, this has been told elsewhere. This is the story of how the flights and fights of a small group of men were affected by the evolution of the first aircraft carriers. I have referred wherever possible to the original memorandum, minutes, operation plans, log books and flight reports. Personal memoirs have been used where they are appropriate, but memory is a fickle friend and all too often we confuse events and telescope or stretch time. Personal diaries, letters and records also have their problems, as the writers were rarely in full possession of all the facts, and they can often be frustratingly incomplete. Therefore, the selected extracts are either anecdotal or can be confirmed from the official records.

Over four years of war the RNAS went from clumsy, underpowered floatplanes to naval versions of landplanes serving over the front lines. The first practical torpedo bomber was entering service and a new generation of reconnaissance and fighting machines were in development. The aircraft-carrying ships had developed from basic conversions of cross-channel steamers, carrying just two or three floatplanes, to the world's first aircraft carrier, whose hangar could shelter over twenty aeroplanes. Aircraft were at sea aboard cruisers and battleships, and two more aircraft carriers were under construction.

No account is given of the anti-submarine war fought by the airships and land based aeroplanes and seaplanes. Not because it was unimportant—it was just as vital in the First World War as it would be a generation later—but because it had little role in the development of ship-borne naval aviation.

All opinions expressed are mine. But I would be remiss in not mentioning and thanking the people and organisations who have assisted me.

My thanks to Kai Jach (www.seekrieg14-18.de) whose encyclopedic knowledge of German naval aviation in the First World War has made this book much less one-sided.

William Casey maintains and updates a web site (www.tondernraid.com) dedicated to his great-uncle Lieutenant Walter Albert Yeulett, DFC; my thanks also for his generous assistance with all aspects of the Tondern Raid and photographs from Toby Yeulett's album.

Chas Mott and Stuart Attrill have provided biographical details of Charlie Attrill, and photographs from his albums.

Adrian Vicary has, for many years, been most generous with images from the Maritime Photo Library collection. Special thanks also to the Orkney Library and Archives and to the Dock Museum, Barrow-in-Furness, for permission to reproduce images from their collections. I have collected images for many years, including from the collections of Chas Schaedel, John Dixon, Stuart Leslie, Eric Harlin, and Cross and Cockade International. I have endeavoured to determine the copyright of the images used, but so many identical copies of wartime photographs found their way into personal albums, or have been copied by collectors, including myself, that this can be a Sisyphean task. Consequently, many photographs are credited to the Author Collection. If I have incorrectly credited any photographs, I offer my sincere apologies.

1

To Ascend From a Floating Base
The Birth of British Naval Aviation

In the spring of 1806 the frigate *Pallas* (32, Captain Thomas Cochrane) was cruising off the Île d'Oléron which protected the approaches to the French naval base of Rochefort. There was a brisk onshore breeze and *Pallas* came closer inshore than was usual. From her deck rose a strange thing, a child's toy, a kite. The breeze carried the kite closer still to the coast. Then a slow match burnt through a string to release sheets of paper to be borne on the wind over and on to the land.

In his biography Cochrane suggests that this procedure was followed on more than one occasion. The papers were propaganda proclamations sent on board by the Admiralty with instructions to distribute them to the French people. Quite how this was to be done was left to the intellect and intelligence of the captain in command. Normally, the papers would be left with the crews of local fishing boats to be taken ashore. The probably illiterate fishermen would certainly have found other uses for the paper. Cochrane, however, was an inventive captain. The previous year he had attempted to use a large kite, assembled from spare spars and sail canvas, to increase the speed of *Pallas* whilst making a transatlantic passage. He devised a smaller kite to carry the leaflets inland.

Cochrane's kites are the first recorded use of a flying device by the Royal Navy. They were not, however, the first time such devices had been discussed in the Royal Navy. Three years previously Rear Admiral Sir Charles Henry Knowles proposed the shipboard use of a spherical balloon. He suggested that the balloon could carry an observer aloft to spy out the harbour of Brest and observe any preparations for the invasion of Britain. Like many ideas before their time his paper was filed and forgotten. Although over the next century the balloon and man-carrying kites would find limited uses at sea, to truly grow and develop naval aviation would have to await the invention of the heavier-than-air flying machine.

There is no reasonable doubt that the Wright brothers made the first manned, heavier-than-air flights on 17 December 1903. They returned to their home in Dayton, Ohio, and patented their method of flight control, fiercely defending it for many years. When they appeared in Europe in 1908 with the Wright Model 'A', it was immediately evident that they had mastered manned flight. Their visit was a catalyst for rapid design and performance-improvements in Europe, which came to terms with the brothers regarding their patent. Back in the USA, the patent tended to stifle innovation. So that when the aeroplane first went to sea, it was little more advanced from the designs of 1903.

Glenn H. Curtiss, attempting to work around or ignore the Wrights' patent, had developed a serviceable pusher biplane. Together with Eugene Ely, a civilian demonstration pilot, Curtiss took the US Navy into the air age. On 14 November 1910 Ely flew one of Curtiss' machines, the *Albany Flyer*, off a sloping ramp built over the bows of USS *Birmingham* moored in Hampton Roads, Virginia. Just over two months later, 18 January 1911 in San Francisco Bay, Ely landed back onboard, this time on a ramp built over the stern of USS *Pennsylvania*. He was flying an improved design, the Curtiss Model 'D' pusher.

Both of Ely's flights were one-off stunts. Whilst they helped Glenn Curtiss sell some aeroplanes, the experiments were not repeated. However, the US Navy was the first to employ naval aircraft in combat. During 1914 Mexico was in the throes of a revolution, into which the US Navy and its nascent air arm was drawn. On 9 April 1914 nine US sailors were arrested by the Mexican government after landing in an off-limits area of Tampico. The sailors were soon released, and an apology issued. But Mexico's failure to apologize in the terms demanded by the US Government ultimately led to the US Navy's occupation of the port of Vera Cruz, from 21 April to 23 November. A limited number of flights were made by two Curtiss aircraft carried aboard USS *Mississippi*. The two machines were a Model 'E' pusher floatplane, AH-3, and a Model 'F' flying boat, AB-3. A flight by AB-3 piloted by Lt (JG) Patrick N. L. Bellinger, on 25 April, to scout for mines in the harbour was the first recorded combat mission by any naval aircraft.

The US Navy was not alone in experimenting with aviation. The navies of France, Germany, Italy, Japan and Russia all experimented with ship-borne aircraft between 1911 and 1918. Russia was particularly active in this sphere, maintaining several seaplane carriers in the Black Sea, but the French were the first to commission a vessel modified to carry seaplanes, the *Foudre* in March 1912. These experiments are beyond the scope of this book but, as we will be encountering it throughout this story, German naval aviation will be discussed in more detail in a later chapter.

In Great Britain studies were leading toward practical experiments in the use and purpose of naval aviation. Throughout the later nineteenth century and the early twentieth century the Royal Navy had experimented with man-carrying kites and balloons. Not all developments were seized with enthusiasm. When, in 1907, the Wright brothers offered to sell their patents to the Admiralty, it was politely refused informing them that '[aeroplanes] would not be of any practical use to the Naval Service.' However, opinions change, and a discussion paper dating from late 1911 outlined the potential duties of naval aviators, one of which read in part, 'To ascend from a floating base [...]'. That would become the underlying aspiration of British naval aviators and the Royal Naval Air Service from their first flights until it was achieved.

On 13 April 1912 the Royal Flying Corps was formed, absorbing all existing military and naval aviation units. As initially set up, the Royal Flying Corps contained Naval and Military Wings, and was to establish a Central Flying School at Upavon on Salisbury Plain. The Royal Flying Corps, Naval Wing was not long in establishing its own unique identity. The title soon disappeared from official documents, The Royal Naval Air Service (RNAS) soon becoming its *de facto* title. Whilst the separation did not become official until 1 July 1914, from its very beginnings the RNAS began extensive, and prolonged, investigations into the problems of naval aviation. Even before the formation of the Royal Flying Corps, Naval Wing, naval officers were training to be pilots and experimenting with take-offs from ships at anchor and underway.

Francis (Frank) Kennedy McClean was one of the founding members of the Royal Aero Club (RAeC). He was an enthusiastic aeronaut, gaining Fédération Aéronautique Internationale Aeronaut's Certificate No. 11 on 18 May 1909. He became interested in heavier than air flying following a flight with Wilbur Wright at Le Mans in 1908. The Short Brothers, who were originally balloon manufacturers, had been appointed by the Wrights to build their machines in Britain. McClean ordered the first copy, Short No. 1, the beginning of a long and fruitful association. McLean bought the ground on which the aerodrome at Eastchurch was built, and leased it to the RAeC for one shilling per annum. After struggling unsuccessfully with the Wright machine McClean purchased the Short-Sommer No. 2 from J. T. C. Moore-Brabazon. Flying this machine he completed the necessary tests to qualify for RAeC Certificate No. 21 at Eastchurch on 20 September 1910.

In its issue of 3 December 1910, *Flight* announced that:

> The Committee of the Royal Aero Club has placed two aeroplanes at the disposal of the Admiralty for the use of Naval Officers at Sheerness and Chatham, at the Club's flying grounds at Eastchurch, Isle of Sheppey. The machines are biplanes, fitted with Gnome motors. Several members have promised to assist in giving practical instruction to the officers.

The machines were made available by Frank McClean, who also arranged for G. B. Cockburn (RAeC Certificate No. 5) to act as instructor. Cockburn had previously been instructing army pilots on Salisbury Plain.

The Admiralty, in announcing the offer in a general order, made it known that 'naval officers piloting them were to be asked to make good any damage done.' It also arranged for Colonel H. S. Massey of the Aerial League of the British Empire to lecture on aviation to the 'Vice Admiral Commanding the Third and

Fourth Divisions of the Home Fleet and the officers of the Fleet and Dockyard at Sheerness' in January 1911. At the end of the lecture officers interested in volunteering for an 'aviation course' were to give their names to the Admiral, the offer was also open to junior officers throughout the fleet. The cost of the course was noted as £20, which might be refunded by the Admiralty, and was expected to last six months. There were over 200 applications for the course. The four trainees, selected from the applicants, were Lt Charles Rumney Samson, RN (RAeC Certificate No. 71, 25 April 1911), Lt Arthur M. Longmore, RN (RAeC Certificate No. 72, 25 April 1911), Lt R. Gregory, RN (RAeC Certificate No. 75, 2 May 1911), and Lt E. L. Gerrard, RMLI (RAeC Certificate No. 76, 2 May 1911). There were three similar Short-Sommer machines available for instruction: Short S.26 (Short-Sommer No. 3) known by the trainees as 'Th'owd Bitch' and other less than complimentary names, Short S.28 (Short-Sommer No. 8) and Short S.34 (Short-Sommer No. 7).

Often overlooked in the list of early British naval aviators is Commander Oliver Schwann. In 1909 he was appointed to *Hermione* at Barrow as Assistant Inspecting Captain of Airships, supervising the construction on HM Airship R1 under Captain Murray F. Sueter. Whilst at Barrow, in June 1911, Schwann purchased a well-used Avro Type 'D' biplane for £700. He intended to use the machine to solve the problems inherent in float design, by testing a series of experimental floats. With the financial support of a small syndicate of his fellow officers from *Hermione* he was, after many trials and tribulations, able to design a set of floats which enabled the underpowered aircraft to take-off from the waters of Cavendish Dock. The importance of Schwann's work was not so much that he produced a workable floatplane, after all most British floatplanes of the period used a completely different design, rather it was that his experiments were officially recorded and acted as a catalyst for further, more scientific, work. Captain Murray Sueter recorded details of the early testing in R&M 69, 'Report of Experiments Carried Out With A Hydro-Aeroplane, With Notes And Suggestions For Further Experiments', published in December 1911 by the Advisory Committee for Aeronautics. After Barrow, Schwann was appointed Assistant Director Air Department in the Admiralty. Here, together with Director Sueter, he helped guide and develop the Royal Naval Air Service. He was promoted to Captain, RN, shortly before the war. (During the war his Germanic name was causing problems in public and, in 1917, he changed his surname to Swann, which spelling will be used in subsequent chapters.) We shall meet him again as captain of *Campania*.

Meanwhile, back at Eastchurch, the four new pilots had set about improving their skills. When McClean returned from a scientific expedition in the South Pacific arrangements could be made for the training of other officers. Lt Arthur M. Longmore recalled that in September the first four, having completed the six month course, were wondering what their future would be.

I was deputed by Samson, who was the senior, to go and find out. The particular Senior Naval Officer at the Admiralty who dealt with our appointments as lieutenants did not seem to know much about us but supposed that, now we had had our bit of fun, we would be resuming our more serious duties in the orthodox Navy that went to sea in ships. I mildly pointed out that as we had been trained and were sufficiently expert to train others it was unlikely that Mr. Cockburn, our instructor, would be willing to spare another six months to do what we could perfectly well do ourselves.

The Admiralty evidently agreed for, after a short leave, Longmore returned to Eastchurch to find that four more officers had been appointed for training. The next step was for the Admiralty to make Eastchurch into a permanent school for flying instruction. At a meeting of the RAeC Committee on 28 November it was agreed that the Admiralty could have the use of the airfield for £150 per annum, with the option to purchase it in December 1918. Thus, more than four months before the formation of the Royal Flying Corps, Eastchurch was established as the Naval Flying School. In May 1912 Lt (Acting Commander) C. R. Samson was appointed Commandant of the Naval Wing.

From this time forward, particularly with Samson's energetic leadership, the RNAS increasingly went its own way. It cooperated with the RFC, Military Wing on the formation of the Central Flying School, but retained the Eastchurch Naval Flying School. It refused to be tied to the products of the Royal Aircraft Factory, sourcing its equipment from private British manufacturers, particularly the Short Brothers and Thomas Sopwith. It also bought aeroplanes from French companies and Glenn Curtiss in the USA. The RNAS forged ahead, particularly in preparing the aeroplane to fit the Royal Navy's specific needs and requirements. Their next task was to take the aeroplane to sea.

Whilst Schwann was working at Barrow, Longmore was also messing about with floats. 'Oswald [Short] was also a great help to us and it was with him that I worked out a scheme for fitting torpedo shaped airbags to the wooden undercarriage skids of a biplane.' Two airbags were installed on the main undercarriage skids of Short S.38, with a third between the two tail skids. Short S.38 (Short-Sommer No. 9), a replacement for S.28 written off during training, was of 'boxkite' design with a pusher 50 hp Gnome rotary engine. In November 1911 Longmore landed, 'or more accurately splashed', on the Medway. After being towed ashore, cleaning the engine and inspecting for damage, he took off and flew back to Eastchurch. Short S.38, which also had a naval serial T.2, complete with Longmore's airbags, deserves to be commemorated at the first British naval aeroplane, being used by Samson and others to fly off ramps from two pre-dreadnoughts.

First to take-off from a ship of the Royal Navy was Lieutenant Charles Rumney Samson, RN, on 10 January 1912. The take-off was made from a sloping track erected over the forward turret and forecastle of *Africa*, moored off Sheerness.

Short S.38 had been lightered out to the ship, hoisted aboard, then, with the ship moored and facing into wind, Samson took off using most of the track and returned safely to Eastchurch. One local newspaper reporter witnessed the flight.

'over the forward turret.'

> When all was ready, the pilot gave word to "Let go all," and with his engine working perfectly he shot down the sloping rails clear of the ship's stern [sic] and was borne upon the air with the grace of some winged creature … Cheer after cheer sounded from the great ship from the moment of the launch.

The aeronautical press also took note, *Flight* 20 January 1912 at the bottom of a long report of events at Eastchurch briefly noting:

> The event of the week was undoubtedly Lieut. Samson's flight from the battleship *Africa*, a feat which the intrepid aviator accomplished with great skill. The start being visible from the shore at Sheerness, this accomplishment has naturally been given some publicity by the Press, otherwise actual photos and details have not been obtained.

On the whole the first take-off was achieved with little fuss or fanfare. The next attempt, which occurred prior to the King's arrival at the Royal Naval Review at Weymouth, was the exact opposite to the first flight, well recorded and attended by senior naval officers.

At the end of April, *Hibernia* was fitted with a track, longer and flatter than that previously installed on *Africa*. During the forenoon of 1 May Short S.38, now with a more powerful 70 hp Gnome engine, and a new tractor float biplane the Short S.41, christened by Samson 'Amphibian', were hoisted onto the track for transportation to Weymouth. *Hibernia* then sailed from Sheerness, arriving off Weymouth at 5.40 a.m. on 2 May. At 5.55 a.m. *Hibernia*'s log book noted the weather as clear with a Force 2 wind out of the west. It then noted, 'Aeroplane T.2 [Short S.38] left ship Cmdr Samson as pilot and flew to Lodmore.' Samson's flying log book was a little more forthcoming. The underlining is Samson's.

> 6 a.m. Flew from Fxle of 'Hibernia' steaming 10½ knots in Weymouth Bay on T.2 (70 hp Gnome) 3 miles off Breakwater flew to Lodmore and landed. 6 miles, 9 minutes rather bumpy. Felt no gusts when leaving ship. T.2 got off in 60 feet I should calculate. 1st time from ship steaming.

A little detail missing from most accounts is the role of boy-seamen from the training ship *Ganges*. A squad had been drafted aboard *Hibernia* to assist with the take-off. They were told to haul on a rope, which would release the restraining toggle, when given a signal by the pilot. Once Samson was satisfied with his engine, he dropped his left hand, and the boy seamen hauled enthusiastically on the rope to release the toggle. With the tension released, the plane flew away and the boys ended up in a heap on the bridge under the feet of the senior officers, much to the latter's amusement.

One minor mystery is where was Short S.41 whilst Samson was taking off? Photographs show that it was transported ahead of Short S.38, so would have to have been moved to permit the take-off. There is no record in *Hibernia*'s log of it having been hoisted out, but Samson recorded flying it on 3 May 'off water in Portland.'

At Lodmore, the Short joined two more aircraft, a Deperdussin monoplane, naval serial M.1, and a Nieuport monoplane, naval serial M.3, which appear to have flown over from Eastchurch. The exact location of the landing ground is not certain but it was probably close to the present day Lodmoor Country Park. This was also the base for famed civilian pilots Claude Grahame-White and B. C. Hucks with their Nieuport and Blériot monoplanes. The 'Amphibian' was lodged on a boat slip at Portland.

In its issue of 18 May 1912 *Flight* recorded:

As soon as word was received on Wednesday of last week [8 May], that the Royal Yacht was within a dozen miles of Admiral Callaghan's flagship, intimation was given to Commander Samson and the other aviators, and all four at once set off to find the *Victoria and Albert*, Commander Samson starting from Portland on 'Amphibian', and Lt Gregory on the Short biplane, Lt Longmore on the Deperdussin and Captain Gerrard on the Nieuport, followed one another in quick succession from Lodmore. All were quickly swallowed up in the fog, and the first to actually find the Royal Yacht was Commander Samson who, after circling above it, returned to his headquarters, having been in the air about an hour. Lt Gregory, Lt Longmore, and Capt. Gerrard also circled above the yacht, the first named during a flight which lasted 1 hr 10 mins.

Longmore flew into a patch of thick fog on his return:

I flew blind for some minutes by compass and nearly ran straight into the cliff near Lulworth Cove. I followed the top edge of the cliff back the few miles to the landing ground, which, incidentally, was so small that some years later I saw it and could not imagine how we had managed to fly out of it at all.

Later that afternoon the airmen were up again. Samson took Short S.41 out to the fleet and landed close to the Royal Yacht. A small boat then transferred his passenger, another naval officer, to the *Victoria and Albert* with a letter for the King. 'After the machine had been resting on the sea for some time, it was restarted and carried out several manoeuvres before returning to its shed.' *Flight* did not mention whether the passenger had returned, other sources suggesting that Samson may have delivered the letter himself. Perhaps he received an invitation to dinner, as he had the honour of being included among the naval officers who dined with the King on the Royal Yacht on the evening of 10 May. All three machines were up again from Lodmore, Gregory flying 'at a safe distance from the Royal Yacht and discharged a dummy bomb, weighing 300 lbs from a height of 500 ft.' Both civilian flyers were also out over the fleet. The air may have seemed quite crowded at times.

Flight asserted:

> The feats performed by the naval aviators, during the King's review of his ships, must have convinced the Naval authorities, if they needed any convincing, of the practical stage attained by aviation, and also that the Navy does not lack officers who are quite competent to rank with any aviators in the world.

Following Samson's take-off the track remained fitted on *Hibernia* for several more days, until 15 May after the ship had returned to Sheerness. During this period more take-offs were made, both Lt R. Gregory, RN, and Lt Cecil J. L'Estrange Malone, RN, have been mentioned as possible pilots. These flights were probably made on 12 May whilst *Hibernia* was returning to Sheerness. The log book noting manoeuvres consistent with those necessary for two flights, but is extremely vague regarding actual events. There is also the possibility of a flight on 13 May whilst moored at Sheerness but, once again, the log book fails to provide actual confirmation.

The final flight in this series of experiments was made by Lt C. J. L'Estrange Malone on 4 July 1912. Relatively inexperienced, his RAeC Certificate No. 195 being dated 12 March 1912, Malone flew Short S.38 out from Eastchurch and landed at sea alongside *London* moored at Sheerness. The Short was then hoisted aboard and placed on the same track that had previously been erected on *Hibernia*. The ship then sailed around the coast towards Portsmouth. When approximately nineteen miles from Portsmouth, Malone took off whilst the ship was steaming at 12 knots into a 10 mph wind, requiring just 25 feet of the track, and flew on ahead to land at the dockyard.

Practical flying from ships underwent a hiatus of a year whilst other problems concerning armament and communications were studied, and the development of improved aeroplane designs pursued. About this time the term 'seaplane' came into use. Flight Commander Richard Bell Davies recalling in his memoirs:

> Up to this time, aeroplanes on floats had been called hydroaeroplanes, but I heard Winston Churchill say, 'That's a beastly word. Let's give then a better name; let's call them seaplane.' And seaplanes they have been ever since.

Seaplanes can be further subdivided into two main groups, flying boats and floatplanes. Essentially, flying boats combine fuselage and boat hull into one structure, whilst floatplanes have separate flotation devices, floats or pontoons, attached by struts to the fuselage or wings.

Late 1912 saw the first stirrings in design for aircraft-carrying ships. In December William Beardmore and Company submitted a proposal to the Admiralty for a 'parent ship for naval aeroplanes and torpedo boat destroyers.' Sir Arthur W. Johns (Director of Naval Construction, 1930–36) in a 1934 paper to the Institution of Naval Architects described the proposed vessel:

> The displacement was 15,000 tons, length 430 feet, beam on waterline 82 feet, and speed 15 knots. The upper or flight deck, 450 feet long and 110 feet wide, had side houses for a length of about 220 feet, through which the funnels, boiler and engine room ventilators, etc., passed, and also housed six aeroplanes with wings spread, each in its own hangar. Four aeroplanes with wings detached were stowed in the forward hold and could be struck down or lifted out by either of the two forward cranes. Between the side houses was an open deck about 50 feet wide which could be closed in at the fore end by hinged inclined gates. If the open forecastle deck proved to be of insufficient length for an aircraft to fly off, it could start in the passageway. Similarly, aircraft landing on the quarterdeck might finish their flight in the passageway. Although in a calm sea very experienced pilots might find the width of passage adequate, yet it was evident that in a seaway a 50 foot width was certainly on the small size, especially with a transverse form of ship whose rolling would be erratic and irregular.

It was a brave attempt which, in the face of future knowledge, was doomed to failure. In addition to the potential difficulties noted by Sir Arthur, disturbed airflow around the two islands would have made landings impossible and the quoted speed appears optimistic for such a barge-like hull. The Admiralty politely refused the proposal, simply stating that 'sufficient experience had not yet been gained with hydroplanes working from a ship at sea to enable naval requirements to be definitely stated.'

The next year, two more proposals were made to the Admiralty. Admiral Mark Kerr, who later in 1914 would become the first British flag officer to become a pilot, is said to have submitted a sketch design remarkable for its prescience, depicting a flat unobstructed deck with offset funnels. In January 1913 Admiral of the Fleet Sir Arthur Wilson suggested that an old cruiser of the 1897 *Eclipse* class could be modified by removing the mainmast and hinging the aft funnel to permit the installation of a landing platform, a take-off platform was to be erected over the foredeck. It would be some years before the RNAS would attempt to land on a ship, so all of these proposals were far-sighted. It is, however, difficult to completely separate Sir Arthur Wilson's proposal from the work soon to be carried out on *Hermes*, an old protected cruiser of the *Highflyer* class originally commissioned in 1899. The *Highflyer*'s were improved versions of the *Eclipse* class with increased armament, the serendipitous class name must surely be accidental.

Hermes re-commissioned on 7 May 1913 as headquarters ship of the RNAS. To fit her for the role as parent ship to two or three floatplanes *Hermes* was provided with a launching platform over the forecastle, suitable booms for hoisting in and out the machines, petrol storage space and a supply of spare parts. Canvas shelters were provided forward of the bridge, at the top of the launching platform, and on the quarterdeck. The launching platform was no improvement on the one used the previous year, the two forward 6 inch guns were actually removed to make room for the platform. As if that were not insult enough, the aft mountings were also landed to provide space for the storage of floatplanes.

The 1913 Naval Manoeuvres were intended to simulate the defence of the East Coast (Blue fleet) against an invading naval force (Red fleet). There was also a trade protection exercise carried out off the west coast of Ireland. Little imagination was required to realise that the Red fleet was meant to represent Germany. A large part of the Home and Atlantic Fleets were involved; 16 dreadnoughts and 24 pre-dreadnoughts, 5 battle cruisers, 58 cruisers and 139 destroyers, plus many smaller craft and submarines. Included in the total were eight seaplanes and *Hermes*. The Report by the Umpire-in-Chief, Admiral of the Fleet Sir William Henry May, makes for dry reading but includes a separate Appendix covering the work of the seaplanes 'as it was not possible to embody it without confusing the narrative, and also because this is the first time aircraft have taken part in the Manoeuvres on the high seas.' The fleet manoeuvres commenced on 23 July 1913 and were terminated by Admiralty order on the evening of 1 August.

The Blue fleet had air stations at Cromarty and Leven with three floatplanes at each base. The Red fleet had *Hermes* with two floatplanes and an air station at Great Yarmouth with four floatplanes. Despite difficulties operating from extemporised bases, off unprotected beaches, all the land-based machines were able to complete a number of patrol and reconnaissance flights. Submarines and other vessels were observed and reported but could not be attacked as the rules defined their role to be entirely that of reconnaissance. These were a foretaste of the unending and frequently tedious patrols flown from shore bases throughout the First World War.

Hermes, based at Great Yarmouth during the manoeuvres, carried two floatplanes; Borel monoplane, serial number 48, and Short Admiralty Type 74 Folder Tractor Seaplane, 81, an improved version of Samson's 'Amphibian'. The Short had folding wings that reduced its 56 foot wing span to only 12 feet, greatly reducing the required on-board space for storage. It was also fitted with an early Rouzet radio transmitter, but no receiver. Commander Samson was aboard *Hermes* with Lt Raymond Fitzmaurice, RN, to act as observer and radio operator. As with the land-based machines, *Hermes* and her floatplanes were considered to be immune from attack, and were not permitted to make attacks themselves. *Hermes* and her machines were intended to represent an airship attached to the Red fleet, as such she was permitted to proceed up to 300 miles from Great Yarmouth, but must return within 48 hours.

On the morning of 23 July, just before the exercise commenced, a full gale was blowing at Great Yarmouth. The Borel, which was stowed on the forward platform, had its right wing torn off. The Short, carried aft, suffered only minor damage from heavy rain. Caudron G.II, 55, an amphibian with wheels partially buried in its floats, replaced the Borel on the forward platform. Its sole contribution to the manoeuvres came on 28 July when, with *Hermes* steaming at 10 knots into a light wind, Lieutenant R. P. Ross successfully flew the Caudron from the platform and went on to land at Yarmouth.

The bulk of flying from *Hermes* fell to the Short, 81, with Samson and Fitzmaurice as crew. Over the ten days of the manoeuvres the Short made seven flights. Radio transmissions were received by *Hermes* during many of the flights. On her final flight, leaving the ship at 9.30 a.m. on 1 August, Samson was to fly out for 50 miles then turn back. A brief undecipherable message was received shortly after the machine had turned back, then silence. The radio staff on *Hermes* were able to estimate a position and a destroyer, *Mermaid*, was sent to search for the missing machine with *Hermes* following as soon as she had raised steam. Fitzmaurice later reported that:

> I had been sending signals by W/T all the time and had just reported a tramp [steamer] on the starboard bow, when the engine suddenly stopped. We unfortunately made a bad landing and completely smashed our undercarriage and part of the lower plane and tail; fortunately, however, the tramp came to our rescue and hoisted us on her poop.

Hermes came up with the tramp, a German timber-carrier *Clara Mennig*, a few hours later and took the floatplane and crew aboard. Investigation found that, 'A piece of tin in the inside of the bonnet got loose and broke four ignition wires, thus putting four cylinders out of action. The engine then stopped and a landing was made.'

Although *Hermes*' floatplanes failed to make any significant contribution to the results of the 1913 manoeuvres, the extended period of operations was a watershed in the development of naval aviation. She continued operating her floatplanes into October, spending some days in Scapa Flow. About 20 further flights were made although only one, again by the Caudron on 3 September, used the platform. Methods of operation of floatplanes were established that, with minor changes, were to stand the test of war. In addition, the way ahead in naval aircraft design was clearly delineated. *Hermes* paid off into reserve at the end of the year.

Following analysis of the role of aviation in the 1913 Naval Manoeuvres the Admiralty decided to include the sum of £81,000 in the 1914–15 Naval Estimates to acquire a dedicated aviation vessel. Rather than start with a blank sheet, the Admiralty decided to take over a merchant ship for conversion. The vessel selected was in an early stage of construction at Blyth Shipbuilding Company at Blyth, Northumberland, probably with just the keel laid and a few frames erected. Originally designed as a typical three-island tramp steamer for use in the Black Sea coal trade, the ship as completed was radically different in appearance. Thus it can justifiably be claimed that when launched on 5 September 1914 *Ark Royal* was the first ship to be designed and built as a seaplane carrier.

The engines and oil-fired boilers, bridge, and officers accommodation were moved to the aft third of the hull leaving over 200 feet of clear deck to the forepeak. Within this space a large hatch, 40 feet by 30 feet wide, provided access to the 'aeroplane hold', itself some 150 feet in length, 45 feet wide and 15 feet high, and workshops. To hoist the seaplanes in and out of the hold and on to the water two three-ton capacity steam cranes were fitted, one each side of the hull. These were simply dockside travelling cranes, with the motive gear removed, installed on a supporting steel framework. *Ark Royal* would spend the entire war at Gallipoli and in the Aegean Sea as a seaplane tender.

Whilst the first ship to be built as a seaplane carrier plays no further part in this story, there were many ships converted to seaplane carriers to hold our attention in the North Sea.

2

The North Sea, Fleets and Bases

It is easy to think of the North Sea as a level battlefield. Whilst it could be so, it is always in motion and frequently hidden in fog or stirred up by storms. To the north, beyond the Orkney and Shetland Islands, it mixes with the cold Norwegian Sea. It is land locked on the east by Norway and Denmark, to the south by the low lying coasts of Germany, the Netherlands, Belgium, and the northern tip of France, and on the west by Great Britain. In the south-west, beyond the Straits of Dover, the North Sea becomes the English Channel. On the east it is joined to the Baltic Sea by the Skagerrak and the Kattegat, separating Norway and Sweden from the Danish Jutland peninsula. The Kiel Canal, passing through the German part of the Jutland peninsula, also joins the two seas.

The North Sea is affected by the lie of the land and seabed. Relatively shallow, averaging less than 350 feet in depth, it is some 700 miles long and, at its broadest, some 400 miles wide. But the sea bed is not flat. There are deep trenches along the Norwegian coast which descend to 2,300 feet. The North Sea is also divided in two by the Dogger Bank, a vast moraine deposit from a previous ice age, in places less than 50 feet below sea level. Starting some 60 miles off Flamborough Head the bank aligns to the north-east pointed at the Skagerrak, it is approximately 160 miles long and maximum 60 miles wide. Along the English coast lie further shallow sandbanks. Closer to the European mainland are the Frisian Islands, a series sandy barrier islands running from the Netherlands to Denmark. Further out, off the German ports, lies the rocky island of Heligoland.

During the war large areas around the German ports, the Straits of Dover and along the coast of the United Kingdom were mined. To the far north by the end of the war a mine barrier, the North Sea Barrage, ran from the Orkney Islands to the Norwegian Coast—all adding further complications to the navigation of large ships and fleets. Radio communications were by Morse code and, whilst basic radio cross bearings were possible, navigation was mostly by dead reckoning and sun or star sights—little changed since the days of sail. Vision was limited to the horizon when fog or smoke from the fleet permitted, radar far in the future. Little wonder then that both the Royal Navy and Imperial German Navy (*Kaiserliche Marine*) welcomed the possibilities aviation offered to see beyond the horizon.

British Fleets and Bases

When war came in August 1914 Admiral Sir John Jellicoe laid out four principle responsibilities for the Royal Navy.

1. To ensure for British ships the unimpeded use of the sea, this being vital to the existence of an island nation, particularly one which is not self-supporting in regard to food.

2. In the event of war, to bring steady economic pressure to bear on our adversary by denying to him the use of the sea, thus compelling him to accept peace.

3. Similarly in the event of war to cover the passage and assist any army sent overseas, and to protect its communications and supplies.

4. To prevent invasion of this country and its overseas Dominions by enemy forces. The above objects are achieved in the quickest and surest manner by destroying the enemy's armed naval forces, and this is therefore the first objective of our Fleet. The Fleet exists to achieve victory.

To achieve these goals the Grand Fleet was formed in August 1914 from the most modern elements of the Home Fleet. The older portions of the Home Fleet, the Second and Third Fleets, comprising older pre-dreadnoughts and old cruisers, were initially allocated to the Channel Fleet or Reserve Fleet. They would later play important roles worldwide in secondary campaigns and sideshows. Under the command of Admiral Sir John Jellicoe the Grand Fleet steamed for its wartime base at Scapa Flow on the commencement of the war. The role of the Royal Navy was considered to be so critical that Jellicoe was said to be the only man on either side who could lose war in an afternoon. Commanding the battle cruisers, Vice Admiral Sir David Richard Beatty would eventually replace Jellicoe after the Battle of Jutland. Supporting, (or hindering depending on the circumstances) at the Admiralty, were the First Sea Lord Admiral of the Fleet Sir John Arbuthnot Fisher, who replaced Prince Louis Alexander of Battenberg in October, and First Lord, Winston Spencer Churchill. Both Fisher and Churchill were to fall after the Dardanelles campaign. Fisher was replaced by Admiral of the Fleet Sir Henry Jackson, the new First Lord being Arthur Balfour.   *and Churchill?*

The Royal Navy was fortunate in having bases capable of supporting major fleet units around the coasts of the United Kingdom and Ireland. For North Sea operations the most important of these were in Scotland. Scapa Flow the main base of the Grand Fleet was located in the Orkney Islands. On the mainland were Invergordon in the Cromarty Firth and Rosyth in the Firth of Forth. Between the Forth and the Thames were a number of smaller ports, the most important of which would be Harwich. Beyond the Thames the first major base was at Dover. Here the Dover Patrol was tasked to prevent enemy shipping, chiefly submarines, from entering the English Channel and to protect the constant flow of troops and materiel from the United Kingdom to the battlefields of France. A mine barrage was the first line of defence, effectively barring German surface ships from the English Channel.

However, the actual situation on the outbreak of was far from ideal as the only fully equipped east coast port was at Chatham which was considered to be too far south to be of use as a major base. Harwich was assigned as the main base for torpedo craft becoming home base for the Harwich Force. The Harwich Force will feature frequently in following chapters. Rosyth, although thought of as a main fleet base, was far from complete and largely unprotected. Admiral Fisher believed Rosyth to be unsafe and badly located upriver from 'that beastly' Forth Bridge, a successful attack on which could trap the fleet in the river Forth. Scapa Flow was a completely unprotected anchorage with no facilities. In time, and with much expenditure, both Scapa Flow and Rosyth would become first class fleet bases.

Invergordon, although having some land defences in position, was relegated to a secondary base set up for oiling, heavy repairs and maintenance with a 31,500 ton capacity floating dock which had been brought up from Portsmouth in September 1914. A second smaller floating dock was added in 1916, and a third by the end of the war. However, the Cromarty Firth was a fine, well-protected, natural anchorage too good to be left under used. Once a submarine defence boom had been provided late in 1914 Jellicoe began basing battle squadrons and supporting cruisers and destroyers at Invergordon. This was, in part, to provide opportunities for land exercise and recreation lacking at the main base of Scapa Flow.

A seaplane station was established at Cromarty in May 1913, for the naval manoeuvres of that year, with Lt Arthur Longmore in command. He located a suitable patch of ground adjacent to the Cromarty Coastguard Station. During the 1913 Naval Manoeuvres, Admiral Sir John Jellicoe, who was at that time Second Sea Lord in charge of Naval Personnel and Training, left his Admiralty desk and took command of the Red Fleet based at Invergordon on the Cromarty Firth. Longmore recalled a visit by Jellicoe, who showed great interest in the machines, then:

> He asked me whether I could just ferry him out to his flagship: I knew what he wanted but hadn't said, so off we went in the Borel. I gave the engine full throttle, took off and flew him round his Fleet, landing him safely close to his ship: a boat collected a very delighted Admiral and nothing was said as to my having exceeded his instructions.

Jellicoe thus became one of the few senior Royal Navy officers to experience flight before the war. The station was reactivated and enlarged during the war and a second station was opened at Fort George, a few miles down the coast on the south side of the Beauly Firth. There was a small landing ground at Delny, two or three miles north-east of Invergordon, for the fleet's aircraft. The adjacent Inverness and Ross-shire Railway was convenient for returning the aeroplanes to the fleet.

Scapa Flow lies in the Orkney Islands, north of mainland Britain. What made it ideal as a naval base was a large sheltered anchorage more than capable of accommodating the entire Grand Fleet. On the outbreak of war the Grand Fleet comprised twenty dreadnought battleships (increasing to twenty-eight by the time of Jutland) and nine battle cruisers, with supporting cruiser squadrons and destroyer flotillas and a myriad of smaller vessels.

For the crews, officers and men based at Scapa Flow there was little to recommend it, for many his ship became his home and his entire life. Flotta Island was set aside for recreation, there was a YMCA hut serving tea and buns and a wet canteen serving beer, there were a few muddy, wind-blown football fields and eventually, for officers only, a golf course. Food for the fleet was plentiful, if often lacking in fresh items:

> Each man was allowed half a pound of meat and a pound of potatoes a day, and lashings of dried peas, haricot and butter beans, cheese, salt fish and eggs. Fruit was very scarce and many men developed blotches and mild scurvy. Bread soon became dry and wooden but the supply was plentiful. The daily issue of rum kept the majority happy.

Another sailor recalled, 'All of us were well fed, our own bakery, distilled water, a good comfortable hammock, complete with warm blankets: in fact, we were really comfortable whilst lying in the Flow.'

The SS *Borodino* was a unique addition to the Grand Fleet. Placed at the disposal of the Junior Army & Navy Stores, Ltd, she was to supply everything required to:

> Ward Room Officers' Messes, Gun Room Officers' Messes and Warrant Officers' Messes. It was intended that the Vessel should be fitted with a Grocery and Provision Shop, a Laundry, and also a Hairdressing Saloon, the working of which the Stores were to undertake and maintain.

The interior was set up as a replica of the firm's London store, complete with white coated shop assistants. Whilst intended for officers only a number of captains requested that the store be made available to their enlisted men. The first time this happened, 'Over 800 men were served, piles of rhubarb, onions, cabbages, &c,

disappearing as if by magic, until our large stock was exhausted.' On a number of occasions the fore deck of *Borodino* was given over to fleet boxing competitions making use of a portable ring provided for the ship. A second welcome addition was SS *Gourko*, a sister ship to *Borodino*, 'named the "Theatre Ship" as her 'tween deck for'ard was utilised for that purpose.' The *Gourko* would moor alongside a warship and that ship's concert party would use the theatrical facilities to stage their entertainment, be it a review or a full-blown three act musical play.

Local leave for an afternoon or overnight having so little to offer, many men preferred to stay on board for months on end waiting for the eagerly anticipated home leave. Long leave (long enough to return home) was only given when the ship was refitting often at either Invergordon or Rosyth. Those lucky to head south faced an endless rail journey on the 'Jellicoe Express' down to London.

As early as 15 August 1914 three Henry Farman floatplanes arrived at Scapa Flow for the protection of the anchorage. Under the command of Flt Cdr Douglas A. Oliver they had been detached from Great Yarmouth air station. There was no established base at this time and the machines appear to have operated from a field of still green oats belonging to the farm of Nether Scapa. The floatplanes were man-handled across a fine sandy beach into Scapa Bay. This detachment appears to have been short-lived, as by the end of August two had crashed and the third is reported at Grain by 20 November. A November gale may have sealed its fate, blowing down tents and damaging the remaining machines. The site, moreover, was considered unsuitable due to the difficulty in launching the floatplanes. However, at a later date, some permanent buildings were erected on the site and a slipway constructed, and it became a base for maintenance, repair and storage.

In 1917 a seaplane station was established at Houton Bay, overlooking the anchorage, enlarging a site where huts and a slipway for seaplanes had already been built in 1916. During 1918 it was further enlarged by the addition of a number of large canvas sheds housing kite balloons. Houton Bay became the main seaplane and flying boat base at Scapa Flow after an inland base on Loch Stenness proved unsuitable.

In 1918 a basic landing field was located at Smoogro, on Swanbister Bay just around the coast from Houton Bay, for the use of the fleet's aeroplanes. The landing field had been in use as a fleet practice station since mid-1917. It was intended to develop the base as an outstation for Houton Bay, work commencing on large permanent hangars, a slipway and a stone and timber jetty with a crane for hoisting out aeroplanes on to and off lighters for transport out to the fleet. Although the buildings were never completed, the jetty and base for the crane still survive.

Following the German bombardment of the east coast towns of Scarborough, Whitby and Hartlepool on 16 December 1914, the battle cruisers were rapidly moved south to be based at Rosyth for the remainder of the war. Scapa Flow was just too far north to permit rapid reaction to German raids. In 1916 the Battle Cruiser Fleet was created at Rosyth, the battle cruisers being joined by battle squadrons formed from the most modern and fast battleships. To get under the 'beastly bridge' the big ships had to strike their topmasts. Over time the sailors, 'got to know the soldiers guarding the Bridge, the Argylls, who would shout down greetings to us whenever we crept under the huge structure.' Rosyth-based personnel had more opportunities to obtain fresh food and, for local leave, Edinburgh was just a short train journey from the fleet anchorage. But, they too had few chances for long leaves.

The RFC airfield at Turnhouse opened in 1915, located about two and a half miles south of Queensferry on the south bank of the Firth of Forth. A second airfield close to the anchorage on Dalgety Bay was opened in 1917, at Donibristle. Turnhouse became the main base for RNAS/RAF aeroplanes operating with the fleet, but Donibristle was better located for deck flying training. Aircraft would fly off then land at Donibristle, from where a railway spur was used to transport the machines a few miles to North Queensferry, under the Forth Bridge, where they could be lightered out to the ships. A third base, East Fortune, became the major aviation establishment in the area. Located in the country south of North Berwick, it was used as both an airship station and aerodrome. It became the main base for the fleet's aeroplanes.

The Dogger Bank served to separate the main operational areas of the Grand Fleet and Harwich Force; the Grand Fleet mostly operating north of the bank, where it had room to manoeuvre. When the Grand Fleet Flying Squadron was operating later in the war, *Furious* would often close the Danish coast to fly her aircraft off over the northern Heligoland Bight. The Harwich Force, mainly light cruisers, destroyers and seaplane carriers, operated in the area contained between Dogger Bank and the Dutch and German coastal islands and as far east as the island of Heligoland.

The *Kaiserliche Marine*

The High Seas Fleet (*Hochseeflotte*) was formed in 1907 by renaming the Home Fleet (*Heimatflotte*). It was the creation of one man, Grand Admiral Alfred von Tirpitz. During the war it had three commanders. Vice Admiral Friedrich von Ingenohl took command in April 1913 until sacked by the Kaiser in February 1915. He was succeeded by Admiral Hugo von Pohl who, dying from cancer, was replaced by Vice Admiral Reinhard Scheer in January the following year. Scheer remained in command until almost the end of the war.

The *Kaiserliche Marine* had less choice for its bases than the Royal Navy but they benefited from powerful coastal defences thanks to the islands of the North Sea coast. There were three main dockyards at Wilhelmshaven, Kiel and Danzig (Gdansk, Poland). The last two named were on the Baltic and used for training and operations against Russia, when ice conditions permitted. The High Seas Fleet made its home port at Wilhelmshaven, Germany's principal North Sea base, on the Jade Bay near Hamburg. Just east of the Jade was the Weser river with its port of Bremerhaven, further north lay Cuxhaven on the mouth of the Elbe river. Inland on the north bank of the Elbe lay Brunsbüttel and the North Sea locks of the Kiel Canal, wide and deep enough to permit the passage of dreadnought battleships. To the west of Wilhelmshaven lay the River Ems and Emden. Emden was connected to the Jade by the Ems-Jade Canal, passable to destroyers. Less than ninety miles separates the mouths of the Ems and Elbe, with the Weser approximately midway between. The island of Borkum protected the entrance to the Ems and the line of islands continues to the mouth of the Jade and Weser, the Schillig Roads anchorage. Further out in the North Sea; the fortified island of Heligoland provided the outer defence. However, the High Seas Fleet could only cross the bars at the mouths Weser and Elbe at high water, for the entire fleet to exit required two tides. Once anti-submarine nets were provided, and protective minefields laid, it became the practice for squadrons of battleships to lay anchor beyond the bars. For this purpose the most frequented anchorage was the Schillig Roads.

Life for the German sailors in the High Seas Fleet was if anything worse than that of their British counterparts. The gulf between the enlisted men and officers was far wider than in the Royal Navy. Their ships were also more uncomfortable and rations poor, especially once the British blockade began to bite. Seaman Richard Stumpf, of the dreadnought SMS *Helgoland*, recorded his views of the main base at Wilhelmshaven:

> Strangers are never impressed with Wilhelmshaven. Even the natives detest the place. There are many reasons for this. First of all, the climate is wet and unhealthy, there is total lack of any natural beauty, and lastly, the population is very ignorant.

He goes on to complain about the lack of shops, restaurants, theatres and book stores. Stumpf was an atypical sailor preferring to spend his spare time reading, writing or at the theatre, rather than drinking and carousing. However, despite being based in mainland Germany with good communications, his opportunities for a long leave were little better than his British opposite number, his diaries only record four home leaves throughout the war. Most telling as the war progresses are the increasing number of diary entries concerning food. This from November 1916 is typical:

> There was much complaining about the food this week. Each day we got a soup mixture which was so thin and weak and so poorly prepared that I always felt hungrier after the meal than before it. As an additional treat, the soup was almost always burned. I pilfered potatoes whenever I could and cooked them over steam at night.

In January 1917 he was recording:

> We only get potatoes once a week. On weekdays we get yellow, red and other
> varieties of turnips, alternating with blue, red and green cabbage. Maybe they
> will increase the bread rations.

Stumpf would be disappointed as no increase in the bread ration was forthcoming.
The sailors were better off than the dockworkers though, the latter being reduced
to begging for food scraps from the sailors.

Wilhelmshaven offered an anchorage for the High Seas Fleet sheltered from
all but the worst North Sea gales and well protected by minefields and outlying
fortifications, it was all but impregnable except by air. Although the High Seas Fleet
was smaller than its British counterpart, at Jutland it had sixteen dreadnoughts,
six pre-dreadnoughts and five battle cruisers, its ships were better armoured and
its armament more efficient, although of smaller calibre than the Grand Fleet.
There were major differences also in the aerial services of the two fleets.

The German Naval Air Service, *Marine-Fliegertruppe*

Founded in 1911 under the patronage of the Kaiser's younger brother, Prince
Heinrich of Prussia, a career naval officer who had learnt to fly in 1910, German
naval aviation initially struggled. Its home base was a small airfield at Putzig
(Puck, Poland), located on the coast some 25 miles north of the Danzig shipyards.
Initial products from the Albatros and Ago concerns failed to impress and
several Avro 503 floatplanes and Curtiss flying boats were purchased. Spurred
by the foreign competition German manufacturers were soon producing efficient
designs. The floatplanes equipping the *Marine Fleigerabteilung* throughout the
war were generally superior to their British equivalents, strong, fast, long ranged
and well-armed. But the service entered the war with less than a dozen operational
machines, mostly obsolescent.

In October 1914 the armoured cruiser, SMS *Friedrich Carl*, was the first German
warship to carry seaplanes. She was the flagship of Rear Admiral Behring, the
commander of the German cruiser squadron in the Baltic Sea. The German naval
command ordered Behring to attack the Russian port at Libau (Liepāja, Latvia) to
prevent it from being used as a submarine base. Two Albatros WDD floatplanes
were attached to the ship, but no special arrangements appear to have been made
and it is probable that they were only being transported. Poor weather conditions
delayed the operation until the 16 November. The following day *Friedrich Carl*
was steaming some 30 nautical miles off Memel (Klaipeda, Lithuania) when
she struck two Russian mines. After the crew was removed, *Friedrich Carl* was
abandoned, taking the floatplanes with her when she capsized and sank. There
were a few more attempts to use seaplane carriers in the Baltic area during the

First World War, the *Kaiserliche Marine* converting a number of merchant ships to seaplane carriers for limited operations in the Baltic Sea. However, the *Marine Fleigerabteilung* was largely shore-based, almost entirely so in the North Sea.

Late in the war the light cruiser SMS *Stuttgart* underwent an ambitious conversion. Armament aft of the funnels was removed and a large steel-framed, but canvas covered, hangar was constructed together with seaplane handling derricks and cranes. She could carry up to three Friedrichshafen FF49c reconnaissance machines. She re-commissioned on 16 May 1918 as a seaplane carrier (*Flugzeugmutterschiff*). *Stuttgart* provided protection and aerial reconnaissance for minesweeping forces in the North Sea.

The *Marine Fleigerabteilung* comprised several major operational units, which in turn were subdivided into specialised units. The First and Second *Seeflieger Abteilungen* were floatplane units reporting directly to the *Reichs Maritime Amt* (Admiralty) in Berlin. *Seeflieger Abteilungen Flandern* was a mixed reconnaissance and fighter floatplane unit based on the mole at Zeebrugge and at Ostend. Finally, the *Marine Landflieger* were landplane units, both single and two-seaters, protecting the Flanders coast and cooperating with the Imperial German Army Air Service.

The First *Seeflieger Abteilung* was based in Kiel for Baltic operations and training purposes. The Second *Seeflieger Abteilung* will concern us most in the following pages as it was based at Wilhelmshaven with *Seeflugstationen (SFS)* on the islands of Borkum, Heligoland, Norderney, and Sylt. Its duties included reconnaissance over the North Sea, its machines being divided into *Aufklärungs Staffeln* (reconnaissance patrol flights) and *Kampfstaffeln* (fighter patrol flights). Reconnaissance patrols were usually flown in pairs, the bombing and fighter flights were often in formations of five or more machines. The machines that equipped this unit were mostly two-seater floatplanes equipped either for reconnaissance or fighting. Of the former the most common throughout the war was the Friedrichshafen FF33, built between the end of 1914 and early 1918, it was the equivalent of the RNAS's Short 184. Unlike the Short, the FF33 was built in both reconnaissance and fighter versions. Both had the same 150 hp six cylinder Benz engine but the fighter version had reduced wing span and a fixed forward firing machine gun and a free machine gun for the observer. A limited number of FF39 variants were built with a 200 hp Benz, a radio transmitter and a single free machine gun for the observer. The FF49 replaced the earlier design from mid-1917, it had the engine of the FF39 and armament of the fighter version of the FF33. The FF33 had similar performance to the Short 184, the FF39 and FF49 were superior in all respects.

The success of FF33 fighter version led to the development of a range of two-seater fighter floatplanes, the most important being the Brandenburg W12 and W19 biplanes, entering service in 1917, and Brandenburg W29 monoplane, entering service in the spring of 1918. The W12 had a maximum speed of about 100 mph with one or two fixed forward firing machine guns and one free machine gun for the observer/gunner. The W19 was a larger, long range (five hours endurance) version of the W12 with two fixed forward firing machine guns and one free machine gun. The W29, the best floatplane fighter put into production during the First World War, could fly at 110 mph with a similar armament to the W12. Either of these machines were formidable opponents for any RNAS machine.

The *Marine-Fliegertruppe*, however, was not solely dependent on heavier than air machines. Its strong second arm was the *Marine Luftschiffabteilung* operating majestic but vulnerable rigid airships. Whilst most were built by the Zeppelin company, at least ten were built by Schütte-Lanz or Parseval. To the British all airships were Zeppelins. Consequently, through constant repetition, the word Zeppelin has come to refer to all rigid airships. Based pre-war at Nordholz near Cuxhaven, additional coastal stations, with their huge hangars and gas generating plants, were built at Tondern, Wittmundhafen (near Wilhelmshaven) and Hage, also at various inland locations. There were two main roles for the airships: scouting flights for the High Seas Fleet and bombing raids on the United Kingdom.

The airships varied in size and design but a typical mid-war craft, L35 a Type R 'Super Zeppelin', was 196.5 metres long and 23.9 metres maximum diameter. It was inflated with almost 55,000 cubic metres of highly inflammable hydrogen gas. Powered by six 240 hp Maybach HSLu engines its maximum speed was just over 100 kph (64 mph). L35 entered service in October 1916 and survived the war. It made 14 scouting flights and five raids on Britain; a remarkable record in comparison to many of its sister ships. The second of the class L31, for example, flew just one scouting mission but eight raids on Britain. She was intercepted and destroyed by 2nd Lt Wulstan Tempest, RFC, flying a BE2c on 2 October 1916 near Potters Bar, north of London. The Zeppelin was commanded Kapitänleutnant Helmut Mathy, who perished with his entire crew of nineteen, many of whom chose to jump to their deaths rather than be burnt alive.

The bases were in general located close enough to the coast to be affected by the storms and fogs for which the North Sea is notorious. The airships were in consequence much subject to the vagaries of the weather. However, the *Marine Luftschiffabteilung* made 971 scouting flights over the North Sea, and 306 bombing sorties (177 reaching England), during the war. Losses were horrendous, fifty-three (of some eighty entering service) airships failed to return together with most of their crews. But they were a major concern to the British Admiralty and Government throughout the war. Their real weaknesses were not realized, and their potential for long range naval reconnaissance and bombing were overrated. However, their mere existence resulted in many attempts by the RNAS to attack them and their bases from the sea, directly leading to developments in ship-borne aviation.

3

Plan Y
Christmas over Cuxhaven

When the First World War commenced the Royal Navy attempted to obtain a warship for conversion to seaplane carrier. Other than *Hermes*, lying in Reserve, none were available. So, on 31 August 1914, she was re-commissioned as an aircraft transport. On 31 October, whilst transporting two Short floatplanes across the channel, the old cruiser was intercepted off Dunkirk by *U27* (*Kapitänleutnant* Bernhard Wegener). The submarine fired a single torpedo at the zigzagging cruiser, which turned away but the torpedo hit aft. Slowing, and beginning to settle, *Hermes* was hit by a second torpedo and sank within a few minutes. Most of her crew were rescued by patrolling destroyers, whilst *U27* slipped away.

Whilst *Hermes* was re-commissioning, two cross-channel packet steamers from the South Eastern and Chatham Railway Company were taken over to be converted into seaplane carriers. On 11 August 1914, *Engadine* and *Riviera*, both 1,675 gross registered tons (grt) and capable of 22 knots, were taken in hand at Chatham Dockyard for conversion. An Admiralty account noted that:

These consisted of wooden platforms surrounded by canvas screens and covered by canvas awnings. The seaplanes were handled by swinging derricks and the vessels' capstans [...] it was only possible with the original arrangements to find accommodation for three seaplanes. The workshops and stores were, moreover, of very modest dimensions.

Engadine was completed on 1 September to be followed by *Riviera* a few days later. After commissioning as ship of the Royal Navy and a brief work-up at Sheerness both seaplane carriers reported to Harwich by early October. A third South Eastern and Chatham Railway Company packet steamer, *Empress* (1,694 grt, 18 knots), was taken over on 25 August initially to serve as an RNAS transport and supply vessel. She was soon sent to Chatham for conversion along the lines of the earlier ships, commissioning at Sheerness on 10 October.

Once completed the seaplane carriers were attached to the Harwich Striking Force, soon to be known as the Harwich Force, commanded by Commodore Reginald Yorke Tyrwhitt. The Harwich Force, although nominally part of the Grand Fleet, would effectively be an independent command throughout the war. Constantly varying in numbers, it typically comprised between four and eight light cruisers, several destroyer flotillas and the seaplane carriers. Its principle roles were to carry out reconnaissance of German naval activities and to screen the Grand Fleet when it was operating in the southern parts of the North Sea, also to escort ships sailing between the Thames and the Netherlands. Harwich Force operations were often supported by distant elements of the Grand Fleet. In addition, Tyrwhitt often had to provide ships to back up the operations of the Dover Patrol.

Also stationed at Harwich was a submarine force under Commodore S (Captain Roger Keyes). At the beginning of the war these submarines were organized into flotillas with a destroyer as leader. The submarine flotillas initially operated as submersible destroyers, putting a screen ahead or on the flank of the surface units. As the war progressed it was realised that the submarines operated more efficiently on independent patrols.

Harwich is located on the estuaries of the Stour and Orwell rivers and is one of the best ports between the Thames and the Humber. Since 1657, when Samuel Pepys was the town's MP and First Secretary of the Admiralty, Harwich had been a naval base. Prior to the war it had been best known for the Great Eastern Railway's ferry services to the Continent. When the war came it reverted to its role of a major naval base. Well provided with the necessaries for refreshment and relaxation of its wartime population, Harwich was one of the more favoured home ports; not that long leaves were any more common than further north. The Harwich Force was often at short notice and 'often, by day or in the quiet night, would be heard the weird signal of the sirens that summoned officers and men on leave on shore to hurry back to their ships, as something was happening on the North Sea that called for the Harwich Force, or a portion of it, to put to sea at once.' Across the estuary lay the small port of Felixstowe; it would become home to the floatplanes and flying boats of the RNAS. There was also a small landing field where pilots from the seaplane carriers could keep in flying practice.

The Battle of Heligoland Bight, the first naval battle of the First World War, fought on 28 August 1914, was a direct result of the Harwich Force setting out to trap German patrols off the north-west German coast. Tyrwhitt had two light cruisers and 31 destroyers under his command, supported by eight submarines. At various distances were Cruiser Force K (five elderly cruisers), as well as Commodore William Goodenough's First Light Cruiser Squadron (six light cruisers) and Vice Admiral David Beatty's First Battle Cruiser Squadron (five battle cruisers). In a confused engagement, fought in poor visibility, the Royal Navy sank three German light cruisers and one destroyer, while damaging three other light cruisers. Tyrwhitt's flagship, *Arethusa*, and four destroyers were damaged. This relatively minor engagement was to have a disproportionate effect of the war in the North Sea. Shocked by the loss of ships, Kaiser Wilhelm ordered the navy to 'hold itself back and avoid actions which can lead to greater losses.' He also stipulated that his permission was required before the fleet could sortie, effectively limiting its operational options. From this time forward the German fleet commanders were always aware that someone was looking over their shoulders. In comparison, both Jellicoe and Beatty suffered minimal political interference and were free to act as the situation merited.

The second important event during this period was the raid by Vice Admiral Franz Ritter von Hipper's battle cruisers on the east coast ports of Scarborough, Whitby and Hartlepool on 16 December 1914. This followed a previous raid on Gorleston and Yarmouth on 3 November. In each case the attackers escaped without damage. A direct consequence of these raids was that Rosyth would become the home base for the battle cruisers from 20 December 1914 until the end of the war. Scapa was just too far north to enable a quick response to these and future raids. A similar raid on 24 January 1915 when the German battle cruisers attempted to destroy the fishing fleet on the Dogger Bank was intercepted by Beatty, resulting in the Battle of the Dogger Bank.

Beatty had been forewarned of Hipper's sortie by intercepted German radio messages decoded by British Naval Intelligence, in Room 40 Old Building of the Admiralty, an advantage British commanders were to enjoy throughout the war. In the first weeks of the war the German light cruiser SMS *Magdeburg* was operating against the Russians in the Baltic Sea. On 26 August she ran aground on the island of Odensholm off the coast of Estonia. Before she could be completely destroyed two Russian cruisers came up and her crew were evacuated by an accompanying destroyer. The Germans believed that all secret documents and code books had been destroyed, but the Russians were able to salvage two copies of the SKM code book. One of which they made available to the British, a gift that was as important as the capture of an Enigma machine would be in the Second World War. Using this document Royal Navy code breakers, in Room 40 OB, were able to begin decoding German naval messages. As with Enigma decodes, the information gained was used and issued with care.

During the battle, the old armoured cruiser SMS *Blücher* was sunk and battle cruisers SMS *Seydlitz* and SMS *Derflinger* badly mauled. The British battle cruisers *Lion* and *Tiger* and destroyer *Meteor* were all damaged. Although the battle was a relatively minor affair, it boosted British morale and caused the Kaiser to remove Admiral von Ingenohl from command of the High Seas Fleet on 2 February, replacing him with Admiral Hugo von Pohl.

On the North Sea coast of Germany, far beyond the reach of land-based bombers, airship sheds were thought to exist at Cuxhaven. Attempts were made by *Engadine* and *Riviera*, supported by the Harwich Force and elements of the Grand Fleet, to locate and bomb this base. In truth, the raids were looked upon as an irritation that might draw out part of the High Seas Fleet to destruction in the arms of the Grand Fleet. Operations mounted on 24/25 October and 23/24 November failed, for a variety of weather-related reasons, to the intense frustration of Tyrwhitt and the airmen. During the November raid the seaplane carriers were recalled by Admiralty command before they could launch their seaplanes. The Harwich Force pressed on and, whilst they failed to bring any German surface forces out, were attacked by several German floatplanes with no damage on either side. The recall of the seaplane carriers appears to have been due to Churchill's interference following a bad weather report, then failing to check with the man on the spot. In his report Tyrwhitt called the day 'lovely, calm and clear.'

However, the next operation planned for December 1914 enjoyed more success. Known officially as 'Plan Y', it has gone down in history as 'The Cuxhaven Raid', the World's first carrier air strike. Planning started soon after the failure of the November raid, the first orders for an 'Operation in Conjunction with Seaplanes (Plan Y)' being sent out by Tyrwhitt on 2 December 1914. Not until 18 December were orders issued by Captain Murray F. Sueter, Director of Air Department, concerning the air attack. The intervening period was probably spent in detailed planning of the role of the floatplanes. Sueter's orders are repeated in full below as they provide an excellent summary of the proposed operation.

ORDERS FOR AIR ATTACK ON CUXHAVEN AIRSHIP SHEDS BY SEAPLANES

Air Department, Admiralty, S.W.
18ᵗʰ December 1914.

It is known that one airship shed has been built at Cuxhaven, 10 miles inland; recent report states that four Zeppelins are now at this place, so probably the station has been added to.

The weather is very unfavourable at this time of year for seaplane work, and to carry out a seaplane attack which involves having a large number of ships is almost impossible because of the notice that has to be given to various units.

Light Cruisers and Destroyers.—Approval has been given for a small number of light cruisers and destroyers to act as a supporting force for the seaplane carriers. The details will be arranged with Commodore (T) [Tyrwhitt].

Submarines.—Approval has also been given for submarines to take part in these operations, for the purpose of protecting the seaplane carriers whilst hoisting in and out the seaplanes, and to rescue the pilots after the attack. The details will be arranged with Commodore (S).

The seaplane carriers will consist of –

"Engadine"— 3 machines.

"Riviera" —   3 machines.

"Empress" — 3 machines.

Cuxhaven Sheds.—All machines will drop their bombs on the Cuxhaven sheds. Should the sheds not be found they are to attack the enemy's ships or any positions of military importance and endeavour to destroy them, after which the "Empress's" three machines will count the ships in Schelling [*sic*] Roads.

SCHILLIG (see P. 40

Kiel.—If possible, "Riviera's" three machines will make a reconnaissance round the eastern end of the bight, and count any ships lying off the mouth of the Elbe.

Wilhelmshaven.—"Engadine's" three machines on returning will count the ships lying in Wilhelmshaven Harbour, taking care to keep out of gunfire.

Norderney Gat.—All machines after completing their attack and reconnaissance will shape course for Norderney Gat, and will be picked up on a line north (mag.) from Norderney Gat.

Bombs.—Each seaplane will carry three 20 lb bombs, it having been proved that one of these bombs will destroy a Zeppelin in a shed.

Murray F. Sueter,
Director of Air Department.

Sueter's last point is a reference to the attacks by RNAS land-based aircraft on airship sheds at Düsseldorf and Friedrichshafen in October. The orders note that sheds were known to be some miles from Cuxhaven, they were actually at Nordholz some eight miles inland.

The final set of orders to be issued, on 21 December, was by Squadron Commander Cecil L'Estrange Malone, captain of *Engadine* and squadron commander of the seaplane carriers. These contained detailed instructions for the conduct of the three seaplane carriers and all pilots, and contained additional information regarding permissible targets and reconnaissance objectives. The island of Heligoland was noted as a possible alternate target: 'where there may be hostile watercraft in the harbour or vicinity.' In his notes regarding reconnaissance objectives Malone provides a different emphasis to Sueter. 'The Admiralty would also *like* [Malone's italics.] to obtain some information on the following points, but attention is not to be paid to this to the detriment of the main objective.'

Each machine was to carry fuel for three hours, and three 20 lb Hales bombs, 'slung from the lower positions and fitted with Bowden cable for releasing.' The only other armament carried was the pilot's service revolver with 'six packets of ammunition.' In addition each pilot was to carry, 'Veries [*sic*] pistol and six cartridges. Perrin's lifebelt and one spare charge. Two electric torch lamps. Box of matches. Knife. Maps and charts. Provisions for 48 hours. First aid dressing.' Finally, each machine would be equipped with a tool kit comprising, 'King dicks [adjustable wrench], pliers, Jet spanner, ignition wire, rubber tubing, tape, copper drift hammer, screwdriver, H.T. wire, special tools and spare plugs, &c., as available.' In short, everything needed to carry out emergency repairs on a failing engine. Each pilot was permitted to make his own decision whether to fly solo or with an observer or mechanic/gunlayer.

All nine machines aboard the seaplane carriers were products of the Short Company. Aboard *Engadine*, there were three Short Type 81, serial numbers 119, 120 and 122, powered by a 160 hp Gnome rotary engine. Two Short 135s aboard *Riviera*, 135 had a 135 hp Salmson radial engine and 136 a 200 hp Canton-Unné radial engine. Finally, four Short C Folders (an improved Type 74), 811, 812, 814 and 815, with 100 hp Gnome rotary engines, 811 was aboard *Riviera* the remaining three on *Empress*. Apart from the engines, and overall dimensions, the Shorts were similar in appearance. They were large single-engined two-seater biplanes, the upper wing of longer span than the lower, with two forward thrusting, flat bottomed, floats. A tail float with water rudder was installed on struts under the rear fuselage, small cylindrical air bags were also fitted under the lower wing tips. Bombs were carried on light racks under the fuselage, located so that the bombs would not foul the float struts when released. Bomb aiming was primitive in the extreme, the pilot looking through a hole in the bottom of the fuselage and releasing the bombs when the target appeared.

The seaplane carriers and their escorts, the light cruisers *Arethusa* and *Undaunted* and eight destroyers, sailed from Harwich on 24 December 1914. Sailing separately, Commodore S in *Lurcher* with *Firedrake* and ten submarines in company, was to establish submarine observation of the German ports ready to make attacks on any vessels coming out to attack the force, and to pick up any pilots unable to return to the seaplane carriers. As in previous operations, elements of the Grand Fleet were to be in the North Sea as distant cover in case the High Seas Fleet sortied. Over 100 vessels from the Grand Fleet at Scapa and Rosyth were involved, concentrated north of the Dogger Bank for the operation.

The Harwich Force spent a quiet night until just before dawn when they ran through a line of German fishing trawlers. Radio messages were heard shortly afterwards and Tyrwhitt, concerned that they had been discovered, came close to cancelling the raid. Shortly before dawn, whilst he was considering what action to take, through the fog lying over the calm sea they saw a light shining in the east, which was eventually identified as the planet Venus. For Tyrwhitt all misgivings disappeared, '[...] I had no doubts or fears. I firmly believe the Almighty arranged for that star [*sic*] to act in this peculiar manner.'

Dawn came cold and still with broken fog patches, nevertheless it was decided to launch the floatplanes. The three carriers came to rest in line abreast, approximately fifteen miles north-east of Heligoland, with *Engadine* in the middle and *Empress* and *Riviera* to port and starboard respectively. Between 6.15 a.m. and 6.45 a.m. all machines were hoisted out. In the cold morning air the air mechanics, precariously balanced on the floats of the assortment of Short designs, attempted to start recalcitrant engines. Shortly before 7 a.m., as the sky was becoming brighter, Malone gave the signal to take-off. The orders had said that the slower 100 hp machines would take-off first followed, after a five minute interval, by the remaining machines. This part of the plan fell apart immediately as none of the machines were ready to go. However, over the next twenty minutes, seven of the nine floatplanes got away and, after taking aboard the two non-starters, the force got underway for the recovery rendezvous.

First away was Flt Cdr Francis E. T. Hewlett from *Riviera* flying solo on 135. He was quickly followed by Flt S/Lt Vivian Gaskell Blackburn with CPO James Bell (Mechanic) on 814 and Flt Cdr Douglas A. Oliver with CPO Budds (Mechanic) on 815. The third machine from *Empress* (812, Flt Lt Reginald J. Bone with Air Mechanic Waters) failed to take-off due to engine failure. The remaining machines got off within a minute or so or each other. From *Engadine* Flt Cdr Robert Peel Ross on 119 and Flt Lt Arnold J. Miley on 120 both flew solo, the third machine (122, Flt Cdr A. B. Gaskell) suffered engine failure and did not take-off. Finally, from *Riviera*, came Flt Lt Charles H. K. Edmonds flying solo on 811 and Flt Cdr Cecil F. Kilner with his observer Lt Robert Erskine Childers were off on 136.

After take-off the crews all had similar experiences. Most reported seeing several trawlers, probably working in the swept channel, they also sighted an airship. Kilner and Childers 'sighted a large German airship of the Schütte-Lanz type on the port bow, steering west. We circled round and endeavoured to get above her with the view of attack, but at 4,500 feet gave up the attempt, her rate of climbing being superior to ours.' Every report of the flight contains descriptions of the poor visibility over land, resulting in all the pilots wandering over an invisible landscape. Flt Lt Miley's report is typical, 'The land was completely covered with a low lying mist, which blotted out everything except what was lying immediately under the machine.' Several of the pilots believed they came close to the sheds, Flt Lt Edmonds not being alone in deciding that even if he found them, 'the bombs when dropped from the altitude at which I was forced to fly would probably not explode.'

Returning to the seaplane carriers the pilots did their best to complete the reconnaissances requested, Kilner and Childers presenting a very complete set of observations. They passed over the island of Wangeroog looking for a reported submarine base. There was no sign of the base but the island did possess two well manned anti-aircraft guns, 'firing a bursting shell of a shrapnel type. The fusing was excellent, bursts occurring frequently just at our level, and in some cases the direction was very nearly accurate. Two drift wires were severed and a chassis strut damaged.' After passing Wangeroog Flt Cdr Oliver passed over Langeoog Island, 'sighted row of red coloured sheds, which might have been seaplane base; houses behind. Flew over and dropped three bombs, second taking effect, and apparently destroying one shed.'

Edmonds was the only pilot to report attacking naval ships:

On leaving the coast I got into clearer air, and sighted on my starboard bow two light cruisers at anchor, with three and four funnels respectively. I decided to attack the latter and climbed to 1,000 feet. When I got close both ships opened fire with rifles, maxims, and anti-aircraft guns. I glided to 800 feet and released my bombs, but could not see the result.

His targets were the SMS *Graudenz* (three funnels) and SMS *Stralsund* (four funnels). German reports account for only two of Edmunds three bombs, the closest exploding 200 yards from *Graudenz*. The anti-aircraft fire was accurate, Edmonds later finding 'five bullet holes and one due to shrapnel.'

Aboard SMS *Helgoland*, Seaman Stumpf's Christmas was disturbed by the British floatplanes:

The extreme heavy fog prevented me from seeing anything but I could hear the noise of their motors quite distinctly. Our ships all fired at the invisible enemy with gusto. One of their dirigibles [*sic*] dropped two bombs on a cruiser escort and a steamer and started a huge fire. Two of the aircraft were later fished out of the sea near Helgoland. We had probably shot them down.

Whilst inaccurate, the 'dirigible' story has the appearance of a rumour exaggerated version of Edmonds attack. The two salvaged aircraft were probably the floating remains of machines that failed to return to the seaplane carriers, which is where we must now turn to complete the story of the Cuxhaven Raid.

After recovering the two floatplanes that failed to take-off, the seaplane carriers and their Harwich Force escort set course for the recovery position north of Norderney Island. Although the squadron had been undisturbed during the one and a half hours they had spent launching the floatplanes, shortly after moving off a Zeppelin (L6, based at Nordholz) was seen approaching from the direction of Heligoland. Following close after the airship several German seaplanes (Friedrichshafen FF19, Marine Numbers 29 and 80, and Friedrichshafen FF29, Marine Number 202) came in to attack the seaplane carriers. Malone reported that he 'was much impressed by the accuracy of their bomb dropping. The German seaplanes flew at a height of about 4,000 feet; it appeared that their sights must be carefully designed as most of the bombs seemed to drop right for direction and speed.'

Lagging behind the squadron, her engines suffering from 'condenseritis', *Empress* was given special attention from the German airmen. The commander of *Empress*, Lt Frederick W. Bowhill, reported the attacks in detail:

The first seaplane attacked from the starboard bow, at a height of about 2,000 feet, after flying close to the Zeppelin which was on the starboard beam, and commenced operations by dropping a star bomb; this signal, I presume, meaning 'am about to attack'.

Crossing over the bows of *Empress* from starboard to port:

> The aviator dropped three pairs of bombs, but made very bad shooting, the
> bombs dropping from 200 to 300 yards away on our starboard bow. A second
> seaplane attacked from the port bow at a height of about 1,800 feet, dropping
> two fairly large bombs.
> This attack was nearly successful, one bomb dropping 20 feet away on port
> beam and shaking the ship severely, and the other 40 feet off the starboard beam.
>   The method of defence adopted was to arm the gun's crews with rifles, and
> volleys were fired at the seaplanes, a few picked shots keeping up independent
> firing. As far as could be judged, the seaplanes were undamaged. I continuously
> kept on altering my course throughout the attacks.

The Zeppelin now made an attack 'by rising to about 5,000 feet on the starboard
beam and coming over towards me. When nearly directly overhead she dived to
about 2,000 feet, and then manoeuvred to get directly above me, slowing down,
and heading in the same direction as myself.' After dropping a pair of sighting
bombs L6 followed up with three large bombs, estimated at 100 lbs each. Bowhill
avoided the bombs by commencing a hard turn, then when:

> I could see her rudders put over to follow me, and directly her head started to
> turn, I put my helm over the other way. I continually repeated this manoeuvre,
> which seemed to worry her, for she was never on a steady course, and I think it
> put her off her aim; otherwise I fail to see how she could have missed us.

About this time heavy shrapnel bursts began to appear around the airship. Tyrwhitt,
seeing the exposed position of *Empress*, had reversed course with *Arethusa* and
Undaunted both cruisers opening fire with their main armament. This drove the airship
off, sped on her way by some shots from *Empress'* 12 pdr guns. When L6 landed back
at Nordholz, during a brief break in the fog and low clouds, the airshipmen found
nine bullet holes in the gas cells possibly the work of *Engadine*'s massed riflemen.

For the present that was the end of German attacks. The seaplane carriers and
escorts reformed and set course for the recovery rendezvous. Shortly after 9.30
a.m. reinforcements in the form of *Fearless* and eight destroyers joined the screen
around the seaplane carriers.

By this time all the floatplanes from the raid were in the area of Norderney and
swinging north for the rendezvous. Some were damaged and several were having
engine problems. Of the seven floatplanes that set out only three returned to
the carriers, one of these being towed by a destroyer. Two of *Riviera*'s machines
returned, Kilner and Childers on 136 landed safely with the damage previously
mentioned, being hoisted in at 10.20 a.m. and Edmonds on 811 five minutes later.
Both machines had been airborne for over three hours and in the case of Kilner and

Childers were returning on only half an engine. The 200 hp Canton-Unné radial engine had two rows of seven cylinders, in effect two engines bolted together, they reported that 'serious engine trouble developed and we were forced to fly on the front engine only for the rest of the flight.' At 10.30 a.m. *Lurcher* brought 119 alongside *Engadine* to be hoisted in. Flt Cdr Ross, after being forced down around 8.30 a.m. to correct a problem with his fuel system, was able to get off with a faltering fuel pump. Spotting *Lurcher* and *Firedrake* at 9.10 a.m. he landed and was taken in tow by the former.

Three of the missing machines, running low on fuel and unable to reach the rendezvous, were able to land alongside the submarine *E.11* (Lt Cdr Martin E. Naismith). First to land was Flt Lt Miley on *120*, after being unable to see anything whilst over land he was able to make some useful observations of ships lying in the Weser and Schillig Roads. At 9.35 a.m. he saw a periscope immediately beneath him; this was *E.11* which surfaced taking Miley aboard and 120 in tow. A few minutes later 814 and 815, both low on fuel landed close alongside. After dropping his bombs on Langeoog Island Flt Cdr Oliver and his mechanic CPO Budds had proceeded towards the rendezvous, spotting 120 in tow of the submarine Oliver decided to land. A few minutes earlier Flt S/Lt Blackburn and his mechanic CPO Bell, had also landed close to the submarine. Whilst over Wilhelmshaven, they had been 'subjected to an extremely hot anti-aircraft fire; one of the shells struck the float, passed through it and carried away the fitting of the starboard chassis strut.' The chassis held together through the landing but whilst taxiing toward *E.11* it collapsed and the machine went up on its nose.

Naismith was now in a difficult position. Shortly before the two machines landed an airship (Zeppelin L5) was seen to be closing, and a submarine which was also approaching was seen to dive and had to be considered hostile. The tow was cast off, all crews taken aboard the submarine and quickly hustled below. Whilst all this was going on the airship was getting close and Naismith took off his cap and waved it in a friendly gesture. With all the crews aboard, and rifle bullet holes through all the floats and petrol tanks, Naismith dived his boat to safety below the waves. Two bombs exploded on the surface as the boat passed 40 feet depth. Safely on the bottom, Naismith and his crew shared their Christmas meal with their guests before returning them safely to Harwich the following day.

The mysterious submarine was another British boat D.6 (Lt Cdr R. C. Halahan). Halahan was closing at full speed to assist Naismith but had to dive when the airship turned toward his submarine. After seeing *E.11* dive safely Halahan surfaced alongside one of the abandoned floatplanes, probably 120, to rescue the crew if necessary. On surfacing, he saw the airship within a hundred yards at a height of not more than 50 feet. A heavy fire, apparently from a machine gun, was opened on the submarine and seaplane. Finding the seaplane abandoned, he dived again at once.

Whilst recovering the three machines which had returned, the seaplane carriers were attacked once again, 'A second Zeppelin and several hostile seaplanes now approached from the southward; all dropped bombs without success.' German records show that only two seaplanes were involved, Friedrichshafen FF19s, Marine Numbers 25 (flown by *Kapitänleutnant* Berthold, commander of the Heligoland *SFS*) and 84. They ignored the seaplane carriers and concentrated their attacks on escorts, without making any hits. The German seaplanes were greeted by everything the British could put up against them, anti-aircraft guns, machine guns and rifles all contributed to the barrage. Returning to Heligoland Berthold's machine 'collapsed entirely' on landing and was written off.

As the attacks ended Tyrwhitt signalled, perhaps ironically, 'I wish all ships a merry Christmas.' By this time Tyrwhitt reluctantly realised that no further machines would be returning. The assembled force shaped course back to Harwich.

The Grand Fleet far to the north had taken no part in the events of Christmas Day, but would suffer more than either the Harwich Force or the High Seas Fleet. Returning to its bases a severe storm blew up. Approaching Scapa Flow at the height of the storm the dreadnoughts *Conqueror* and *Monarch* collided. The stern of the latter was stove in and the stem and bow of *Conqueror* badly damaged. Both ships required extensive dockyard repairs. The battle cruisers returning to Rosyth also suffered storm damage, but it could be quickly repaired by the dockyard.

There remains one floatplane unaccounted for; it would be early in the New Year before Flt Cdr Hewlett could tell his story. After leaving *Riviera* on 135 he set course directly towards Cuxhaven. Passing over the anchorage in the Elbe, partially hidden in the thick mist, he was spotted and fired upon by several ships. Now over land he sought the sheds, but could not see any land marks:

At 8.5 a.m. I should have been very near the sheds, and as I could see nothing above 150 to 200 feet I realised that it would be useless to drop my bombs. I therefore altered course for the return journey at 8.8 and at 8.20 I ran out of the mist and found myself clear of the land with nothing in sight.

At 8.40 a Zeppelin airship [probably L5] came out of a cloud quite close to me, 1,500 feet above and inshore of me. She opened fire apparently with rifle or small gun, but the machine was not hit. As I could not climb above her and we were of about equal speed I altered course to the westward again and soon got out of range.

As I had sighted no islands or land since 8.20 a.m. I considered it time to alter to N. at 9.12, calculating that I should be on the correct bearing for meeting the seaplane carriers and flotilla, *i.e.*, N. of Norderney Island.

At 9.25 the engine began to misfire slightly, and the revolutions dropped, and I noticed that the oil pulsations in the sighting glasses were becoming very feeble. In a few minutes the glasses emptied and the engine was obviously overheating.

Looking around he saw a small trawler flying a Dutch flag. Landing alongside he was able to taxy over and tie up astern. There was no engine oil aboard the trawler, the

Maria van Hattem, and Hewlett was unable to restart the engine. The fishermen took the floatplane under tow but, at the end of a long day as it was growing dark and the wind rising, Hewlett reluctantly punched holes in the main floats and shot holes in the tail float using his revolver. The machine sank by the bow, dragged under by the heavy engine, until just the tail surfaces were above water and had to be abandoned in that condition as the remarkably patient trawler men had a living to earn. Hewlett was landed at Ymuiden on 31 December 1914. It was important that Hewlett be officially recognized as a shipwrecked seaman by the Dutch authorities, that way he could avoid internment and be repatriated. The British Vice Consul was able to start this process and a few days later, in the British Embassy in the Hague, Hewlett sat down to write his report. He arrived back in Harwich on 3 January 1915. Hewlett was the first RNAS pilot to benefit from the shipwrecked mariner ploy, he would not be the last.

Safely returned to Harwich, those involved settled down to writing their reports. Tyrwhitt's report, dated 27 December, contains many observations and initial lessons learned. The airships did not impress him, declaring that attacks could be avoided with little difficulty, 'an 8 point turn places them out of action for a considerable period, observing that ships must not be in line ahead,' echoing the practical experiences of Bowhill in *Empress*. Lt Bowhill also believed, 'that had an anti-aircraft gun been on board we could not have failed to bring her down, as the target was so large, and that any ship so fitted would always bring a Zeppelin down in daytime, should she attack.' That may have been the case on that particular Christmas Day, but airships would quickly learn to keep at a safe distance from any Royal Navy ship. Eventually, the only way to attack the airship was by a single-seat fighter launched from one of the ships. Generally, the attacks by the German airships and seaplanes were not viewed too seriously:

It was generally necessary to wait to see if the seaplane in question dropped a bomb before opening fire, which at times caused considerable merriment amongst the ships' companies, who could not be induced to look on the attacks from Zeppelins or seaplanes in any light except that of a chance of firing a weapon of any sort.

Tyrwhitt concluded:

I am quite convinced that, given ordinary sea room, our ships have nothing to fear from seaplanes or Zeppelins.

The commanders of the seaplane carriers, all qualified pilots, had a number of professional observations and recommendations. Squadron Commander Malone, *Engadine*, being particularly perceptive:

In conclusion, I look upon the events which took place on 25th December as a visible proof of the probable line in the development of the principles of naval strategy. One can well imagine what might have been done had our seaplanes, or those which were sent out to attack us, carried torpedoes or light guns.

The only machines to return directly to the seaplane carriers came from *Riviera*. Perhaps this was in part due to her captain, Lt E. D. M. Robertson, ordering 'my pilots to take four hours petrol instead of three.' The machines coming down alongside *E11* had been in the air for less than three hours and were almost out of fuel, whereas those returning to *Riviera* had been in the air well over three hours. He praised the 200 hp Short 135 Folder, for:

> Possessing very good climb, high speed, big fuel endurance, and when more fully known, a reliable engine, this machine appears to stand out well above the other types used, and I strongly recommend that further machines of this type should be ordered and sent to the carrier.

Similar versions would be produced by the Short Brothers in the near future. The Short 166 was slightly larger than the Short 135 but retained the 200 hp Canton-Unné engine, an improved design the Short 827/830 followed. The Short 827 having a V8 Sunbeam 155 hp engine, the Short 830 a 135 hp Salmson radial engine. Finally, the Short 184, with 225 hp V12 Sunbeam engine, was being developed and would become the most widely used British floatplane of the war.

So what had the raid achieved? On the face of it the British losses of four floatplanes to one German was poor return for the effort. Also, the Grand Fleet lost the use of *Monarch* for one month and *Conqueror* for two and a half months. Due to the persistent fog little intelligence had been gained. The airship sheds had not been located. Only one pilot, Flt Lt C. H. K. Edmonds, succeeded in aiming his bombs at identified targets, the light cruisers *Stralsund* and *Graudenz*, the nearest of which missed by 200 yards. However, the morale ascendancy of the Royal Navy over the German Navy had moved up another notch. The small, weak force had been operating for several hours within fifty miles of the German coastline. Other than the seaplanes and airships, which had the good fortune to discover them, it had been unmolested by the second largest fleet in the world. Materially, although four were lost, the Short floatplanes generally performed well and received some praise.

Flight in its issue of 1 January 1915 commented:

> The Cuxhaven raid marks the first employment of the seaplanes of the Naval Air Service in an attack on the enemy's harbours from the sea, and, apart altogether from the results achieved, is an occasion of historical moment. Not only so, but for the first time in history a naval attack has been delivered simultaneously above, on, and from below the surface of the water.

Which is as fair a judgement as you can give.

4

Operations with the Harwich Force, 1915

The Cuxhaven Raid had shown up the weaknesses of the seaplane carriers, which were far from perfect. It was recognized that the arrangements were of a temporary nature, something that would shortly be addressed, and they were all on the small size, future conversions would need to be larger. Their speed was adequate for operations with the Harwich Force but, if they were to operate with the Grand Fleet or battle cruisers, something more would be needed. *Empress* particularly suffered in this respect, having already lagged behind whilst off the German coast. On the return to Harwich Bowhill noted that:

> I had some difficulty in keeping up with the fleet, and also had a lot of trouble to keep steam, […] necessitating the employment of all the engine room ratings for the whole time. The air mechanics also assisted the stokers.

They were also inadequately armed for self-protection. The next seaplane carrier to arrive at Harwich would begin to address many of these problems.

As early as 25 October 1914 discussions were taking place concerning the requisition of additional steamers for conversion to seaplane carriers, including one for the Grand Fleet. The debate was given added impetus with loss of *Hermes* a few days later. On 27 November 1914 the Admiralty bought the old Cunarder *Campania*, saving her from the scrap yard, with the intention of making her into a seaplane carrier fit to accompany the Grand Fleet. Then, in January 1915, *Ben-my-Chree* was requisitioned from the Isle of Man Steam Packet Company, for use with the Harwich Force. We will return to *Campania* in a later chapter, for now looking at the conversion of *Ben-my-Chree*. Pre-war, she had been a crowd favourite during the summer holiday season between Liverpool and the Isle of Man. Launched in 1908 she was the third ship to bear the name, *Ben-my-Chree* or 'Woman of my Heart'. Designed to be fast, she made over 24 knots on trials, and comfortable for her 2,549 passengers, she was 390 feet long and 2,250 grt, significantly larger than *Engadine*, *Riviera* and *Empress*. She was handed over to Cammell, Laird and Company, Birkenhead, where the conversion was to be carried out.

The first task was to strip *Ben-my-Chree* of most of her peace time comforts. The ship's cabins and saloons were converted into officers' accommodations, ward room, a wireless office, intelligence office, and sick bay. The wheel house was completely rebuilt and enlarged. On the lower deck, first class saloons in the fore part of the ship were transformed into stokers and seamen's mess decks, and a large sick bay. Instead of lifeboats *Ben-my-Chree* now carried three motor launches (20 foot, 25 foot and 30 foot), needed to assist with towing floatplanes, a 28 foot whaler and two 18 foot cutters. Two 12 pdr quick firing guns were mounted on the forward end of the promenade deck. Between the guns was space for a single floatplane, which was to take-off from a simple removable take-off platform running over the bows from the promenade deck, the foremast was fitted with a suitable boom to handle the machine.

All structure aft of the second funnel above upper deck level was removed. On to the space thus created a large-slab sided hangar was constructed. Measuring 80 feet by 40 feet, and some 18 feet high, it could accommodate several floatplanes, the exact number varying according to the type carried. The usual mix was two or three large, folding-wing Shorts and two, or more, smaller Sopwith single-seat floatplanes. The aft end of the hangar could be closed off by two steel roller blind type doors, with a removable central post. The main mast, which had been removed during the surgery to create the hangar space, was stepped and rigged on top of the hangar. Between it and the fore mast were rigged wireless telegraphy aerials. At the forward corners of the hangar roof two 3-pdr anti-aircraft guns were installed on raised platforms. There remained 65 feet of open deck aft of the hangar. Of this only 40 to 45 feet was relatively unobstructed and available for handling the floatplanes. At the aft end of this space a kingpost, and boom powered by a steam donkey engine, was stepped for lifting the floatplanes. The width of deck tapered from 40 feet at the hangar doors to 30 feet at the kingpost. Aft of the kingpost were an emergency steering position and two more 12-pdr guns. On the main deck below the hangar, the space once occupied by the second class saloon became an aviation workshop. Fully equipped, it boasted three lathes, two drill presses, a shaping machine and a circular saw, in fact just about everything necessary to build the wooden aeroplane structures of the day. Large components could be lowered into the workshop through a 10 foot by 5 foot hatch in the hangar deck. One deck further down, in what used to be the second class dining saloon, were located aviation store rooms and accommodation for the Air Department ratings. Below the forward mess deck, space was found for magazines, bomb and torpedo rooms. Hoists for the munitions pierced through all decks to reach the upper and promenade decks. Fuel for the ship was also a problem that had to be solved. Built for short daily round trips, her bunkerage was insufficient for extended operations. So, additional bunkers were built along both outboard sides of the main deck, over the engine and boiler rooms, providing coal capacity sufficient for five or six days operation at cruising speed. The additions increased *Ben-my Chree*'s displacement by almost 700 tons, some of which was ballast added forward to counteract the mass of the aft hangar structure. The hangar caused another problem, the big side area 'acting like a spanker, made her tricky in a strong wind at slow speed', otherwise she was reported to handle like a destroyer.

It all took time and on 10 February, well before the work was complete, *Engadine* arrived on the Mersey to be followed by *Riviera* four days later. They both went into Cunard's docks at Liverpool, on the other side of the river, to receive similar refits to *Ben-my Chree*'s. The three ships shared more than engineering experience. From *Engadine* came *Ben-my Chree*'s commanding officer, Squadron Commander C. J. L'Estrange Malone, and her intelligence officer, Lt Robert Erskine Childers, RNVR. Some of the seamen and many of the engineering staff were ex-Isle of Man Steam Packet Company, including the chief engineer. Engineer Lieutenant G. Robinson, RNR, had been with *Ben-my-Chree* since 1908, and was to remain aboard throughout her commission. Included in the ship's company of over 200 were the Air Department which averaged 40 officers and ratings of the RNAS.

Ben-my-Chree commissioned as a ship of the Royal Navy on 23 March 1915, and finally left dockyard hands four days later. Following a brief work-up at Calshot, she arrived at Harwich by the end of April. Her entrance into Harwich was far from triumphant, running aground on a well-buoyed sandbank. She had to await high tide and a tug before working free, fortunately without damage to the hull. Already tied up at their buoys off Parkstone Quay were *Engadine*, with her new commander Flt Cdr Robert Peel Ross, and *Riviera*, fresh from their refits. Retaining their original crews, they required less working up. The last of the original trio, *Empress*, had sailed a few days earlier to Liverpool for her conversion.

The Christmas Day operation was the last conducted by the Harwich Force carriers before *Engadine* and *Riviera* departed for their conversions. *Empress*, the sole remaining carrier, with two or three Short floatplanes under her canvas shelters, made two attempts on 20 and 23 March 1915, to attack an important wireless station at Norddeich, near Emden, that it would be very advantageous to have eliminated or disabled. Both attempts were foiled by bad weather, the first by a 'lumpy sea and strong wind' the second by thick fog. During the attempt on 23 March the two escorting cruisers, *Arethusa* and *Aurora*, each carried a Sopwith Schneider single-seat floatplane, the operational introduction of the type.

The next operation to be attempted appears to have had its origins in a proposal submitted by Flt Cdr Ross to Squadron Commander Malone. Dated 4 April 1915, Peel suggested an ambitious attack on Kiel using 'fast machines of Schneider cup design,' an alternate was offered for the Shorts to attack the wireless station at Norddeich. Malone forwarded the proposal to the Director Air department two days later noting that:

It will be remembered that the attack on Kiel Canal was the first scheme proposed by me.

With the seaplanes then available, this was not feasible, at any rate with much chance of success.

The advent of the small high-speed seaplane has made this scheme more practicable.

Possibly Malone's 'first scheme' was a now lost proposal for the attempts that preceded the Cuxhaven Raid. He continues:

I see no reason why each ship should not carry FIVE or SIX tabloids [The Sopwith Schneider was a development of the landplane Tabloid.], and each tabloid carrying, say, six 20 lbs bombs.

If these were all concentrated on the lock gates, considerable damage might be done, the effect on the ships would be less.

But, again, if the Canal is to be the objective, surely it would be better to attack the gates at Brunsbüttel, or even one of the massive high level railway bridges, which would be considerably nearer.

The proposal probably seemed too ambitious, possibly unrealistic, to the Air Department at the Admiralty as the Operation Order sent to Harwich was for a much less exacting task based on Peel's alternate for the Shorts.

The Air Department's Operation Order No. 1.D.12 set an objective:

To obtain photographs of the Island of Borkum whilst deluding the enemy that the objective is solely bomb dropping.

It was proposed that photographers and cameras would be carried by two Shorts and a camera by one of the Schneiders. Additional machines, carrying 100 lb and 20 lb bombs, were to attack the wireless station at Norddeich and 'the Airship Shed at Norden' (actually located at Hage a few miles east of Norden), then carry on to make a reconnaissance of Emden Harbour. The three available seaplane carriers, *Ben-my-Chree*, *Riviera* and *Engadine*, escorted by the Harwich Force were to take part. Initial plans indicate that as many as six of the new Short 184, 225 hp, floatplanes might be available, although only orders to send the first two machines, 184 and 185, to *Riviera* exist, in the end neither would be available as both were involved with prototype testing at the Isle of Grain and Felixstowe. The first production machine would not be ready until late in May. Later events suggest that the carriers may have had a mix of Shorts and Sopwith Schneider floatplanes aboard.

The operation was attempted on 3 May 1915, early that morning, the take-off platform was rigged over the bows of *Ben-my-Chree*, and Schneider 1445 taken forward where it was mounted on a wheeled trolley ready for use, Flight Sub Lt A. S. Maskell being selected to pilot it. Shortly thereafter the Harwich Force sailed with the three carriers and a covering force of four cruisers and eight destroyers. The force ploughed across the North Sea in the hope of better weather, but the following morning the sea was too rough and the raid abandoned.

At 5.00 a.m. on 6 May *Ben-my-Chree* slipped from her buoy in a fog-enveloped harbour. Four minutes later, the destroyer *Lennox* was glimpsed through the fog crossing her bows from port to starboard. Having bare steerage way, the former was unable to avoid the destroyer and rammed into her starboard quarter. The destroyer captain, in his fury, was heard to swear that it was just his luck to be run into by a 'bloody Saturday afternoon battleship,' a pointed reminder of his assailant's origins. Because of the low speeds involved, little damage was done to either ship, *Ben-my-Chree* suffering a few sprung plates and the bow rudder jammed, all of which was quickly repaired. Of the three carriers available only she was involved, together with *Arethusa* and *Undaunted*, both of which were carrying Schneiders. It seems likely that an attempt to raid Norddeich with a small, fast force was planned. The collision put paid to the plan, and when the fog cleared in the afternoon *Ben-my-Chree* returned to her buoy.

Schneider *1445* was again sitting on the take-off platform on 11 May when all three carriers sailed at 6.40 a.m., with the same objectives and covering force as 3 May. At 4.10 p.m. that afternoon an airship was sighted in the distance. *Ben-my-Chree* pulled out of line, turned into wind and attempted to launch the Schneider. The engine could be started from the cockpit by turning a handle, however, when attempted on this day there was an explosion, after which the engine backfired, briefly ran backwards and then caught fire. The fire fortunately burnt out once the fuel which had collected in the bottom of the cowling had been consumed. More serious was the damage caused in the cockpit. When the engine backfired, the handle used to start the engine had been ripped out of Maskell's hand breaking his wrist, then proceeding to smash all the instruments in the cockpit as it continued to rotate with the engine. So ended the first, and last, attempt to use the take-off platform. Now *Engadine* fell out of line and, covered by four destroyers, stopped to launch three Schneiders all of which got off safely. However, they soon flew into fog and turned back, only one being able to alight alongside *Engadine* before the fog completely enveloped the force. Of the two remaining machines one, 1443, spun in, killing the pilot. The other, 1444, smashed up on landing although the pilot was rescued by one of the escorting destroyers, the remains of the machine also being taken aboard. Once again bad weather, and discovery by the airship, forced abandonment of the raid, the force returning to Harwich.

With this failure, the carrier squadron was dispersed. The break-up of the squadron may be seen as a tacit admission that the floatplanes currently available were not adequate for conditions in the North Sea. Whilst it is true that the Schneiders would prove to be extremely fragile, the larger Shorts, especially the new 184's, were much more seaworthy. However, pressing requirements for the seaplane carriers elsewhere was the most probable cause of the dispersion. *Engadine* was sent north to join the Battle Cruiser Squadron in the Firth of Forth, *Riviera* went to Dover, and then on to Dunkirk, as base ship for the RNAS floatplanes operating from those ports. *Empress* remained at Harwich for a while, later moving to southern Ireland to conduct anti-submarine patrols and then moved on to Egypt. *Ben-my-Chree* was destined for Gallipoli and the Dardanelles.

For the remainder of May and June the only machines taken to sea were single Sopwith Schneiders carried on the light cruisers of the Harwich Force. It was intended that they should be used in an anti-Zeppelin role. On 2 June an airship was sighted approaching the Harwich Force. *Arethusa* came to a stop and the Schneider (probably 1441) was hoisted out and, despite damage to the floats, successfully took off. At 1,800 feet it was seen to be climbing well when the pilot suddenly turned back and landed, causing further damage.

The pilot claimed that he had mistaken smoke made by one of the accompanying destroyers for a recall signal. Some of *Arethusa*'s officers saw things otherwise, blaming 'the utter incapacity of the pilot alone, for failing, as they expressed it, to pick off one of the VC's which were simply hanging on to this Zeppelin. They described him as a child.' Harsh words, but it should be noted that the Schneider was relatively new to service and there were no fully experienced pilots available. Reviewing the attempt, Tyrwhitt was of the opinion that they were 'too small and too difficult to handle.' Time would prove him correct.

At the beginning of July *Engadine* and *Riviera* were recalled to Harwich, a new scheme, Operation G, was being planned. The Admiralty had received reports that transports were being collected in the Ems river. The floatplanes were required to reconnoitre the area of Emden and Borkum island off the mouth of the Ems river, if the airships could be drawn out and attacked that was all to the good as well. At dawn on 4 July the force arrived some thirty miles north of Ameland island, about sixty miles north-west of Emden. For once:

> . . . the sea was calm enough for seaplanes to be operated. The two carriers stopped and hoisted out their seaplanes, while destroyers from the flotilla circled around to keep off any submarines which might be in the vicinity.

'Hoisted out their seaplanes,' what did that involve? Gerald Edward 'Gerry' Livock, then a Flt S/Lt on *Engadine* but attached to *Riviera* for this sortie, describes the evolution in his memoirs:

> Four Short seaplanes, which had folding wings, were pushed in and out of the hangar on trolleys. The procedure for launching was as follows. The seaplane was first wheeled out of the hangar on to the after deck, where the wings were

spread. When the pilot and passenger had embarked, the plane was hoisted off its trolley and over the ship's side. As soon as the floats touched the water the engine was started and the passenger slipped the crane hook. The pilot then taxied the seaplane away from the ship and, if the engine was running properly and the sea wasn't too rough, he took off. To return to the ship, the pilot taxied up to the crane hook, which was hung out over the ship's side, and the passenger fitted the hook into slings on the top plane—not a very easy manoeuvre, especially in a strong wind or rough sea.

Single-seater pilots of course had to pick up their own hooks, and could be as busy as the proverbial one-armed paper hanger at such times.

Engadine had a Short 830, 819 (Flt S/Lt Sorley), and three Schneiders, 3711 (Flt Lt D'Arcy Levy), 3712 (Flt Lt Moon) and 3714 (Flt Lt F. J. Rutland), aboard for this operation, whilst *Riviera* carried four Short 830s, 1335, 1337, 1338 and 1339. At 2.30 a.m. the carriers began hoisting out their seaplanes. It was not *Engadine*'s day, none of her machines were able to get away and all three Schneiders were lost. Sorley was having engine problems, 'CPO Mech Brooks was sent to assist. Having started the engine, Brooks jumped overboard from the seaplane and was picked up by the dinghy. Seaplane 819 then proceeded to taxi, but getting in the wash of a Destroyer, split her propeller and had to be subsequently hoisted in.' This is not the only time a mechanic, having cured an engine problem, jumped into the sea to be pulled out by a ship's boat. They were skilled and dedicated craftsmen, working long hours and taking risks to ensure the machines were in the best possible condition.

Each of the Schneiders suffered float failure, *Engadine*'s commander Flt Cdr Ross commenting:

> With regard to the floats, it is of interest to note that these machines were quite new, the only flying they had done was their acceptance trials. Nevertheless when brought on board two pairs of floats had to be changed, the original ones being split and broken after one flight.
>
> The cause of failure was undoubtedly due to very weak construction of floats.

Unfortunately, this would not be the last time poor construction would affect the Schneider's performance with further reports of float failures coming from shore bases. Eventually, the problem would be solved but the Schneider was gaining a poor reputation. The weak floats was not a problem limited to the Schneiders, it was endemic to British float design at the time. Attempting to make them as light as possible, the designers had also made them too weak. Although the Short floats stood up to North Sea conditions quite well, in warmer climes the floats were known to disintegrate if not carefully maintained. At least all of her pilots were safe, although they suffered a ducking in the North Sea.

Riviera had a little more success. All four machines were able to take-off by 2.50 a.m. and set off eastward towards the German coast. Just twenty minutes to get four floatplanes launched and in the air was an impressive performance, especially when compared to the Cuxhaven Raid. Livock recalled:

I was given Short Type 830 No. 1335, which was armed with four 16 lb bombs, a revolver and a Very pistol. Considerations of weight did not allow an observer to be carried.

None of the Shorts carried an observer this day. Livock passed by Borkum and crossed the coast whilst at 1,600 feet:

Then the engine faltered. In a state of panic I turned round and steered back towards the ships with the engine popping and banging, but luckily maintaining just sufficient power to keep me in the air.

Four airships had been drawn towards the ships and Livock had to fly right under one to get back to his carrier. 'I suppose the Zepp must have spotted me, for he slowly turned, stuck his nose in the air and climbed away.' The cruisers were by this time firing their main armament at the Zeppelins, some of the bursts coming too close to Livock for his peace of mind. Landing and taxiing up to the ship:

... much too fast, missed the crane hook and hit the ship's side with a splintering crash, which shattered the propeller. The handling party, however, heaved a line to me and I was hoisted on board.

Squadron Commander Francis E. T. Hewlett, promoted since the Cuxhaven Raid, returned a good twenty minutes before Livock. His Short, 1338, had also suffering from engine problems.

Flight Lieutenant E. I. M. 'Dicky' Bird on 1339 failed to return. After setting out with the others he had flown over Juist and Borkum but failed to find the carriers on his return. The operational instructions had been clear on the conduct expected under these circumstances:

If possible, Pilots should fall into Dutch hands and claim the privilege of a shipwrecked mariner, i.e., they should not on any account admit being a prisoner of war liable to internment, but demand repatriation.

With his engine oil and petrol running low he was forced to land alongside a Dutch trawler. He got the trawler's skipper to run down and destroy his machine then take him on to Holland. Here he was registered as a shipwrecked mariner and, after a few days, returned to his ship.

Not suffering from engine troubles, the fourth pilot Flt Lt Harry Stewart, on 1337, made a good flight. He made a reconnaissance of the islands and of the Ems river, finding no transports in the area. He dropped one of his bombs on a battery located at Knock Point (deep into the Ems estuary close to Emden) and two more on torpedo boats lying close to the mouth of the Ems. He then flew on to take a look at the seaplane station on Borkum. Not lingering, as he had spotted a German seaplane climbing up towards his Short, Stewart headed out to sea to find *Riviera*. He was now at 3,500 feet, above the clouds and had lost his pursuer. Seeing four airships in the distance, he realised that they were observing the movements of his ships and dived below the clouds to look for them. He soon located *Riviera* and her escorting destroyers. Remembering to drop his remaining bomb well clear of the ship, he landed alongside and was hoisted in after a flight of just over three hours.

Lt Cdr E. D. M. Robertson, his commanding officer on *Riviera*, was full of guarded praise:

Being a Direct Entry Officer, he has not had the experience in navigation or any extensive experience in observation such as a Naval Officer in his position would have had. In carrying out this reconnaissance as far as Knock Point, he performed a more extended observation than had been ordered, and his report, without naval training, appears to me to be very complete and concise.

Robertson was displaying the regular naval officer's distrust of the part time sailors beginning to flood into the wartime Royal Navy and Royal Naval Air Service. Indeed, about this time Really Not A Sailor entered the slang of the salthorses of the Navy for the RNAS. Whilst their training in the maritime arts might have been skimped, time would show that as in times past and to come the well-trained part timers were quite capable of performing the duties of the regulars. More than a handful of RNAS flyers would qualify as officers of the watch during their time with the fleet. The training of RNAS personnel was also becoming more complex as the war progressed.

5

Personnel and Training

Manning the converted seaplane carriers required a mix of regulars, reserves, wartime volunteers and Merchant Navy personnel. The commanding officer was whenever possible a prewar Royal Navy officer with RNAS experience, usually as a pilot. Under him as ship's officers were a mix of RN, RNR (often the prewar ship's officers) and, as the war went on, RNVR officers. The enlisted crew were a similar mix with, particularly in the engineering department, a number of Merchant Navy seamen and stokers recruited on T.124 papers (i.e.; although subject to naval discipline they were paid at Merchant Navy rates.). Added to this were the RNAS party. *Engadine*, for example, had a nominal crew (officers and men) of 197 including an RNAS contingent of 53. The RNAS contingent could not come from the prewar regulars, there were too few. The training schools had to provide the men for the seaplane carriers, shore stations and later the growing number of flying platforms with the fleet.

At the start of the First World War the Royal Naval Air Service comprised 128 officers and warrant officers, and just under 600 enlisted men. All were regulars. On 1 April 1918, when amalgamated with the Royal Flying Corps to form the Royal Air Force, the RNAS had over 55,000 officers and enlisted men, mostly wartime volunteers. In a highly technical service these all required special training.

Pre-war Training

Typical of the prewar flyers was Squadron Commander Cecil John L'Estrange Malone, RN, who we first met as a lieutenant flying off *London*, then as a wartime commanding officer of *Engadine* and later *Ben-my-Chree*. He entered the Royal Navy in 1905, passing through the Royal Naval College at Dartmouth in one of the first terms to use the newly completed college buildings, instead of the old 'wooden wall' *Britannia*. He followed the typical career path of a Royal Navy officer spending time in battleships, including *Dreadnought*, and cruisers followed by the lieutenants' course at the Royal Naval College, Greenwich, and command of a torpedo boat, *TB81*. Promoted lieutenant on 15 December 1911 he was selected to take a course of flying training at the Naval Flying School, Eastchurch, following which, as we have already noted, he became one of the first RNAS pilots to fly from the deck of a ship. Since that time he had been actively involved with many aspects of naval aviation, including the early development of torpedo aircraft. He was appointed to command *Engadine* in August 1914, shortly after his promotion to Squadron Commander, and was in overall command of the seaplane carriers with the Harwich Force.

Once the Central Flying School was established at Upavon initial pilot training for both the RNAS and RFC was undertaken there. It was soon recognised that once the trainee had learnt the essentials of flying, the requirements of his service were quite different, as one historian of the Central Flying School has noted:

Psychologically, the two Services were poles apart. The Navy was run on personal initiative; the Army on regulations. The Navy was a technical service in which the equipment was the prime factor and the personnel simply a means of operating it efficiently. In the Army, the man was the prime factor and the equipment merely a means of making him more efficient. The Navy's task was to sink ships; the Army's to kill men.

Once the basic training was completed the RNAS pilots were posted to the Eastchurch Naval Flying School for finishing as naval aviators. If the candidate had previous flying experience, particularly if he had already had his RAeC Certificate, then the officer concerned would be posted to Eastchurch without going through the CFS. Lieutenant Richard Bell Davies (later Vice Admiral, VC), for example, had taken his ticket at Hendon in 1911 gaining RAeC Certificate No. 90. He then spent time on the China Station before obtaining his transfer to the RNAS in 1913, being posted directly to Eastchurch to refine his flying skills.

In June 1914 a paper by Captain Murray Sueter, Director of Air Department, was circulating in the Admiralty looking at the training requirements for the RNAS following its independence on the first of the next month. It discussed the formation of a Royal Naval Air Service Reserve and looked at the instruction required for officers 'in the higher problems relating to their profession,' in other words preparation for higher rank. Most interesting, however, is a section looking forward to how the RNAS could be expanded by direct recruitment, it being anticipated that expansion could not be supported solely through volunteers from the fleet. The section on the 'Training of Civilian Officers' is particularly relevant to the rapid expansion that would soon be forced on the armed services. With some adjustments, and contraction, it provides the pattern for training during the early part of the First World War. The paper assumes that almost all of the required training will be carried out at the Sheerness Air School, located in buildings within the dockyard, the airfield at Eastchurch and a new seaplane establishment at the Isle of Grain on the opposite side of the Medway.

The paper laid out a training regime that initially emphasised discipline, drill and Royal Navy history. The candidate would then pass on to the elementary flying course at the CFS.

In summer routine flying instruction will be confined chiefly to early morning or evening hours. In winter routine to such daylight hours as are suitable. The first week's instruction will be entirely on the ground and will consist of the general rudiments of the art of flying. After this passenger flights will commence, flights in dual control machines, taxiing, straights, etc., until by the end of the fifth week the pupil should be competent to carry out all simple turns by himself. He will also be instructed in the finesse required for the execution of vol-planes [engine off gliding], vol-piques [nose dive, as after a stall], spirals, etc. By the conclusion of the three months course he should be a competent but inexperienced aeroplane pilot.

Classroom and shop work filled the non-flying hours. 'Elementary theory of flight, Theory of internal combustion engines and practical details of principal aero-engines, Aerial navigation and reconnaissance, Meteorology, Strength of materials, Practical work in the Carpenter's, Engineer's, and erecting shops.'

Pilots passing these courses were then posted to Grain, Where they would be first taken up on the dual control school seaplanes, then passing on to advanced seaplane training. The whole prewar course, including naval officer training with the fleet, was to last over a year. During the war the course was accelerated, cut to the essentials, and the time with the fleet removed from the programme.

Wartime Pilot Training

With the coming of war the main flying schools at Eastchurch and the Central Flying School were completely inadequate to cope with the growth of the two flying services. When Claude Grahame-White came to the Admiralty on 4 August 1914 and offered the use of his machines, factory and airfield at Hendon it was accepted with alacrity. The Grahame-White Flying School was taken over in its entirety by the RNAS and placed under Naval command. Whilst Grahame-White was the main user of Hendon, there were two additional flying schools based there. The Beatty School, owned by an expatriate American George William Beatty, used aeroplanes of Wright design. The second school was run Mr W. H. Ewen for the British Caudron Company. These continued to operate as civilian schools training pilots for the RNAS, and RFC, but under supervision of the commanding officer of RNAS Hendon. Around the country, the remaining civilian flying schools were taken over to train military pilots.

Grahame Donald and Gerry Livock were interviewed and accepted for the RNAS in late September 1914. They were sent to Hendon in October for their initial training, Donald at the Beatty School and Livock with Grahame-White. Both had remarkably similar experiences; neither had any significant ground school instruction, and both spent most of the day hanging around hoping to get a few minutes instruction. Donald, 'It was all dual, dual control. Beatty wasn't going to risk his sacred Wright biplane solo until you were ready for your certificate. People didn't realise at that time you took your certificate on your first solo.' Livock recalled he was lucky to get 'a flight of about ten minutes every few days, weather permitting. Every morning we rushed to the anemometer to check the wind strength, for if it was over five or six miles an hour instruction was off.'

There was no such thing as air traffic control, the Grahame-White and Beatty schools flew circuits in a different direction and flew straight line flights directly from in front of their hangars. As these were located at opposite corners of the airfield the tracks crossed in the middle of the aerodrome. Somehow, major accidents and incidents were avoided, though both recalled some lucky escapes.

As mentioned the Beatty School used Wright biplanes with chain driven twin propellers, pupils were always wondering what would occur if one of the chains broke. Then one day it actually happened.

> Fortunately it happened just about thirty feet up.... The pilot was a little engine mechanic called Virgilio, an Italian, a very excitable lad. Suddenly one of the chains cracked; we were all standing just almost below it, and we heard it go. The plane just did a complete flat spin of about one turn and dropped like a pancake right in the middle of the [empty] car park—and broke nothing. Didn't even hurt Virgilio. But the funniest thing was, on the way down he stood up in his seat and screamed the most beautifully coloured Neapolitan cuss I've ever heard. He stood up and screamed '*Tonnerre de Dieu*—GORBLIMEY!!' And everybody collapsed in heaps and then went up to have a look at the 'plane— there was nothing wrong with it.

Livock was also lucky to escape a very dangerous situation. He was flying dual on a Grahame-White Boxkite looking over the shoulder of his instructor Marcus D. Manton:

> After a couple of circuits, Manton aimed for the middle of the aerodrome and, blipping the engine on and off, glided down to land. Just as we were touching down, Manton for some reason glanced back over his right shoulder. Letting out a wild yell, he put everything hard over to the left to make a bumpy landing at right angles to our original course, allowing a Caudron biplane to land on the very spot he had selected for his touchdown. I had looked round at the same time as Manton, and was only mildly surprised to see the Caudron's spinning prop

aimed straight at the back of my neck, and only about ten yards away. How he missed us I don't know. Nor did the pilot, who had committed the cardinal error of only looking out over one side when coming in to land, and he had never even seen us.

After about three months both were able to take their 'ticket' over the winter of 1914–15:

What you did, you took the 'plane off and you made five figures of eight covering the entire airfield. You didn't get very high, probably a matter of 150 feet or so, but it did make sure that you could do both left and right hand turns and keep her more or less round what we called pylons which marked the edge of the aerodrome. And after you had done your five figures of eight you'd bring her into the centre of the airfield and land her and come to rest within a given distance of a mark—which was the test inspector's oil skin coat. Then you went up again and did another series of five figures of eight and made another landing, stopping within a specified distance. And having done that, your test was now two thirds complete.

Then they tied an altimeter on to the passenger seat so that you'd know what height she was going to, with instructions to take her up to five hundred feet, which seemed a colossal height. And having reached five hundred feet you were supposed to do a 'vol plané descent', which meant with the engine totally cut off. Which was quite tricky on the Wright, because you had to push her nose well down with the engine full on before you dare switch it off otherwise you just stalled and fell out of the sky. However, you got the nose down into a nice dive, just slightly above five hundred feet, shut the engine off and kept it shut off and then you had to land her without touching the engine again within a specified distance of the mark.

Having got their 'tickets' (Livock, No. 1004, on 20 December 1914 and Donald, No. 1061, on 30 January 1915), the schools took no further interest in them. If they wanted to fly, they had to beg, borrow or steal a machine until posted to the next stage of training.

Donald was posted to Eastchurch early in February, having sent a telegram to the Admiralty advising them of his success. He learnt to fly floatplanes at the Isle of Grain and given ground instruction along the lines specified in the 1914 paper. He was posted to the Naval Air Station at Eastbourne at the end of February, flying coastal anti-submarine patrols until posted to Dundee, and later *Engadine* at Rosyth in October 1915. Livock was initially sent to the Central Flying School, for a short advance course in flying, then to the Isle of Grain to learn to fly floatplanes. He was posted to *Riviera* at Harwich in June 1915, where we met him in the previous chapter. We will meet both of them again in later chapters.

This rather haphazard training system continued until early in 1916, although additional schools and training establishments were added during 1915, including a Preliminary Flying School at Eastbourne. This had two separate flights, an *ab initio* flight with Maurice Farman pushers and the advance flight equipped with Curtiss JN-3 tractor biplanes. However, a new RNAS Central Training School opened at Cranwell on 1 April 1916, and a scheme of standardized training came into force at the same time.

> *Aeroplane pilots.* After a disciplinary course at the Crystal Palace, pupils were to be posted for preliminary flying training (20 to 24 hours solo) to the Schools at Eastchurch, Chingford, Eastbourne or Redcar. They were then to pass on to Cranwell for advanced training in cross-country flying, navigation, engines, aerial gunnery, bomb dropping, photography, and wireless telegraphy. *Seaplane pilots.* Pupils were to pass from the training schools to the seaplane stations at Calshot, Felixstowe or Killingholme. They were then to go on to Cranwell, where they were required to graduate in all subjects except [landplane] flying.

The training received was thorough by the standards of the day but its weaknesses were evident when the newly trained pilot reported for service.

> I beg to report that the junior pilots being sent to *Campania* seldom have sufficient flying experience to permit of their being put on to reconnaissance work and flying from deck immediately they arrive. A particular point is that practically none of them have ever taken up a passenger when they arrive. […] I find that pilots have very little familiarity with the use of the compass. […] The pilots also have very little knowledge of starting their engine, throttling down and stopping their engine, and this lack of knowledge constantly leads them into difficulties and causes damage to the seaplanes in *Campania*.

This was just part of a letter written on 9 August 1917 by Captain Oliver Swann to Commodore Godfrey Paine, Director of Air Services at the Admiralty. To which Paine replied on 21 August.

> It is not practicable, at present, to lengthen the period which is spent by pilots at schools, though this may be possible when the additional schools, which are under consideration, have been provided. In future, all officers will be appointed to patrol stations after graduating at Calshot, and they will thus be able to obtain familiarity with the use of the compass, to take up passengers, etc. Vacancies for seaplane pilots in carriers will be filled from patrol stations.

Gradually the requirement for seaplane pilots to serve with the fleet reduced, the need being for land plane pilots familiar with single-seat and two-seat landplanes to fly from an increasing number of small flight decks. Many of these pilots would not go through the seaplane training at Calshot. Their course at Cranwell included instruction in engines, signalling, passenger, and cross country flying. From Cranwell they were posted to East Fortune which acted as a depot for future carrier pilots. Their progress from this point on will be discussed later.

By the middle of the war the training of flying officers for both services had reached such a peak that pocket books, such as *Hints for Flight Sub-Lieutenants*, were enjoying healthy sales. Published in 1916 this anonymous little book contains a wealth of information and good advice for 'the Flight Sub-Lieutenant RNAS who has just received his first appointment from civilian life.' All aspects of service from 'How to obtain a Commission' to 'Pensions and Gratuities' are covered in its 46 pages. It contains many useful admonitions, such as, 'The attention of all officers under training is called to the fact that the words "joy stick", "joy ride", "bus", etc., are never to be used in the Royal Naval Air Service.' To ease the new officer into the Naval family he is particularly advised that, 'When you receive your first appointment as Probationary Flight Sub-Lieutenant you will become entitled to wear practically the same uniform as a Sub-Lieutenant, RN, and you must not forget that in the Navy this takes an immense amount of hard work and some years to attain.'

Leaving Tiffin Boys School in Kingston-on-Thames in 1915, Walter Albert 'Toby' Yeulett obtained a position as a student engineer with Gordon Watney and Company in Weybridge, Surrey. Before the war Gordon Watney and Company had specialised in coach building bodies for Mercedes and De Dietrich chassis imported into the UK. During the war the company's workshops were converted into the manufacture of aero engines, principally Clerget rotary engines. After gaining workshop experience in the construction of engines, Yeulett began working in the firm's drawing office. On attaining the age of eighteen he applied to join the RNAS. The next step, according to *Hints for Flight Sub-Lieutenants*:

> You will then be told to attend at the Admiralty to appear before the Selection Committee, who are a Board of Officers on the RNAS ordered to examine candidates for Commissions. They will simply ask you questions about yourself, and what you have done up to now in the way of Motoring or Motor Bicycling, or in fact anything that is likely to have tested your nerve, and shown that this will not be wanting in the air.

With his engineering background he would have been an ideal recruit for the RNAS, probably narrowly avoiding being sent for training as an engineering officer. Toby was appointed a Probationary Flight Sub-Lieutenant on 22 July 1917 and ordered to report to the Crystal Palace for basic training.

The Crystal Palace was an extraordinary place, a massive building in glass and metal, reconstructed in 1854 on Sydenham Hill from the original temporary building erected in Hyde Park to house the Great Exhibition of 1851. At the beginning of the war it was taken over for training new recruits for the Royal Naval Division and renamed *Victory VI*, but generally referred to as the Crystal Palace. Early in 1916 the Royal Naval Division vacated the site which was taken over by the RNAS as a depot for the basic training of recruits. The course lasted three or four weeks including lectures on Naval history and procedures, followed by a steady diet of daily physical training and drill. Posting to the flying school would come as a relief at the end of the course. It would be a matter of luck to which school the Probationary Flight Sub-Lieutenant would be posted, Yeulett was posted to the Preliminary Aeroplane School at RNAS Chingford.

Airfields of the period were little more than large fields, hopefully flat but not always so. The CFS at Upavon was notoriously located on the top of a hill. Chingford was flat, but had other problems. One of the trainees, Charles P. O. Barlett, recalled:

> Chingford was not an ideal beginner's aerodrome. Innumerable streams traversed it and were boarded over with wooden [railway] sleepers. The hangars backed on to the main Chingford to Ponders End road, immediately beyond which was a large and deep reservoir extending northwards for rather more than two miles.

In time the reservoir would gain a reputation almost as unsavoury as the infamous Brooklands sewage farm. A fully crewed navy whaler was kept ready whenever flying was in progress.

The new trainees, 'Quirks' in the slang of the day, initially spent time in lectures and at the end of flying helped the air mechanics stow the machines in the hangars. After two weeks, weather permitting, they commenced flying training on the Maurice Farman Longhorn. After a brief period of dual control the trainees were sent off solo, frequently with a bare two hours instruction. A few more hours solo flying would see the trainee transferred to the advanced flight on the Avro 504 trainer. The Avro 504 was A. V. Roe's principal contribution to the war effort, and what a magnificent one it was. From 1913 through to just before the Second World War, RNAS, RFC and RAF pilots learned about flying on this machine. Over 10,000 Avro 504s were built in an alphabet of variants, not only did they teach the British flying services but they could be found in military service throughout the World. A few hours on the Avro then a few on a more operational type, the Royal Aircraft Factory B.E.2a or B.E.2c, and training would be over. Having followed a military training course few bothered to take the tests required for their Royal Aero Club tickets. There is no record of Toby Yeulett having taken his ticket before being posted to Cranwell, for advanced training, on 13 October 1917.

When Yeulett was at Cranwell the trainees arriving from Chingford and other Preliminary Aeroplane Schools were assumed to have a basic grasp of piloting an aeroplane. So, other than a few dual flights required to convert them to new types, all flying was solo. After a number of climbs to a given height, and circuits, the trainees would be sent off on cross country flights. If these were satisfactorily completed the pupil would be led out to a Bristol Scout, a single-seat scout with sensitive controls, have the handling explained and sent off for solo circuits. If the trainee was lucky, and had not damaged the Bristol, he might be permitted a few flights on a Sopwith Pup. On completion of the course at Cranwell, Toby Yeulett was sent on a brief machine gun and bombing course at Frieston, on the coast of the Wash near Boston. The airfield was right on the coast, barely ten feet above high water, and subject to flooding. But, the mud banks of the Wash were ideal for use as a bombing and machine gun range; several targets were set up, at least one of them being an old and unserviceable aircraft. Now a fully-fledged Temporary Flight Sub-Lieutenant, Yeulett returned to Chingford to fly a number of other aircraft types prior to finally being posted to his operational unit at East Fortune in January 1918. All reserve or wartime only officers were considered temporary, but the prefix was usually dropped in service. Toby Yeulett will re-enter this story in a later chapter.

So far all the entrants for flying training have been from Britain itself. However, the Empire also brought forward many volunteers for the two flying services. Many of these came by ship from their homelands to volunteer and be trained in the United Kingdom. Canadian, and American, volunteers had an alternate option open to them.

The RNAS recruiting procedure in Canada required applicants to appear for an interview and medical examination in Ottawa or at one of the naval bases located on the east coast at Halifax, Nova Scotia, or west coast at Esquimalt, British Colombia. If the applicant was judged suitable, he was accepted as a candidate for the RNAS, but he then had to gain a pilot certificate from a private flight school in either Canada or the USA. With this document he would be commissioned as a Probationary Flight Sub-Lieutenant and sent on to the UK for service training. The cost of obtaining the certificate (approximately $400 in 1915) fell on the applicant, but partial reimbursement would be made following commissioning as a Temporary Flight Sub-Lieutenant after training in the UK.

Stuart Douglas Culley was a typical transatlantic recruit. He was born on 23 August 1895 in Omaha, Nebraska, to an English father and Canadian mother, from Thetford Mines, Quebec, but who claimed strong Yorkshire roots. Culley always thought of himself as 'English and not in any way American or Canadian.' On 9 March 1917 he applied to join the RNAS and was interviewed in Ottawa. Although accepted as a suitable candidate, it was not clear whether he would actually be appointed to the RNAS:

It is perfectly true that the RFC were at that time opening up schools in Canada. But we were lucky in a way as, after a lot of argument between Ottawa and

London it was finally agreed that a final batch of 50 Canadians would be accepted for the RNAS and a special school was put up for them under canvas at Manston. There were also another 50 odd applicants on the list for RNAS who were however arbitrarily transferred to the RFC.

So, Culley was sent to Britain for all his training at Manston then Cranwell. On completion of the Cranwell course he was selected for 'Special Service'; deck flying with the Grand Fleet.

The number of flying platforms with the fleet was rapidly increasing at this time, also the aircraft carrier *Furious* was in service and there were the new ships being prepared for service. The need now was for pilots. Culley recalled receiving additional training for deck flying, mentioning flying Sopwith Pups from a mock deck marked out on the airfield. A dummy deck 200 feet in diameter, so that it was not subject to wind direction, had recently been laid out on the airfield at Grain for experimental trials and training:

Aircraft were flown from this deck by means of a quick release gear which consisted of a trestle to hold the tail in the flying position, on top of the trestle there being a groove to guide the tail skid. The pilot opened the engine of the aircraft full out and pulled a toggle in the cockpit which operated an ordinary bomb release anchored to the deck at one end and engaged with a cable attached to the aircraft.

Following this basic deck training, Culley spent a few weeks at Calshot for seaplane training, before being posted in January 1918 to Rosyth for actual deck flying training. Here he completed three actual deck take-offs before being posted to the light cruiser *Cassandra*.

The first challenge for all pilots was taking off from a small deck. *Nairana* and *Pegasus* were two seaplane carriers, whilst they will be fully described later for now all that needs to be understood is that in addition to the aft seaplane hangar both had been provided with a small forward flight deck and hangar for land planes. The routine for the carriers was load up with Sopwith Pups or Beardmore WB.IIIs, one already on the flight deck and a full load in the forward hangar and under the flight deck, then sail out through the boom and out into the Forth to an area off the island of Fidra, North Berwick. Here the trainees would take their turn to fly off the fore deck and return to land at Donibristle. Once all the machines were away the ship returned to the anchorage, the machines were lightered out and taken aboard, and the whole exercise repeated the next day. Each pilot had to complete three flights to gain his 'flying off' ticket.

The crews of the two seaplane carriers were well aware that the leave train for Edinburgh left South Queensferry station at 1.55 p.m. each day. Unfortunately, the ship was usually still outside the boom by that time. So, flying off exercises began to be conducted inside the boom and those with leave were able to catch the train. Lt Cdr Kinnersley Saul was navigating officer on *Pegasus*, and recalled that: 'From this it was but a small step to "flying off" at anchor, using the engines to hold the ship accurately into the wind, and easing them off in lighter and lighter winds until we finally let them go in a dead calm.' There was always one of the ship's motor launches standing by with a photographer and sick berth attendant just in case something went wrong. Though Saul noted that in 'the training of pilots, mostly boys in their teens from Canada and Australia, in "flying off" I should hazard a guess that we turned out over a hundred without a single accident of any kind for service with the Grand Fleet.' That represents around three hundred take-offs without an accident, an admirable record.

Training to land on was conducted at the Isle of Grain using the dummy deck. The trainees would make landings on the deck, which was fitted with a primitive form of arrestor gear, using Sopwith Pups fitted with skids, instead of wheels, and hooks to engage the wires. The Pups were mostly well-used examples, some of which had seen service with squadrons on the Western Front. Flt Cdr Geoffrey Moore recalled that:

It was not difficult to take-off on a grass aerodrome without wheels; to start moving we rocked the machines back and forth and they soon gathered way.

It can safely be assumed that not all pilots found this so simple, hence the selection of well-used machines. The great need was for pilots capable of taking off from small decks, so the actual number of pilots undergoing deck landing training was probably quite small. All indications being that only those actually posted to *Furious* were sent to Grain for training.

Observer Training

The RNAS had no recognised Observer Officers, with appropriate training, until 1916. Prior to that the second seat had been occupied by enlisted engine mechanics or locally trained observers.

Lt Robert Erskine Childers was the only officer 'observer' to fly on the Cuxhaven Raid. Most pilots had chosen not to carry a passenger, those that did had a senior mechanic with them. Not surprisingly, therefore, the best reconnaissance report was produced by Kilner and Childers. Childers sailed with *Ben-my-Chree* for the Mediterranean and, whilst the ship was the flagship for the East Indies and Egypt Seaplane Squadron, he organized an observers school in Port Said. Most of the trainees were army officers, as the EIESS mainly operated in support of the Army this was an advantage. However, for operations with the fleet naval officers were essential.

Based at Rosyth in 1915, *Engadine* had four trained pilots but no observers. Gerry Livock recalled that they recruited ship's officers and trained them as observers. These first observers were Assistant Paymaster G. S. Trewin, Lt Swan, RNVR and three RNR midshipmen. The training was basic in the extreme, 'Many hours were spent circling around the Firth of Forth while our homemade observers jiggered about with unreliable W/T sets. We did practically no navigational exercises or ground training.' *Campania*, also at Rosyth, trained her own observers who were RNR midshipmen volunteers. They were excellent material, but they had all been told they could eventually transfer to pilot training. So, as soon as they were becoming useful observers they went off to train as pilots. The obvious solution was to select men specifically to train just as observers. As the midshipmen's weakest point had been in signalling it was decided to ask for volunteers from the fleet's signal yeomen, who were informed that if they passed the course they would be advanced to warrant officer, RNAS.

Finally, in 1917, an Observers School was established at Eastchurch. It gave a four month course in subjects including seamanship, wireless telegraphy, navigation, intelligence organisation, bomb dropping and aerial gunnery.

Enlisted Technical Training

The roles open to enlisted personnel were largely concerned with the maintenance and armament of the aeroplanes. Once enlisted, they followed a similar basic training course at the Crystal Palace then went on for training required for their speciality. If they entered with a suitable civilian trade, such as engine mechanic, they would follow that speciality in service often without additional training. Those without an existing or useful trade were sent for basic aptitude testing then sent on the appropriate course. Courses would last anything from two weeks to two months depending on the technical complexity. Once qualified the men were posted to ships or air stations as required. Not all two-seaters required observers, a select few enlisted men were selected for training as Gunlayer, manning a machine gun in the second cockpit.

6

Vindex with the Harwich Force, 1916–1918

The Harwich Force, without its own carrier since the middle of May 1915, had made no sorties with a seaplane carrier since Operation G at the beginning of July. On 14 November 1915 *Vindex*, a new seaplane carrier conversion, arrived at Harwich to join the 5th Light Cruiser Squadron, to become part of the Harwich Force.

Vindex was another converted Isle of Man Steam Packet Co. turbine steamer (350 feet long, 1,957 grt, 22 knots) originally named *Viking*. Converted by the Cunard Company, Barrow, *Vindex* had the usual large aft hangar for seaplanes that could house four two-seater and one single-seat floatplanes. However, she differed from previous conversions by having a small forward flight deck. The flying off deck was short, barely 64 feet long, tapering in width from a maximum of 28 feet as it followed the curve of the bow. A steam jet was provided to give a visual indication that the ship was headed into wind prior to take-off. A forward hangar, 25 feet by 15 feet, could accommodate two disassembled single-seat scouts. The aft edge of the flying off deck was some 6 feet higher and 20 feet ahead of the hangar, two derricks were provided to lift the machines on to the flight deck. The bridge and wheelhouse were rebuilt above the hangar. As completed, *Vindex* was capable of operating up to seven aircraft, both wheel and float equipped. She was the first of what would retrospectively become known as Mixed Carriers, a term coined by Maurice Prendergast, an editor of *Jane's Fighting Ships*. The layout would be repeated in three later conversions; *Manxman*, *Nairana* and *Pegasus*. The problem was that once aloft the pilot could not return. At best they faced coming down into the sea close to an escorting destroyer, and hope to be plucked from the frigid water.

Up to this time any take-offs from a platform or track mounted on a ship's foredeck had been little more than stunts. The task now was to develop a repeatable method that was within the capabilities of quickly-trained wartime pilots. With *Vindex*'s new, but small, flight deck this task became urgent. When her conversion was completed, she was detailed to Nore Command at Sheerness, ostensibly for patrol purposes. Actually, she was required for the final stage of a series of experiments leading to a take-off from her flight deck.

The experimental program was carried out in three separate phases; experiments on land, with the ship alone at sea and with a machine on the ship. The land-based phase was to establish the shortest distance the pilot required for take-off and to develop 'any accessories [that] are desirable to assist him in getting off or to enable him to keep direction in the confined area available.' The experiments with the ship concerned mainly ship handling. The final phase aboard ship had two aims, namely that of making a trial flight and to establish how quickly such a flight or series of flights could be made.

The land-based flights were made from an asphalted surface at Eastchurch between 27 September and 7 October 1915. Two Bristol Scout Cs were employed, 1255 and 1246, although the latter made only one flight. Flight Commander B. F. Fowler was the pilot for all experiments.

The initial flights were made with the aeroplane restrained by a quick release cable attached to a peg driven into the ground. With the engine running the pilot was able to lift the tail into the correct flying attitude using the elevator, he then released the machine. Three problems became immediately apparent: The machine had an inherent tendency to wheel round to the left; the tail dropped at the moment of release and, owing to the tail blowing about in the air stream from the propeller, the machine was seldom pointing into the wind at the moment of release. The first problem was due to the engine and propeller-induced torque. Attempts were made to overcome it with elastic cords attached to the rudder bar, but ultimately it was left to the pilot's skill to control the machine. The remaining problems were ultimately solved through the development of a tail guide arrangement. The tail guide arrangement devised for use aboard *Vindex* comprised a long, initially 15 feet, slotted tube fastened, slot facing out, to the side of a wooden trestle. The height of the trestle was arranged to support the aeroplane in flying attitude with a ball end fitting, clamped to the side of the tail skid, fitted into the well-greased tube. With the engine running the pilot could slip a quick release cable and the ball sliding through the tube guided the aeroplane during the initial part of its run. The tail guide trestle became standard equipment aboard aeroplane equipped ships, although the slot was often moved from the side to the top of the tube. Using the tail guide trestle an average run of 88 feet was required against a four knot wind before the Bristol rose into the air. On one occasion against a ten knot wind only 63 feet was needed. Using this data as a basis it was recommended that take-off from *Vindex* should be attempted into a 25 to 27 knot wind; this to be achieved through a combination of ship's speed and wind speed.

The experiments with *Vindex* were to calibrate wind speed measuring apparatus and to ensure there was no excessive air flow disturbance over the flight deck. Finally, experiments were tried in handling the ship to avoid running down the machine if it crashed into the sea on take-off.

With this comforting thought Flt Cdr Fowler prepared to make the first take-off from *Vindex*'s deck. The first flight was accomplished at 7.50 a.m. on 3 November 1915. With a 27 knot wind over the deck, *Vindex* steaming at 12 knots into a 15 knot wind, Fowler flew Bristol Scout C 1255 off the deck with a run of only 46 feet. The Bristol commenced to swing to the left immediately on leaving the tail guide but Fowler was able to correct this towards the end of the run, he then flew on to land at Eastchurch. As the small forward hangar necessitated aeroplanes being stowed disassembled, forty-five minutes were required to prepare one for flight. With two machines rigged for flight, one on deck and one in the well immediately behind, it was estimated that two flights could be made within ten minutes. However, it is not clear whether this claim was put to the test. Tests completed, *Vindex* sailed for Harwich.

Exercises and aborted raids on the German coast punctuated *Vindex*'s first few months at Harwich. On 4 December two of her Shorts, including 8036 flown by Flt S/Lt Grahame Donald with Mid D. L. Ridson as observer, were wrecked off Felixstowe whilst familiarising the Harwich Force with flying operations. Donald's experience shows just how willing and forgiving a Short 184 could be:

> Well, first of all there was a new pattern of bomb. Didn't like the look of them very much; sort of bomb that was inclined to go off if you gave them a cross look. We'd to carry four 112 pounders and about eight twenty-five pounders which actually with an observer was an overload. Found that out later. Didn't like the feel of her on the water let alone in the air. But the thing was we'd to try take-off and climb.

It was a day of glassy calm and sea haze, but the Short got off and Donald was able to coax the overloaded machine up to 3,000 feet. The haze became a thick fog over the sea and far inland. Donald had taken off with a low fuel load, sufficient for about an hour and a half, so he had to come down. Setting the Short up in a very gentle glide he began to descend.

> But with the fog we had it was very difficult and so I started on a very flat glide and because of that load of beautiful bombs aboard I wasn't the least bit keen on hitting anything unduly hard. Set her on a course just about north which should keep England on one side and the Fleet on the other and getting lower and lower and lower, and it was very thick. I remember seeing a destroyer's mast whiz past about three feet off my wing tip [...] And I was getting pretty near the water now and began to flatten out a bit, the engine ticking over nicely, keeping her pretty flat. You couldn't see a thing, not even a mermaid, in spite of the fact that the altimeter was registering minus two hundred feet and the observer looking out in all directions. And suddenly we saw just a glint of light on the water; it was marvellous. At that moment a horrible great brown mass appeared right in front

of the 'plane. Theoretically you can't stop a seaplane doing sixty five knots; you can't stop her dead. I can assure you this one did. Turned out later on that it was a sandy cliff. The dear old Short by jove—what a 'plane!—she zoomed neatly up the cliff, only hit the very top. Spread herself over about half an acre in the middle of a very comfortable Army fort. And not one bomb went off; not one bomb. It really was miraculous.

Donald and Ridson were remarkably lucky, a mild case of concussion apiece and a few days in hospital would see them right.

Throughout January 1916 attempts by the Harwich Force to search out their enemy were being frustrated by bad weather. Tyrwhitt complaining , 'We shall develop into the limpet fleet if we don't get a move on soon. We have not been outside for ten days!' But there are no records of the Harwich Force ships ever having to have the weeds scraped off their hulls, unlike the German High Seas Fleet stuck in port due to the Kaiser's caution. Finally, on 18 January 1916, *Vindex* escorted by the Harwich Force set out on her first raid, Operation ARH, an attack on the Zeppelin base at Hage. The operation was cancelled when the force ran into thick fog approaching Heligoland Bight. A second attempt was made on 28 January, *Vindex* had just come to a stop to hoist out her floatplanes when a torpedo narrowly missed Tyrwhitt's flagship *Arethusa*. Since the enemy was obviously on the alert, *Vindex* was ordered to recover her machines and get underway, and the Harwich Force retired at full speed. On 6 February, whilst preparing to launch floatplanes off Borkum, *Vindex* was narrowly missed by a torpedo fired by a U-boat. This, again, caused a hurried cancellation of the proposed reconnaissance and the force returned to Harwich.

Commodore Tyrwhitt now planned an ambitious raid, Operation HRA, on the Zeppelin sheds thought to be at Hoyer. Admiralty approval was given for the raid to take place on 25 March. The Harwich Force, escorting *Vindex*, was in turn covered by Vice Admiral Sir David Beatty's Battle Cruiser Fleet from Rosyth. At dawn *Vindex* was in position approximately 40 miles north west of Hoyer, whilst the battle cruisers were 45 miles west of Horns Reef.

Three Short floatplanes and two Sopwith Babys (improved versions of the Schneider) were sent off at 5.35 a.m. One and a half hours later a Short and a Sopwith were seen returning through snow squalls. Their crews reported finding no sheds at Hoyer although one machine had flown further inland and discovered them at Tondern; an attempt to bomb the sheds failed when his bombs jammed in their carriers and had to be brought back. The second machine reported bombing a large factory at Hoyer and leaving the building on fire. The Harwich Force spent some time in a fruitless search for the missing floatplanes. During the morning *Vindex* was bombed by several German seaplanes and, according to some reports, three Zeppelins. Eventually Tyrwhitt ordered the carrier and her escorting destroyers back to Harwich, which they reached at 4.47 p.m. on 26

March. It was subsequently discovered that the crews of the missing floatplanes were safe as prisoners of war. All three machines had been forced down after suffering magneto failure.

The raid sparked a series of fleet movements that briefly looked as if a major engagement might result. Vice Admiral Hipper sailed from Wilhelmshaven with his battle cruisers supported by two battle squadrons of the High Seas Fleet. Situated between the two fleets, Tyrwhitt spent a hectic night of gales, snow storms and collisions. During a brief encounter with German destroyers, SMS *G194* was rammed and sunk by *Cleopatra*, which was then rammed by *Undaunted*. Both cruisers were still able to steam and slowly made their way back to Harwich. Beatty spent 27 hours in the vicinity of Horns Reef hoping to meet Hipper, but prepared to fall back on the Grand Fleet (which had sailed from Scapa Flow at dawn on 26 March) if the High Seas Fleet came out. The German heavy units were at sea through the night of 25–26 March but did not venture beyond Sylt. At about 6.30 a.m. on 30 March they were forced to retire because of exceptionally rough weather. About noon the British forces turned back.

The Admiralty summary of the operation concluded: 'As an air raid it was not much good, except to show that there were no airship sheds at Hoyer'. However, noting the reaction by the High Seas Fleet, Jellicoe was pressed to use further raids to draw out the Germans and force a fleet action upon them. He was opposed to this, arguing that:

> The raid must take place at daylight, otherwise the force would be reported approaching and five seaplanes would certainly not succeed in achieving anything with a mass of Zeppelins and aeroplanes against them. It also involves our hanging about for a whole day in a bad locality expending fuel… If we could stir them up at dusk and catch them coming out next morning, matters would be different, but I can't see how to do that… At the same time an air raid as a minor operation, especially if combined with some minelaying, is all to the good.

At dawn on 4 May *Vindex*, temporarily on loan to the Battle Cruiser Fleet at Rosyth, and in company with *Engadine*, was in position off the island of Sylt preparing to launch an attack on the sheds at Tondern. They had sailed from Rosyth the previous day escorted by the 1st Light Cruiser Squadron and 16 destroyers. Also in the offing were Beatty's battle cruisers, the Harwich Force and the Grand Fleet. Despite Jellicoe's opposition, Operation XX was mounted with the intention of inducing the High Seas Fleet to come out. *Vindex* was carrying two Bristol Scouts and seven Sopwith Babys, aboard *Engadine* were a further five Babys.

The carriers were being led by *Galatea*, then *Vindex* and *Engadine*, followed by four more light cruisers, the whole screened by four divisions of destroyers. At 3.00 a.m. the launch signal was given, the cruisers turned to port and the two carriers to starboard, coming to a stop to launch the floatplanes. The weather was good with a slight wind and smooth sea. As the launch commenced the cruisers were stationed astern of the carriers, steaming at eighteen knots in close order line ahead, apparently following a race track pattern, the destroyers were circling the carriers at ten cables (i.e.; one nautical mile) and ten knots.

Gerry Livock, back in *Engadine*, recalled that:

> Soon after dawn we reached the rendezvous and started hoisting out the Sopwith Babys as quickly as possible, with the *Vindex* doing likewise half a mile away. We each carried one 65 lb bomb. There was an oily swell, which wouldn't have worried a Short but was clearly going to be a nasty problem for the Babys. I was the last of our five to be launched, but before I touched the water and unhooked from the crane, I saw that the sea was littered with damaged seaplanes, some on their noses, some sinking and others bounding about over the swell trying desperately to get into the air. My engine started at the first pull of the handle and I settled down and opened up to see what I could do. A cloud of spray shot over everything as I breasted the first swell. Bump! Into the second and more spray. I was momentarily airborne. Bump! Crash! The engine raced madly as my prop disintegrated into matchwood and flew in all directions.

None of *Engadine*'s Sopwith was able to take off. Grahame Donald was also on *Engadine*; he recalled the scene after all the attempted take-offs:

> But the main thing I remember about it was seeing at least seven or eight fins and rudders sticking up out of the water with 'Sopwith Aviation Company, Kingston upon Thames', written on them—that was all that was visible of the Sopwith Schneiders.

Vindex launched six machines, only three of her floatplanes were able to get into the air. The first machine, 8159, Flt S/Lt John A. Sadler, capsized and the second, 8167, Flt Lt Harold F. Towler, suffered a broken propeller when he taxied into a heavy sea. Sadler had clambered onto the tail of his machine and was rescued by *Vindex*'s motor boat and taken over to a destroyer *Goshawk*. The third and fourth machines away, 8158, Flt S/Lt C. L. Scott, and 8145, Flt S/Lt Warren MacKenzie, were similarly disabled by the heavy seas. Tragically, the next away, 8143, crashed into *Goshawk*'s mast and Flt Lt O. N. Walmesley was killed. It is possible that the pilot did not see *Goshawk*, which had just crossed *Vindex*'s bow intending to assist the recovery of Sadler's machine. Walmesley:

> . . . flew straight towards *Goshawk* which was lying about 300 to 400 yards on our port beam bow to bow. The machine did not alter course and hit *Goshawk*'s aerial with her floats I think and her right wing hit the mast. The machine immediately nosedived to the left into the sea.

The ship's motor boat, having delivered Sadler to the destroyer had returned to 8159 to attempt to salvage the machine. When Walmesley crashed the boat:

> . . . immediate left that machine and went to the assistance of the Flight Lieutenant. The boat was within 30 or 40 yards and not more than 1½ or 2 minutes could have elapsed before she arrived at the wreck. The Sub Lieut in charge of the boats and the boats crew went overboard but could find no signs of Mr. Walmesley.

The final Baby was 8179, piloted by Flt Lt L. Openshaw:

> I was hoisted over the side at 3.23 a.m. and left the water two minutes later. I proceeded to carry out operations and returned to *Vindex* 1 hr 55 mins later. My machine flew perfectly throughout. On returning to the ship I came alongside and was hoisted in without mishap.

The Germans spotted Openshaw over Tostlund 20 miles north of Tondern, and alerted the anti-aircraft guns and local defence flight at the base. But Openshaw had wandered off over Danish territory, only a few miles north of Tostlund, and dropped his bomb on neutral Denmark, causing no damage.

Around 9.30 a.m. an airship was sighted to the south and the cruisers *Galatea* and *Phaeton* opened fire at maximum range. The Zeppelin, L7, was hit by a shot from *Galatea* and forced down on to the sea near the submarine *E.31*. Quickly manning her 12-pdr gun the submarine opened fire and set the Zeppelin on fire. The submarine rescued seven survivors from a crew of twenty, bringing them back to Harwich after evading a night attack by a German cruiser. The British forces cruised around until early afternoon hoping for the arrival of the High Seas Fleet. At 2.00 p.m. the ships turned for home. The party guest had declined to accept the invitation.

All in all the raid must be considered a disaster for the Sopwith Baby, as will be discussed further in the next chapter. For the RNAS it meant that no further floatplane raids were attempted in the North Sea. Not until the summer of 1918 were the sheds at Tondern again visited by naval pilots of the RAF. Instead the floatplanes were used for reconnaissance flights, anti-submarine patrols and to search for pilots after they had launched from the fleet's flight decks.

Vindex was now long overdue for a refit and sailed for Hull on 24 May. She returned to Harwich on 17 June, assuming the role of anti-Zeppelin guardship. This essentially involved sweeps into the North Sea on nights when raids were expected. She had been out for two nights running, 31 July–1 August and 1–2 August, having just returned to harbour only to be ordered to sea again. Sailing, with the light cruiser *Conquest* and four destroyers in company, during the afternoon of 2 August. The force took up a patrol position fifty miles off Lowestoft.

At 6.05 p.m. an airship was sighted from *Vindex* and as the force manoeuvred to keep it in sight Bristol Scout 8953, armed only with two containers of Ranken Darts (twenty-four per container), was prepared for take-off.

Leaving *Vindex's* deck at 7.50 p.m., with less than two hours of daylight remaining, Flt Lt Charles Teverill Freeman headed the Scout to intercept the Zeppelin:

> I climbed to about 5,000 feet, steering South-East, and when at that height lost sight of all shipping, owing to mist. I saw two Zeppelins, one at 8,500 feet, about 10 miles away, and the second at a slightly higher altitude, about 10 miles further off. Both were steering in a South Westerly direction. I proceeded to attack the nearest Zeppelin altering course as necessary in order to attack down sun from her.

The airships seen by Freeman were two of six which had set from their bases earlier that day to bomb towns along the East coast. The one he was shaping to attack, L17, was based at Nordholz and commanded by *Kapitänleutnant* Herbert Ehrlich.

> She did not sight me until I dropped a container of Ranken Darts, which apparently missed. I was, at this time, about 500 feet above her, and turned back to attack a second time, dropping half a container, but she altered course and succeeded in avoiding them. I therefore attacked the third time and dropped the remainder of my darts. One of these apparently hit as I saw a small puff of smoke and the Zeppelin almost immediately dropped to 5,000 feet. Throughout this period I was subjected to fire from a machine gun mounted at the forward end of the upper surface of the ship.

Freeman believed he had damaged the airship and forced it to turn back. But after he flew away L17 returned to its course and headed towards the English coast. Later that night L17 was over Norwich and was hit several times by shrapnel from anti-aircraft shells, causing over a hundred rents in the gas cells, but was able to return safely to base. There is no record of Freeman's attack having caused damage. It is possible that the puff of smoke he reported was exhaust smoke from a suddenly throttled up engine.

Freeman, meanwhile, had his own problems. After completing his attacked he set his course to locate the ships. Whilst diving after the airship he had switched off his engine, attempting to restart he found that he had lost fuel pressure and was unable to get it going again. He had to come down on the North Sea. He fired a single white Very light just before landing at around 9.10 p.m., the Very pistol was lost on landing:

> Shortly after landing I heard a siren which I took to be that of the *Vindex*, I therefore cut out the remaining Very's Lights and set fire to them with my

matches, which being in an inside pocket and above my waist, had fortunately remained dry.

When he failed to return to the ships, *Vindex* and her consorts spent the night searching in the vicinity of the North Hinder light vessel. *Conquest* finally located the remains of Scout 8953 early the following morning. When the wreckage was recovered there was no sign of Freeman. The force returned to Harwich, Freeman's fate remained unknown for a few days longer.

He spent an hour and a half clinging to the tail of his machine. The weight of the engine had dragged the nose under, but flotation bags kept the tail above water:

> I saw a steamship coming in my direction and as a last resource I lit a few letters that were in my pocket as a flare, at the same time firing with the contents of my Webley Scott. The steamer eventually acknowledged my signal and approached me. She circled around regarding me with a considerable amount of suspicion, but eventually lowered a boat, a proceeding which took about 20 minutes. I was then taken off and to the side of the ship, which proved to be the S.S. *Anvers* of Antwerp.

Anvers was a steamer chartered on behalf of the Commission for Relief in Belgium, carrying foodstuffs from the USA to the Netherlands for distribution within Belgium. Freeman was landed at the Hook of Holland at 5.00 a.m. the next morning. After a brief detention by the Dutch authorities, the British Consul was able to obtain his release and confirm his status as yet another RNAS shipwrecked mariner. Freeman reported to the Admiralty in London on Sunday 6 August 1916.

It is pleasant to be able to report that the actions of Captain Potvleiger of the *Anvers* were well-received by the Admiralty. At their request a message of 'special thanks' was delivered to him by the British Consul General at New York on 23 August.

Freeman was awarded the DSO:

> In recognition of the gallantry and skill displayed by him on the night of the 2nd August, 1916, when he made a determined attack on a Zeppelin at sea, only abandoning the attack when he had exhausted all his ammunition. As darkness was approaching at the time, and his chances of being picked up were problematical, his courage and devotion in returning to the attack a second and third time were exemplary.

One of the new weapons in the Royal Navy's arsenal were small high speed Coastal Motor Boats (CMB), designed to be carried on the boat davits of light cruisers. An attack was proposed on the German Fleet at anchor in the Schillig Roads. The plan had all the makings of a suicide mission. Before it could take place a detailed reconnaissance of the area was required to ensure there were no booms or other obstacles and to locate various fleet units. The Harwich Force was ordered to make the attempt, Operation R.C.2, on 22 October 1916.

Vindex sailed from Harwich on 21 October in company with light cruisers *Centaur* (Flag, Commodore Tyrwhitt), *Carysfort*, *Conquest*, *Penelope* and thirteen destroyers. The light cruisers were also to recover the returning floatplanes, *Vindex* being under orders to retire immediately after launching them. The cruisers *Aurora* and *Cleopatra* with seven destroyers were to provide additional cover.

At dawn the following day the force was in position 70 miles from the coast. Two Short 166, 9757 and 9760, were to make the reconnaissance. Each carried four 16 lb bombs and the observer had a Lewis gun. The first was crewed by Flt Cdr Harold Frederick Towler (pilot) and CPO Alexander Blackwell (observer), the second by Flt Lt Francis Neville Halstead with Lt Erskine Childers as observer. Childers, who had recently returned from Egypt and was working with the CMBs, had been selected for his extensive knowledge of the area having sailed there prior to the war. The two floatplanes were safely away by 6.00 a.m., from a position about sixty miles west of Heligoland. According to plan *Vindex* then departed for Harwich, escorted by two destroyers *Druid* and *Ferret*.

Towler and Blackwell, on 9757, were first away at 5.45 a.m. followed by Halstead and Childers eleven minutes later, both steering south-east towards the German coast close to Wangeroog. Both crews sighted an airship around 6.30 a.m., but were inconsistent regarding the course it was following. Shortly after the sighting, whilst approaching the coast, Towler and Blackwell encountered fog banks. After attempting to either fly below or climb over them Towler turned back and landed at 7.32 a.m. just seaward of the fog bank. After talking the situation over with Blackwell they decided to make another attempt taking off five minutes after landing. Still unable to get through the fog, Towler set course towards Heligoland. They sighted a trawler patrol close to the island then ten unidentified vessels steering SSW. Towler brought the Short back to the squadron and landed astern of *Centaur* at 9.05 a.m. and was hoisted onboard.

Halstead and Childers were a little more successful in avoiding the fog banks. Climbing to 4,000 feet they sighted the island of Norderney at 6.45 a.m., having failed to allow sufficiently for the strength of the wind. Passing over the island they steered eastward and over the next islands in the Frisian chain; Baltrum, Langeoog and Spiekeroog. However, after the latter they too ran into the fog bank. Descending to eighty feet they attempted to reach Wangeroog, sighting an anchored destroyer estimated to be four miles ENE of the island. Shortly after 8.00 a.m. they abandoned the attempt and climbed above the fog bank heading towards Heligoland, sighting the island at 8.15 a.m., and turned towards it intending to make a thorough reconnaissance.

Only a few small craft were observed in the harbour. Two seaplanes were observed to rise from the harbour and give chase. They did not however come within range of our gun, but pursued us for about 40 minutes. At 8.37 a.m. we sighted ten enemy destroyers in two lines abreast and one Torpedo Boat, steering in a South East'ly direction. We manoeuvred to observe them more closely, and at 8.50 six more Destroyers were sighted steering the same course.

The following seaplanes having turned back, Halstead set course for the rendezvous and landed alongside *Conquest* at 9.30 a.m. and was hoisted onboard.

The various destroyer movements noted by both crews were part of a general move by the Germans to reinforce Zeebrugge. Two flotillas of destroyers were detached from Heligoland to make attacks on the forces guarding the entrance to the Dover Straits. The attacks were to assist Flanders based U-boats penetrate the screen and attack cross-channel shipping beyond as part of an upsurge in submarine activity leading to the declaration of unrestricted submarine warfare in January 1917.

The operation had been carried out exactly as planned, only the unpredictable weather had prevented success. A few days later the Lords Commissioners of the Admiralty informed the two crews that they had 'engaged their Lordships approbation' for 'a well-executed operation.' The proposed CMB raid was called off.

For the remainder of 1916 and through 1917 *Vindex* was far from active, taking part in only four operational sweeps with the Harwich Force during 1917. The first two, 20–21 April and 27–28 April, were uneventful trips to cover minelaying forces in the Heligoland Bight and off Terschelling respectively. The third, on 15–16 August, was a reconnaissance of the German coast north of Terschelling. The final trip, 24–25 September, was an anti-Zeppelin patrol in the Terschelling area.

Sopwith Pups had begun to replace the Bristol Scouts early in 1917. The Pups were fitted with a Lewis Gun and a new anti-Zeppelin weapon. The Le Prieur air-to-air rocket had been used with some success against observation balloons on the Western Front and it was hoped that it would be effective against Zeppelins. They were unguided explosive devices looking like overgrown Guy Fawke's Night fireworks. Electrically fired by the pilot, the five foot long stick stabilized a warhead loaded with 200 grams of black powder, the rockets were inaccurate much beyond 100 yards. However, a number of the first batch of Beardmore built Pups, ordered by the Admiralty for naval use, were factory modified to carry a single rocket on each pair of interplane struts. To protect the fabric from the rocket flame aluminum panels were fitted to both the upper and lower wings. The rockets were electrically launched by a button on top of the control column. The single Lewis gun was angled upward to fire through a cut out in the centre section. Aboard *Vindex* local modifications were made to the armament. The angled Lewis was replaced by a vertically mounted weapon immediately forward of the cockpit; the centre section cut out was plated over and permanent lifting slings installed.

At this time, Flt Cdr Bertram Denison Kilner was commanding the RNAS detachment on *Vindex*. Kilner joined the RNAS in October 1914, learning to fly at the Royal Naval Flying School, Eastchurch he gained RAeC Certificate No. 1072 on 1 February 1915. Posted to the Mediterranean he contracted dysentery at Malta and was repatriated for treatment to Royal Naval Hospital Haslar at Gosport. When recovered he was posted to Great Yarmouth seaplane station in February 1916. On 25 April he pursued a Zeppelin fifty miles out to sea in Bristol Scout 1256 but had to abandon the chase. Then, on 12 July, with Air Mechanic Money as his gunlayer, he was flying Short 184, 8222, on a routine submarine patrol. Just off Smith's Knoll they sighted a submarine, which dived as Kilner flew in to dropped his bombs on the target. No wreckage was seen. Finally, on 23 September, on Short 184, 8074, this time with CPO Rose as gunlayer, Kilner set off after another Zeppelin. Rose reported by wireless that they had unsuccessfully attacked the airship 45 miles east of Great Yarmouth. Shortly afterward engine failure forced the machine down and the pair spent a cold night adrift on the North Sea. They were rescued by a patrol boat the following morning and returned to Great Yarmouth. Early in 1917 Kilner was stuck down with Chicken Pox and treated at Shotley Naval Hospital. After recovering he was posted to *Vindex* on 15 February 1917.

On the morning of 25 September *Vindex* was at sea in the Terschelling area on an anti-Zeppelin patrol. At 3.45 a.m. an airship was sighted and shortly afterwards Flt Cdr Kilner took off from *Vindex* in Sopwith Pup, 9927, to intercept it. He had two Le Prieur rockets, and a fixed vertically-mounted Lewis Gun, with six additional 47 round ammunition pans on racks in the cockpit. Shortly after his take-off the ship stopped to launched a Short 184, N1232, piloted by Flt Lt E. G. Hopcroft with Petty Officer E. J. Garner as observer, to follow and pick up Kilner if required.

The Short was unable to make contact with either the Pup or the Zeppelin, but continued to search until about 30 miles north of Borkum. Concerned about his fuel supply Hopcroft turned back and began searching for *Vindex*. He sighted a convoy of three ships with destroyer escort, one of which turned towards the Short. Later, spotting two German seaplanes, Hopcroft prepared to defend himself but reported that they showed no inclination to attack. Failing to find *Vindex* he was forced to land, out of petrol, near the Haaks light vessel after a flight of six hours. Hopcroft and Garner were rescued by the Dutch trawler *HD47*, and the Short taken in tow. They were landed at Den Helder, where the Short was taken into Dutch naval service as K1. It is recorded as being at *Marinevliegkamp* (Naval Air Station) Schellingwoude in 1918. It is believed that both Hopcroft and Garner were interned, probably at the *Engelse Kamp* (English Camp) in Groningen. This was one of the rare occasions that the shipwrecked mariner ploy failed.

There was some routine patrol activity from Borkum *SFS* that morning. A single-seat Albatros W.4, 960, flown by *Flugobermaat* Pönig, had set out early and became overdue from a patrol, three two-seaters were sent out to search for him. A Friedrichshafen FF33J, 1096 (*Vizeflugmeister* Bönninger and Eisenbeiss), and two FF39, 1133 (*Flugmaat* Harsch, *Fähnrich zur See* Heintz) and 1136 (*Flugzeugobermaat* Nagorsnik, *Leutnant der reserve* Liebug). The two FF39s encountered a Short biplane between 8.30 a.m. and 9.00 a.m. GMT. The Short was flying eastward a few miles off the coast of Vlieland and Terschelling, this would have been Hopcroft. Both FF39 reported brief battles with the Short which had to be terminated due to lack of fuel (1133) or mechanical problems (1136). Whilst returning to Borkum Nagorsnik and Liebug may have seen Hopcroft again flying back along the coast searching for *Vindex*. A little later a Curtiss flying boat was chased by Bönninger and Eisenbeiss, they gave up the chase as the Curtiss was the faster machine. *Flugobermaat* Pönig and his machine were found and recovered later in the day.

Kilner was never seen again.

Vindex rounded out the year by colliding with the trawler *Kalmia* on 23 December. She had only the day before completed a refit at North Shields, where a startling new camouflage scheme had been applied. Perhaps the trawler's skipper had been dazzled by her appearance. *Vindex* proceeded to Hull to repair underwater damage and was in dry dock until 9 January 1918. After completing repairs she sailed for Sheerness where the next three months were spent on trials. On completion of trials she received orders for the Mediterranean. Delayed by a refit it was 4 June before she arrived in Malta with Short 184s and Sopwith 1½ Strutters embarked. Later, whilst based in the Aegean on convoy patrol and escort duties, the Strutters were replaced by Sopwith 2F.1 Camels.

With the departure of *Vindex* the Harwich Force also ended its association with seaplane carriers. However, the Harwich Force had not yet finished with naval aviation.

7

The Problem of Performance—
Seaplanes versus Landplanes

The failure of the Sopwith floatplanes on 4 May 1916, as described in the previous chapter, caused Courts of Enquiry to sit. In summary, of the eleven Babies prepared for the raid eight failed to leave the water. Four broke propellers, four had engine problems including one of the three that took off, one was capsized by the wash from a passing destroyer and one crashed killing the pilot. The one that got away achieved nothing.

As *Engadine* was attached to the Battle Cruiser Fleet at Rosyth and *Vindex* to the Harwich Force, two separate Courts sat on 11 May and 10 May respectively. The *Engadine* findings were brief and to the point, 'We find that no blame is attributable to anyone, on the contrary, great credit is due to the Pilots for the continual efforts they made to rise under very trying conditions.' The main blame was put on the weather, 'i.e. swell with a very light wind.' The *Vindex* court appears to have made a more thorough investigation. After taking testimony from all surviving pilots, *Vindex*'s commander, executive officer and RNAS engineering officer, an informed conclusion was reached:

> We are of the opinion that the failure was due primarily to the lack of experience of some of the pilots; though it would appear probable that a contributory cause was the wash made by the vessels in the vicinity, which rendered their task more difficult.

Of all the pilots, on both *Engadine* and *Vindex*, Flt Lt L. Openshaw had the most time, about 50 hours, on the Sopwith floatplane. Most of the pilots had less than ten hours on type, Flt S/Lt John A. Sadler less than four.

The little Sopwith floatplane was never designed to be a fighting machine, being developed from a racing machine. Before the war, Thomas 'Tommy' Sopwith had put all his company's skills into designing a small racing biplane the Type St. B, popularly called the Tabloid. One was completed as a single-seat floatplane, Type HS, to compete in the 1914 Schneider Trophy race, to be held at Monaco, which it won convincingly at an average speed 85.8 mph. The Tabloid floatplane caught the attention of the RNAS, and a slightly modified version was ordered as the Sopwith Schneider floatplane which began to enter service in the spring of 1915. It was a compact biplane, wing span 25 feet 8 inches and length of 22 feet 10 inches, powered by a 100 hp Gnome rotary engine. An improved version, fitted with a 130 hp Clerget rotary engine, was known as the Sopwith Baby.

There are very few pilots' memoirs of the Sopwith Schneider/Baby. Gerry Livock recalled that they 'were considered to be very difficult to handle', particularly on the water. However, he also noted that, 'They were lovely little things to fly and, at 80 knots, were quite fast for those days.' Flight Sub-Lieutenant G. F. Hyams, who was completing his training at Hornsea Mere in 1917, recalled his first encounter with the Sopwith Baby, 'They were absolutely perfect! They had Clerget engines [...]. They would all handle most beautifully and were really a delight to fly; you could turn them on a sixpence.'

In service they were intended to protect the fleet from attacks or observation by German airships and floatplanes. Though it is doubtful that a successful attack could have been made on an airship as it lacked the performance required to climb above it to drop bombs or Ranken explosive darts with which they were usually armed. Attempts to fit a machine gun had an element of W. Heath Robinson about them. It was a willing horse, however, and could often be found with a Lewis gun or two pointing out at odd angles, or overloaded with bombs. However, they were slower than most enemy floatplanes and landplanes and, despite Hyams' praise, their manoeuvrability was adversely affected by the inertia of the floats.

As the results might indicate the raid was the swan song for Sopwith's little floatplane in northern waters. They continued to provide stalwart service at bases around the coast, operating from relatively sheltered waters. Overseas they were used for a little longer from the seaplane carriers of the East Indies and Egypt Seaplane Squadron, which had no choice but to use the Schneiders as escorts to the Short 184s. On 17 September 1916 two Schneiders were escorting a single Short engaged in spotting the fire of two monitors on the German airfield at El Arish. A two-seat Rumpler C.I from *Fliegerabteilung 300* rose in defence, intent on attacking the Short. When the two Schneiders attempted to protect the Short, one was shot down in flames and the second forced down on to the sea. Given time to escape, the Short was able to reach the protection of the anti-aircraft guns of the ships off shore.

The small seaplane carriers in future would operate only single-seat aeroplanes from their flight decks, retaining the larger, stronger and more seaworthy Short floatplanes for open sea operations. The advantages of the landplanes over the floatplanes are immediately obvious. Although both types had fixed undercarriages, the latter's were much heavier and created more drag, seriously affecting all aspects of performance. As the battles over the Western Front grew in intensity, the frontline aircraft were constantly evolving and improving. There was no similar impetus over the North Sea, and the number of aircraft required was much less. Consequently, it was simpler to adapt existing designs for use at sea.

For two-seater machines the RNAS had two major designs. Both, within their limitations, were excellent designs. One was a floatplane the other a landplane, they can be considered complementary designs as both remained in service until the end of the war.

The Short 184 floatplane was the product of a process of evolution over several years, benefiting from the first lessons of war, this large single-engined two-seater was the most widely produced and used British floatplane of the war. It was intended as a multi-role reconnaissance, bomber and torpedo aircraft. Close to 1,000 examples were built by several manufacturers, of which over 300 remained in service at the end of the war.

The basic design remained little altered throughout its long production run. The only major changes made were installation of different engines of increasing power, from 225 hp in the prototype to 275 hp at the end, and minor changes in armament. Early models were powered by a 225 hp side-valve V-12 Sunbeam Mohawk water-cooled engine. A large box-shaped radiator was located on top of the fuselage ahead of the wing, obstructing the pilot's forward vision. The observer's cockpit, behind the pilot, had no provision for armament in the early production machines, but it did provide storage for all his paraphernalia—navigational board and charts, W/T transmitter, Very pistol and flares, sea anchor and, on some North Sea operations, a basket of carrier pigeons. A torpedo could be carried, on two arched spreader bars, between the forward thrusting, flat bottomed floats. Alternatively, racks for bombs could be installed under the fuselage and between the floats. A tail float with water rudder was installed on struts under the rear fuselage, small cylindrical air bags were also fitted to protect the lower wing tips. Spanning 63 feet 6¼ inches the Short's wings could be folded back alongside the 40 foot-7½-inch-long fuselage, reducing the width to 16 feet 4¾ inches. Ailerons were installed on the upper and lower wings. The Type 184 had a large, shapely fixed fin with a cut-away ahead of the rudder hinge line to accommodate an aerodynamic balance surface on the rudder itself. A conventional tailplane with hinged, rubber sprung elevators completed the assemblage.

Flt Cdr A. H. Sandwell, writing long after the war, affectionately remembered the 184:

I was formally introduced to the Short 225, [it was] the pilot's dream for putting in hours—docile, stable, obedient, and thoroughly deserving its affectionate nick name 'Home From Home.'

It was a physical impossibility to fly a Short at much more than 75 miles an hour. If you tried to dive it steeply it would start taking the control away from you at, say, 65 mph, and would have flattened itself out before it picked up another ten miles an hour. No pilot was strong enough to hold the wheel forward so that it would continue to dive, and if he had been he would probably have broken the control wires, or the horns on the elevators themselves. Consequently, even if you had the height to spare, you could not get anywhere in a hurry on a Short by stuffing its nose down as you could on most land machines.

The Sopwith 1½ Strutter first flew in December 1915, and entered RNAS and RFC service early the next year. The upper wings (which joined on the centreline with no centre section) were connected to the fuselage by a pair of short struts and a pair of longer struts, forming a W when viewed from the front, this giving rise to the name 1½ Strutter. The pilot's cockpit was located under the upper wing, the observer's, or gunlayer's, cockpit was under the trailing edge with a good field of fire. The Strutter was apparently a very stable machine, requiring a lot of strength to put it into a dive, which may be why the type was fitted with an adjustable tailplane. It also had a reputation as a good glider, too good as it was sometimes difficult to get it to land, again this may explain the flaps fitted on the lower centre section which lifted upward only to act as air brakes. For naval use as the Ship Strutter the design had very few changes mainly the addition of flotation devices and, on some machines, a W/T set in the rear cockpit. No attempt was made to have any part of the machine fold for storage. If a W/T set was installed, the fixed forward firing Vickers gun was often removed to save weight. It became the principle ship-borne two-seater for the remainder of the war.

The single-seater machines were intended as airship hunters, where the maximum speed was less critical than their ability to climb, and protection of the fleet from aeroplane attack. Here the landplanes had a marked advantage over the floatplanes. The flying qualities of the single-seaters varied enormously, some were a delight, others gained a vicious reputation.

The Bristol Scout, much lighter and handier than the Schneider, had a short career with the RNAS and RFC on the Western Front before being used at sea. Like the Schneider it began life as a prewar racing design, but was always a landplane. It had the reputation of being a pilot's aeroplane, light and crisp handling and a reasonable turn of speed. When retired from front line service it became the treasured possession of instructors. It weakness was its lack of armament; all sorts of weapons were carried by its pilots, Webley revolvers, Holland and Holland Aero 12-bore shot guns, which were adapted to fire cartridges loaded with miniature chain shot. On some machines a Martini Henry rifle was lashed to the centre section strut firing at an angle of about forty-five degrees from the line of flight of the aircraft, this later being replaced by a similarly installed Lewis gun. Aboard *Vindex* the armament was limited to two boxes of incendiary Ranken Darts which had to be dropped from above the airship to be effective. Geoffrey Moore described the Ranken Dart in his memoir.

The darts were carried in a container, the bottom of which was hinged to release them, and each container held a dozen darts. The dart was nose heavy to make it drop nose first and to steady up its flight, and instead of the conventional bomb fin it had a dual purpose arrangement at the tail end. This was like the ribs of an umbrella which opened up on being released from the canisters. These ribs steadied the flight, but their main purpose was to detonate the explosive charge in the dart. On the dart penetrating the fabric of an airship the ribs would catch in the fabric and detonate the dart in the same way that a Christmas cracker is detonated.

Although used with some success against moored observation balloons on the Western Front, the darts were to prove unable to bring down an airship. The single occasion they were used to attack a Zeppelin, 2 August 1916, the attack had failed. It was generally felt that if the Bristol Scout had been armed with a machine gun and incendiary ammunition, rather than the Ranken darts, Flt Lt C. T. Freeman would have succeeded in destroying the airship. In consequence *Vindex* was ordered to equip each of her scouts with a machine gun. Some Bristol Scouts, including 8979 which served aboard *Vindex*, were fitted to carry a single Lewis gun above the centre section to fire over the propeller arc.

However, a better solution soon became available. The Sopwith Pup came about through the Admiralty's search to replace the Bristol Scout, the order for a prototype being placed in April 1916. The resulting machine was one of the finest single-seat scouts of the First World War. Most pilots would probably agree with Arthur Gould Lee's opinion:

> At last, I did my first solo on a Pup, and at once realised that of all the machines I had flown till now were indeed just machines, even the Avro [504]. For the Pup was a dream to fly, so light on the control, so effortless to handle, so sweet and amenable, and so eagerly manoeuvrable that you found yourself doing every kind of stunt without a thought. And she was just as manoeuvrable up high, at 15,000 feet and above.

Whilst not vice less, it tended to be forgiving to the careless and inexperienced. When taken to sea early in 1917, as an airship hunter, the fixed forward firing Vickers machine gun was replaced by a Lewis gun arranged to fire upwards into the belly of the airship, using incendiary bullets.

Less successful was an attempt to make the Pup into 'folding' machine to fit into a tiny space aboard ship. The resulting machine, the Beardmore WB.III, looked like a Pup from a distance, close up it looked like a badly assembled and rigged Pup. In order to get the wings to fold back alongside the fuselage it had been necessary to remove the stagger between the upper and lower wings, the dihedral of the wings was also rigged out so that from the front they appeared flat, small lower stub wings and a reduced width centre section were fitted to permit folding. Paired interplane struts linked the stub wings and centre section, these were joined across the fuselage by horizontal struts. To accommodate the folded wings the fuselage was lengthened to avoid fouling the tailplane. On the early aircraft the undercarriage was arranged to retract up into the fuselage, consequently it was very narrow, later machines were fitted with a jettisonable undercarriage of wider track. Despite all this the speed was not much affected, but the handling suffered.

Flt Cdr William Geoffrey Moore has been mentioned previously, and will feature frequently in the following pages, so it is time to look at his career up to this time. He learnt to fly at Hendon and the Central Flying School gaining RAeC Certificate No. 983 on 26 November 1914. After a brief posting to the Isle of Grain he was sent out to Zanzibar and East Africa, for a period he was a 'One-man Air Force for General Northey' far from the sea in Rhodesia and Nyasaland. After many adventures, amusingly recounted in his memoir *Early Bird*, Moore arrived back in Britain and was posted as second in command of the RNAS unit on *Furious*. He was a natural pilot excelling in aerobatics. He recalled the Beardmore WB.III from his time on *Furious*:

> . . . they did not handle quite as nicely as the standard [Pup]. I used to give little exhibitions of aerobatics for the entertainment of the fleet, but was never really happy when doing this in a 'folder' on account of some lack of response in the controls and I was always wondering whether, if subjected to exceptional strain, they would 'fold' in the air!

Most pilots who had to fly the Beardmore probably considered Moore insane to even attempt aerobatics.

The Sopwith Camel is probably the iconic British fighter of the First World War, but it was fittingly described as 'a fierce little beast.' Whilst being supremely manoeuvrable it was unforgiving and could turn and bite even the most experienced pilot. The naval Sopwith 2F.1 Camel differed from the classic F.1 Camel of Western Front fame in many ways. Essentially, the 2F.1 was designed so that the fuselage could be broken into two parts aft of the pilot's cockpit to ease storage, as the wings could not be folded. The wing centre section was reduced in span by about a foot and had a cut out between the spars on the centreline for an Admiralty Top Plane Mounting for a Lewis Gun firing over the wing, the mounting allowed the Lewis Gun to be lowered for firing upward or to replace the magazine, which most pilots found impossible in combat. The lower wings were reduced in span to match the upper wing. A single forward firing Vickers machine gun, offset to port, replaced the pair of the F.1 Camel. Small bombs could be carried below the fuselage, the only known RNAS use being for the Tondern Raid of July 1918.

As an experienced pilot Moore loved the Camel. He was, however, well aware of its dark side, considering it 'a death-trap for an inexperienced pilot.' For a skilled pilot, such as himself:

. . . it was like having a pair of wings strapped on to his shoulder blades. Once you knew them you could do anything you liked with them and turn their peculiarities to advantage.

With the Camel, he continued to give 'little exhibitions of aerobatics for the entertainment of the fleet', often at suicidally low altitudes. It was arrogant and cocky behavior, but he survived.

8

Campania and the Grand Fleet

The growth of aviation with the Grand Fleet, and the ultimate development of the aircraft carriers, owes much to the support of the two Commanders in Chief, Admiral Sir John Jellicoe and his successor Admiral Sir David Richard Beatty. Both were supporters of naval aviation, Jellicoe more in the background and Beatty more publicly. Without their ongoing support, through good times and bad, naval aviation, given the insatiable demand for support on the Western Front, could have withered on the vine.

Jellicoe whilst serving as Second Sea Lord, in charge of Naval Personnel & Training, in 1913 became an early supporter of aeroplanes over airships and he was strongly in favour of RNAS independence from the RFC. He later proposed that direct entry of civilian flyers to the RNAS should be encouraged, and was active in discussions on all matters concerning the expansion of the RNAS and provision of land bases around the coast.

On assuming command of the Grand Fleet on the outbreak of the First World War his active support of the RNAS had, of necessity, to be curtailed. Jellicoe was deeply involved in preparing the Grand Fleet for battle, providing secure bases and maintenance facilities, and myriad of details involved in the command of the largest fleet in the world. Brought up on stories of Nelson and British naval power and invincibility, the public expected Jellicoe to bring the German High Seas Fleet to battle and destroy it in another Battle of Trafalgar. However, Jellicoe did not have an overwhelming numerical superiority in 1914 and was unwilling to risk his fleet unnecessarily. His constant need was for intelligence before sailing and scouting once at sea. Intelligence came from many sources, with increasing importance being given to the code-breaking efforts of Room 40 Old Building at the Admiralty. At sea he relied on the advance flotillas of destroyers, cruisers and battle cruisers to keep him informed. He envied the High Seas Fleet's access to airborne observation through the airships of the *Marine Luftschiffabteilung*. Whilst the Royal Navy's obsession with the airships was subsequently shown to be misplaced, Jellicoe considered:

The German Zeppelins, as their numbers increased, were of great assistance to the enemy for scouting, each one being, in *favourable weather* [Jellicoe's italics], equal to at least two light cruisers for such a purpose.

Given his prewar interest in the development of naval aviation, it is not surprising that Jellicoe sought to enlist it to assist the Grand Fleet, to provide reconnaissance and observation far ahead of the fleet. As early as September 1914 Jellicoe was writing to Captain Sueter, Director Air Department, requesting a large ship, capable of 20 knots and fuel capacity for several days steaming at that speed, for conversion into a seaplane carrier. Accordingly, on 6 September, Capt. Murray F. Sueter, Director Air Department, sent an urgent request to the Director of Transports for a suitable ship.

> C. in C. Home Fleet [*sic*] requires a large ship to carry seaplanes. Can one be provided capable of steaming 20 knots, and with sufficient coal capacity to keep with Fleet? A seaplane requires the following stowage:—
>
> 35 [feet] x 15 [feet] x 15 [feet]. (Petrol stowage is also necessary).
> As many as possible should be carried.
> Can this be treated as very urgent please?

Initially all that could be made available were either too small, too slow or required too much conversion. One memo clearly pointing out that:

> Generally speaking, ships of a speed approaching that mentioned by D. A. D., *viz.* 20 knots, are not readily adaptable for the service required, i.e., for handling and stowing seaplanes requiring the stowing dimensions stated by D. A. D. Vessels of this speed are built more particularly for passenger service and have small hatches, a height 'tween decks generally not exceeding 8 ft., and a depth of lower hold often not more than 10 or 12 feet.

A few days later the same official in the Director of Transports' office thought of *Campania*.

In 1891 the Cunard Company ordered two sister ships, *Campania* and *Lucania*, for use on their transatlantic service. The two ships were partly financed by the Admiralty, incorporating Admiralty requirements for potential conversion to armed auxiliary cruisers. This included strengthening to mount eight 4.7 inch guns. Built by Fairfield Shipbuilding and Engineering Company of Govan, Scotland, *Campania* was capable of maintaining an average speed of over twenty knots for six days whilst crossing the Atlantic. On her second transatlantic crossing she won the Blue Riband for a west bound passage at over twenty-one knots between 18–23 June 1893. *Campania* commenced her 250th Atlantic crossing on 25 April

1914, returning to Liverpool from New York on 6 May. On arrival at Liverpool the ageing ship, (Cunard now had three 'ocean greyhounds' *Lusitania*, *Mauretania* and *Aquitania* on the transatlantic service), was chartered to the Anchor Line for five round trips from Glasgow to New York. With the outbreak of the First World War two of Cunard's greyhounds, *Aquitania* and *Mauretania*, were requisitioned. *Campania* was therefore recalled to Cunard service, but completed only three transatlantic round trip voyages, her last crossing started from Liverpool on 26 September, 1914, before she was to be sold for scrap.

The Director of Transports' office recommended purchasing the ship outright. Sueter agreed on 21 September that purchase of the *Campania* should be approved. At this time the ship was still in service on the Atlantic. The final minute in the collection reads, over indistinguishable initials, 'Very Well. Let us make the best terms we can.' The Admiralty finally purchased her from the shipbreakers, T. W. Ward Ltd., on 27 November 1914 for £32,500.

There is no doubt that on paper at least *Campania* was a good choice. Designed for year round service on the Atlantic Ocean, and capable of steaming for six days at twenty knots or more, she should be well able to accompany the Grand Fleet on the North Sea. But after more than two hundred and fifty Atlantic crossings her engines were long past their best, her hull was over twenty years old and built with insufficient watertight bulkheads. But she was available.

Campania was towed to Cammell, Laird and Company at Liverpool, across the Mersey from where the same company was working on *Ben-my-Chree*, one of the packet steamer conversions, and soon to be joined by *Engadine*, *Riviera* and *Empress*. Compared to them *Campania* was a giant, 622 feet long and 12,950 grt, but the conversion was on a similarly grand scale. A large hangar was created between the two funnels by removing the first class saloons and lounges down to the main deck, one deck below were created aviation and engine workshops. The hangar over 200 feet by 50 feet was fully enclosed and served by a hatch 45 feet by 30 feet which permitted folded floatplanes to be hoisted up to the boat deck and then onto the water using the two derricks provided. The hangar could house up to seven Shorts. A flight deck was constructed extending aft from the bow ending under the bridge, it was inclined down towards the bow at a very shallow angle of less than 1 degree. The bridge was raised to permit maximum take-off run by placing the tails of the machines under it. Moving one of the large folded floatplanes from the main hangar to the flight deck whilst at sea was an impossibility, so a shelter for four assembled smaller single-seat floatplanes or aeroplanes was created on the foredeck under the flight deck. Access to lift the machines onto the flight deck, using either of two derricks located one on each side forward of the bridge, was provided through a small hatch. When closed, the hatch cover was flush with the flight deck and permitted a take-off run of approximately 160 feet. Finally, the eight 4.7 inch guns provided for in the original design were installed. The conversion completed, *Campania* commissioned on 17

April 1915, commanded by Captain Oliver Swann, and sailed to join the Grand Fleet in Scapa Flow.

After working up, *Campania* was ready to commence work with the Grand Fleet in June. Unfortunately, the ensuing operations were not the success hoped for. Between June and October she sailed with the fleet on seven occasions, the first between 11–14 June. During a series of battle exercises for the Grand Fleet her floatplanes were to attempt to follow, observe and report the movements of several squadrons of the Grand Fleet. Persistent problems with W/T and engines dogged the attempts of her airmen, but Jellicoe remarked that 'an improvement in the scouting work of the sea-planes was noticeable' by the end of the exercises.

Early in July she made her first visit to Pierowall Harbour, Westray (One of the northern Orkney islands.), to act as a mobile seaplane base cooperating with anti-submarine forces in the Fair Isle Channel between Orkney and Shetland. After a visit of four days *Campania* returned to Scapa Flow for more exercises with the Grand Fleet. This time her floatplanes were unable to take-off in the swell. She then returned to Pierowall Harbour for a few more days, then back to Scapa Flow for more attempts to work with the fleet.

At the end of July, Jellicoe complained that 'no seaplane has yet succeeded in flying off *Campania*'. He regretted that the fleet would continue to be vulnerable to Zeppelins, no means of defence being available 'unless it be by means of *aeroplanes* [Jellicoe's emphasis] rising from the deck of *Campania*.'

On 6 August 1915, Flt Lt William L. Walsh flew Sopwith Schneider, 1559, fitted with droppable wheels under the floats, safely off her deck. The ship was steaming at 17 knots into a wind of 13 knots.

> The seaplane was placed on the top of the forward seaplane hatch with the tail right up close against the fore bridge supports. The wheels of the seaplane were then 152 feet from the bows. The engine was run at 1,050 revolutions and, with the tail float of the machine resting on the hatch, the seaplane was released at a given signal. As is usual with the 100 hp Monosoupape Gnomes the engine spluttered a little as the seaplane moved ahead; it soon picked up and on the whole pulled well.

One wonders if Walsh was a sanguine as his commanding officer. The tail float ran along the deck for as much as thirty feet before lifting, at which point the machine began to turn to the right as Walsh over-corrected for an anticipated swing to the left. Again over-correcting the machine then swung a little to the left. Swann commented that, 'A proposal to keep the wheels of the seaplane running between rails or in grooved recesses is now finding favour amongst the pilots.' The seaplane left the deck with more than thirty feet to spare, Walsh allowing the machine to fly itself off when sufficient speed was attained. The total run, including the distance with the tail float down, was measured as 113 feet. The flight was purely experimental, no armament was carried and only 30 lb of fuel. It is notable that this flight preceded that of Flt Lt Fowler from *Vindex* by almost three months.

Walsh repeated his exploit on 4 November, shortly before *Campania* returned to Liverpool for additional work. This time two differently loaded Schneiders were used. Walsh flew 3709 with fuel for 2¼ hours and Flt Lt R. E. C. Penny had 3707 with the same fuel load plus a war load of two 16 lb bombs. *Campania* was making over twenty knots, but the actual wind speed is unrecorded, both got off without difficulty. Penny later repeated his take-off with four bombs.

For ten days after Walsh's first take-off *Campania* was based at Cromarty, assisting the seaplane base, searching for mines. The weather did not cooperate, clear weather being required to spot a mine from the air, and none were spotted. Then a return to Scapa Flow for more exercises. But, from October on, she remained at anchor as a floating base for seaplanes, whilst her future was discussed.

There was no denying, that in her present state, *Campania* was not working. Swann admitted as much in a letter, dated 8 October 1915:

In reviewing the work carried out by *Campania* during the last six months, I think the view cannot fail to be taken by some that the ship has not proved of sufficient utility to the Grand Fleet as a seaplane carrier to justify continuing to employ her as such. I beg therefore to be permitted to submit the following remarks, which may perhaps bring forward some point which might otherwise be overlooked.

Swann goes on at some length about the problems experienced, many of which could be echoed by the commanders of the seaplane carriers attached to the Harwich Force. Namely, difficult sea conditions, problems with the machines and W/T sets and a lack of trained ship's personnel and observers. However, he does state that with experience many of these problems were being overcome; although the difficulty of operating floatplanes in a seaway would never go away:

Flying from *Campania*'s deck is limited at present to very small light machines, suitable for the attack of airships but not for Fleet scouting work. To enable scouting machines to fly from the deck it is also necessary to carry out alterations to the ship.

Swann felt that, 'if alterations to the ship were carried out, the number of days on which seaplanes cannot be sent out would be considerably reduced.' He concluded by saying, 'I therefore beg to submit that I think it would be unwise to disband *Campania* or her personnel on the strength of the results of her first six months work.'

The letter was forwarded by Jellicoe to the Admiralty with the comment, 'It would be a great mistake to payoff *Campania*.' Jellicoe also enclosed a copy of an earlier letter from Swann dated 26 August, containing suggestions for further work compiled by his pilots and ship's officers. The letter suggested that the flight deck be lengthened and the inclination be increased to aid acceleration. Swann himself recommended moving the bridge back against the fore funnel so that a lengthened flight deck, sloped at 5 degrees, could be constructed.

Finally, it was decided to maximise the length of the flight deck to permit both single and two-seater machines to take-off. Essentially this involved splitting the forward funnel into port and starboard halves, increasing the flight deck inclination to 4 degrees and lengthening it to 245 feet. The main hangar and hatch remained unchanged. A second fully enclosed hangar was installed on the main deck under the flight deck, which now began at the forward edge of the main hangar hatch. The forward hangar had a flush fitting hatch, 40 feet by 25 feet, through the flight deck. The hangars could house up to twelve machines depending on type and size. The existing bridge structure was demolished and a small navigating platform built on a light structure between the twin forward funnels. With this large scale reconstruction approved, *Campania* sailed back to the Mersey at the beginning of December, to Cammell, Laird and Company at Birkenhead, where the work would be carried out. During the conversion a proposed aft hangar was cancelled and, at Jellicoe's insistence, a kite balloon hold, winch and a hydrogen generating plant substituted. To accommodate these two of the 4.7 inch guns had to be removed.

The reconstruction was not without its dangers. During the removal of the original fore funnel, it slipped out of the lifting slings and crashed into the seaplane hangar. A few minutes earlier the RNAS contingent had been assembled there for evening quarters but, having just been dismissed, the hangar was clear and there were no injuries. Nor was it without a few problems. Although a navigating position was built on a framework between the two funnels above the flight deck, the wheelhouse remained below it. So, in order to see out, the helmsman was provided with a periscope that projected up through the flight deck.

The reconstruction was completed by 21 January 1916 and *Campania* entered dry dock for hull cleaning, repairs and repainting. Refloated on 5 February the ship undertook trials and exercises in the builders' hands until she re-commissioned on 12 April 1916. Whilst retaining some of her previous officers, including Captain Oliver Swann, and crew there would have been many new faces. Her engineering department, however, was largely unchanged. Like most converted merchant marine vessels in naval service, the engine room staff were largely RNR, professionals to the core, many with experience with the ship in prewar days, which would be important in a few weeks' time. *Campania* sailed for Scapa Flow the following day.

April and May were spent working with her floatplanes and kite balloon. Often she would be in company with the balloon ship *Menelaus*, which also provided her kite balloon, probably a Caquot Type P capable of lifting two observers. On 4 May the kite balloon was successfully towed at 20 knots.

The kite balloon section of the RNAS attracted members of the stage and the police. The senior kite balloon officer in *Campania* was Stanley Bell who had been stage manager to Beerbohm Tree at His Majesty's Theatre for many years. The handling party were nearly all London 'bobbies'. When not in use the balloon was normally kept flying at short stay and the balloon well was available as a deck hockey pitch.

An improvement on later aircraft carriers was where the hockey ball, puck or rope ring was frequently lost overboard.

On the morning of 29 May she was exercising within the Flow and, over a short period of time, launched five Sopwith Babies on trolleys from the forward flight deck. The ship was steaming at 19 to 20 knots. She returned to anchor at Buoy 5 in Scapa Bay at noon. In the afternoon her crew transferred 450 tons of coal from the collier *Gardenia* in just under four hours.

On 30 May *Campania* sailed for the Pentland Firth to exercise her floatplanes and kite balloon in observation and spotting. Short 184, 8069, was sent on an anti-submarine patrol over the eastern entrance to the Firth. The exercises were completed at 3.50 p.m. and *Campania* returned to her berth at 5.15 p.m. Having expended 122 tons of coal she had over 2,800 tons remaining in her bunkers.

At 5.40 p.m. Jellicoe sent the Grand Fleet, including *Campania*, a preparatory signal for leaving Scapa Flow.

9

Jutland—A Lost Opportunity

The Battle of Jutland was the greatest naval battle of the First World War and the greatest of the Dreadnought era. Arguably, it was also the most indecisive. The battle brought together 58 dreadnought battleships and battle cruisers, countless cruisers and destroyers, and a single seaplane carrier. There could, and should, have been two seaplane carriers. Both *Campania* and *Engadine* are usually relegated to a footnote or a brief paragraph. This chapter uses, wherever possible, original documents and memoirs to try and construct a comprehensive account of the seaplane carrier's battle.

By 28 May 1916 it was becoming clear to the staff at Room 40 OB that the High Seas Fleet was preparing a major operation. On the morning of 30 May, the code breakers had sufficient decodes to be confident that the High Seas Fleet would be sailing that evening. At noon Jellicoe and Beatty were warned that the High Seas Fleet were expected to put to sea early on 31 May. At 5.40 p.m. the Admiralty instructed the two commanders that, 'You should concentrate to Eastward of Long Forties ready for eventualities.' The Long Forties, is an area in the North Sea of uniform 40 fathoms depth, lie between Aberdeen and the south west coast of Norway. In anticipation of the Admiralty telegram, at 5.40 p.m. Jellicoe sent the Grand Fleet a preparatory signal for leaving Scapa Flow, at the same time he signalled Beatty, 'Urgent. Raise steam.' At Cromarty Vice Admiral Sir Martyn Jerram, commanding the 2nd Battle Squadron, was also sending a preparatory signal for leaving Cromarty to all ships under his command.

Although the fleet at Scapa was using local Summer Time (GMT + 1 hour), all times quoted are GMT as per the signal log and ship's logbooks.

Campania

At her anchorage in Scapa Bay, *Campania*, received the preparatory signal. Swann immediately ordered steam for full speed at two hours' notice. He then called for four Sopwiths to be sent out from Nether Scapa seaplane station, located at the head of Scapa Bay. When they were hoisted aboard she carried three Short 184s, three Sopwith Babies and four Schneiders. *Elsewhere, "baby's".*

Early Admiralty accounts blame *Campania*'s failure to sail to engine defects. This calumny, which still surfaces from time to time, was challenged by one of *Campania*'s RNR Engineering officers in 1925 shortly after it was included in the Admiralty publication *Narrative of the Battle of Jutland*. The claim was thoroughly investigated, both Swann, by then Air Vice Marshal commanding RAF Middle East, and Jellicoe gave their opinions. Ship's log books, engineering records and signals were all consulted. A correction to the Narrative was later released by the Admiralty, in June 1926, calling the engine defect theory 'erroneous' and detailing the signals and events culled from the above sources.

The events of the next few hours are best told in the signals addressed to *Campania*.

6.37 p.m.: C in C (Jellicoe) signalled *Campania* and *Blanche* (a light cruiser attached to 4th Battle Squadron), '*Campania* will follow *Blanche* and be last to leave.'

7.11 p.m.: C in C signalled *Campania*, 'Raise steam for full speed.' The Engine Room Register at 8.00 p.m. notes, 'Steam for full speed at ½ hrs notice.'

8.07 p.m.: C in C sends a General (i.e. to all ships.) signal by flags, 'Fleet will leave by D.T.3 method at 9.30 p.m.'

8.15 p.m.: C in C repeats the 8.07 by semaphore adding routes to be followed by various squadrons and units. This included the 4th B.S. to which *Campania* was attached. *Campania*'s Engine Room Register notes, 'Reported ready to proceed 8.15 p.m.'

Sunset on 30 May 1916 was at 9.00 p.m. and dusk, which occurs when the horizon can no longer be distinguished, at 10.20 p.m. Between those times semaphore and flags would have become increasingly difficult to read and signal lights would become necessary. The last flag message sent by the C in C was timed at 8.56 p.m. General, 'Fleet will leave by D.T.3 method at 9.30 p.m., speed 17 knots after passing obstruction.' All subsequent messages were sent by wireless or signal light.

10.31 p.m.: *Campania* sends by W/T to C in C, 'Ready to Proceed.'

At this time the fleet was proceeding to sea through the Hoxa Gate.

10.54 p.m.: As the flagship *Iron Duke* was approaching the boom, the C in C sent a signal by flashing light to *Campania*, 'Take station astern of *Blanche*.'

IT WAS

Iron Duke and *Blanche* were recorded as passing the boom at 11.00 p.m. This key stationing, or sailing, signal was not received by *Campania*. *W H-1   NO T?*

From her anchorage at Scapa Bay to the Hoxa Gate was approximately seven miles. The weather was good that day with light winds and broken cloud. By 11 p.m. the fleet had been passing out for almost two hours. As Jellicoe was to write in 1926, when asked about *Campania*:

> I cannot conceive that the departure of the earlier ships was not seen on board the *Campania*. The 3rd B.S., *Chester* and *Canterbury* weighed at 8.50 p.m. and in passing the rounding buoy were within 4½ miles of the *Campania*. Bow lights too were in use on departure from the anchorage, in the case of ships leaving later.

At this distance in time we can only speculate on what actually happened. There appear to be two possibilities, either the signal staff on *Campania* missed the message or the signalman on *Iron Duke* sent the flashing light message to the wrong ship. Wherever the fault lay, the fact remains that *Campania* did not sail when she should have. Ultimately the responsibility lies with her captain. Quite how the lookouts on *Campania* could have missed the parade of ships passing towards the Hoxa Gate has never been explained; visibility was good and the ships commenced passing in daylight. *Campania* was also well aware that she was to sail that evening, as per the 10.31 p.m. message.

> 11.20 p.m.: As the fleet was only a few miles away from Scapa heading to the south-east to rendezvous with Beatty, *Blanche* asked Commodore F (Commodore, Destroyer Flotillas, Grand Fleet: Commodore James Rose Price Hawksley, in *Castor*), 'Can you see *Campania*?' Reply: 'No, I am asking last Destroyer.'

> 11.23 p.m.: Commodore F to *Mons*, 'Can you see *Campania*?' Reply: 'No.'

> 11.58 p.m.: *Blanche* to C in C, '*Castor* reports Destroyers can see no sign of *Campania*.'

To Jellicoe the signal indicates only that *Campania* was not on station, hence the two following signals.

> 11.59 p.m.: C in C to *Campania*, 'Speed from obstruction 17 knots. Course from Skerries 84° until 1.30 a.m. then 90°.' This signal was received on board *Campania*.

> 12.42 a.m. (31 May): C in C to 2nd i/c 4th B.S., S.O. 4th B.S., S.O. 1st B.S., 2nd i/c 1st B.S., *Iron Duke*, *Campania*. '6th subdivision alter course in succession to 90° at 1.30 a.m. without further signal. Remaining subdivisions conform.'

From these two signals it is clear that Jellicoe believed that *Campania* had sailed but was proceeding independently and he was providing course details to enable her to rejoin.

Meanwhile, back at Scapa Bay, at 11.45 p.m. R.A. Scapa (Rear Admiral Francis S. Miller, aboard *Cyclops*) having been informed by the boom guard ship *Royal Arthur* that *Campania* had not passed the boom, enquired, 'Are you leaving tonight?' This message must have caused some consternation aboard *Campania*, especially as it was followed soon afterwards by Jellicoe's 11.59 p.m. signal.

Campania weighed anchor at 12.40 a.m. 31 May and 'Proceeded as required for booms' at 12.46 a.m. She passed through the outer boom at 1.15 a.m. and set course 'S72E. Full speed.' Realising that maximum effort was required her engine room staff were able to work her up to 20.5 knots, possibly a little more, putting the lie to the engine defects tale. She was over two hours behind the Grand Fleet, approximately thirty five miles with the fleet maintaining 17 knots. It would have taken her about twelve hours to catch up; with hindsight, ample time to join the fleet before the battle.

1.45 a.m.: R.A. Scapa to Admiralty and C in C, '*Campania* has sailed.'

This message was received by Jellicoe around 2.00 a.m., and was probably his first indication that *Campania* had not sailed with the fleet.

Jellicoe had been informed by the Admiralty that enemy submarines were active in the North Sea. Also, attacks on ships of the Harwich Force had been reported. Accordingly, now knowing that *Campania* was proceeding without escort and not knowing when he would meet the enemy, Jellicoe ordered *Campania* at 4.37 a.m. to 'Return to base.' She reversed course and slowed to 19 knots, passing the through the boom at 8.35 a.m. 31 May, almost six hours before Beatty's ships sighted the enemy. She came to anchor at 9.04 a.m. back at Berth 5 off Scapa Bay.

Whatever happened on *Campania*'s bridge that evening as the Grand Fleet was sailing out was ultimately Swann's responsibility. He must have had an uncomfortable interview with Jellicoe shortly after the Grand Fleet returned.

Engadine

Following the 4 May 1916 Baby debacle *Engadine* returned to her duties at Rosyth. Her normal berth was close to the harbour of Granton, near the mouth of the Forth. *Engadine*'s captain at this time was Lt Cdr Charles Gwillim Robinson, RN, and his second in command was Lt Handcock, RNR, her prewar captain. She was attached to the 3rd Light Cruiser Squadron, Rear Admiral Trevylyan D. W. Napier, a mixed squadron of several classes of light cruisers. *Falmouth* (flag), and *Yarmouth* were Weymouth Class (eight 6 inch guns), *Gloucester* (Bristol class—

two 6 inch and ten 4 inch guns) and *Birkenhead* (originally ordered for Greece as *Antinavarchos Kountouriotis*, but taken over in August 1914—ten 5.5 inch guns), all were capable of at least 25 knots. Capable of only 22 knots *Engadine* was one of the slowest units of the Battle Cruiser Fleet.

On the morning of 30 May all hands were called and commenced coaling, taking 350 tons aboard in just two hours. At 6.01 p.m. Napier signalled his squadron, including *Engadine*, to raise steam for 22 knots and report when ready, he indicated that *Falmouth* would be ready by 8 p.m. At 8.50 p.m. Beatty signalled the Battle Cruiser Fleet to begin leaving harbour at 9 p.m. Eight minutes later Napier informed *Engadine* that the '3rd L.C.S. will pass [the Forth] bridge at 9.35 p.m., form astern of *Gloucester*, 4th ship.' They were passing the Isle of May at the mouth of the Firth of Forth by 11.30 p.m., joining the Battle Cruiser Fleet steaming easterly at 16 knots, later increasing to 18 knots.

For the next ten hours *Engadine* proceeded in company with the cruisers, approximately ten miles ahead of the main Battle Cruiser Fleet. At times the seaplane carrier was leading the fleet, although well protected by the light cruisers around her. She was located between *Inconstant*, 1st L.C.S., to port and *Falmouth*, 3rd L.C.S., to starboard, in an area of less disturbed water and well positioned to send her floatplanes to scout ahead of the fleet. In her aft hangar were two Short 184s (8029 and 8359) and two Sopwith Babies (8175 and 8182), she had no forward flight deck. Early in the morning the weather was unsuitable for flying but at 11.25 a.m. *Engadine* signalled directly to Beatty 'Conditions suitable for large and small machines.'

Leading Signalman H. Y. Ganderton, stationed on *Engadine*'s bridge recalled:

By 2.20 p.m. we were approaching enemy waters, and everyone was on the alert. *Inconstant* and *Cordelia* had drawn a little ahead of their former position, when smoke was observed on the horizon, and very soon the masts and funnels of two vessels hove in sight on our port bow, just topping the skyline. The captain levelled his glasses at the strange ships and remarked that they appeared to be warships, when a shout came from the lower bridge, and a hurried scatter of feet as the Yeoman of Signals pushed his way past and ran up the ladder to the Captain with the message: 'Enemy in sight, Sir. The signal flag is flying at the masthead of *Inconstant*.' 'Thank you,' was the quiet reply.

These were probably the German large destroyers SMS *B109* and SMS *B110* which had been sighted a few minutes earlier by the cruiser *Galatea* and identified as cruisers.

Shortly afterward, at 2.31 p.m., Napier ordered *Engadine* to 'Close Battle Cruisers.' He repeated this with more emphasis six minutes later, 'Two enemy Cruisers sighted about East. Take cover near battle cruisers.' Robinson, possibly reluctantly, turned *Engadine* to the north towards the main fleet, and increased speed to 22 knots. Undoubtedly relieved to be rid of his impediment, Napier was now free to head into danger. Just a minute after Napier's first signal Beatty had ordered the Battle Cruiser Fleet, 'Alter course leading ships together the rest in succession to S.S.E.' *Engadine* and Beatty were now closing at over forty knots.

Galatea meanwhile was shadowing the two vessels she had earlier reported. At 2.45 p.m. she signalled Beatty that the 'Enemy apparently turned North.'

At 2.46 p.m. Beatty ordered *Champion* (Capt. James Uchtred Farie, Commodore (Hull) (D) in command of the Battle Cruiser Fleet destroyers), flotilla leader of the 13th Destroyer Flotilla, to 'Send two Destroyers to *Engadine*.' Farie detached *Onslow* (Lt Cdr John Cronyn Tovey, later Admiral of the Fleet Sir John) and *Moresby* (Lt Cdr Roger Vincent Alison), they joined *Engadine* about 3.30 p.m.

At 2.47 p.m. Beatty ordered *Engadine*, by searchlight, to 'Send up Seaplanes to scout N.N.E. Am sending two Destroyers to you.' He appears to have been acting on *Galatea*'s signal and wanted the floatplanes to scout along the reported track of the German ships. *Engadine* was now passing between the two battle cruiser squadrons that were Beatty's main force. The two ships of the Second Battle Cruiser Squadron, *New Zealand* and *Indefatigable*, were to her starboard and once past *Indefatigable*, Robinson turned the seaplane carrier quickly across her stern and headed north-east looking for calmer water before launching the Short.

The pilots on *Engadine* flew according to a rota and on this day it was the turn of Flt S/Lt Grahame Donald. As the enemy came into sight on the bridge, he was:

> Sitting in the cockpit, waiting for instructions, engine warming up, clad in flying gear, chain hooked on ready to hoist—we'd have been in the water and away in about a minute and a half. And just as I got my engine nicely warmed up unfortunately our Senior Flying Officer, Flight Lieutenant Rutland, appeared, waved me down and my observer and told me that he'd got the Captain's sanction that he was to go. So my old Short Seaplane 8359 away she went—but without us.

Robinson reported:

> When in company with the Battle Cruiser Fleet, Seaplane No. 8359 was hoisted out at 3.07 p.m. with Flight Lieutenant Frederick Joseph Rutland, R.N. as pilot, and Assistant Paymaster George Stanley Trewin, R.N. as observer, with orders to scout N.N.E. for Hostile ships, in accordance with your signal received on board at 2.40 p.m. The delay in hoisting out Seaplane was caused through the Ship having to keep clear of the Cruisers.

Engadine's clocks were out of synchronisation with *Lion*'s, a not uncommon occurrence when reading through the signal records.

Rutland:

I steered N. 10 E. and after about ten minutes sighted the enemy. Clouds were at 1,000 to 1,200 feet, with patches at 900 feet. This necessitated flying very low. On sighting the enemy it was very hard to tell what they were and so I had to close to within a mile and a half at a height of 1,000 feet.

Trewin reported:

The clouds were very low, which necessitated low flying and therefore reduced the range of visibility which varied from nil to four miles, except for one short spell when it was about 7–10 miles. During this brief break in the mist clouds, I sighted 3 Cruisers and 5 Destroyers at about 3.20 p.m. We closed this Fleet and from their position and composition it appeared to be hostile.

The exact location of Jellicoe's Grand Fleet was not clearly known and the ships seen could have been from his scouting forces. Any doubts were soon dispelled: however

When we had closed them to about 1½ miles, flying at a height of 1,000 feet, I saw more Destroyers, and then heard the reports of bursting shells and saw shrapnel bursts around us.

The appearance of the Short came as a surprise to the Germans. *Leutnant zur See* Heinrich Bassange on SMS *Elbing*, a light cruiser attached to the II Scouting Group of the High Seas Fleet, had already been involved in the first exchange of fire in the Battle of Jutland, coming to the support of the two destroyers *B109* and *B110* which were being fired on by *Galatea* and *Phaeton*. With two more German cruisers, SMS *Pillau* and SMS *Frankfurt*, coming up to support *Elbing*, the British cruisers retired on the battle cruisers and the brief action was broken off. Around 3.30 p.m. (GMT):

. . . a little enemy seaplane came up from the south east. We were much taken aback it was not known that there were any enemy planes at this time, it must have been kept aboard an enemy ship. We had never thought of this idea. The whole manoeuvre took about two minutes. The aircraft inspected us from front to back in length and then disappeared into the mist.

Rutland:

When sighted they were steering a northerly course. I flew through several of the columns of smoke caused through bursting shrapnel. When the Observer had counted and got the disposition of the enemy and was making his W/T report, I sheered to about three miles, keeping the enemy well in sight. While the Observer was sending one message, the enemy turned 16 points. I drew his attention to this and he forthwith transmitted it.

Trewin:

In the middle of my sending a W/T message, timed 1530, I saw the hostile Fleet altering course to due South. On completion of that message, I transmitted another, timed 1533, giving their alteration of course. The Seaplane altered course to the Southward and stood off them about 3 miles, in order to watch their movements and verify their composition, sending messages timed 1545 and 1548.

Rutland, on spotting the battle cruisers during a brief break in the weather, believed that their messages had got through owing to the dispositions and course of the ships. *Engadine* certainly received the messages, but she was the only vessel to read them. The sad tale is reported by Robinson.

The following signals were received from the Seaplane:

1530.—Three enemy Cruisers and 5 Destroyers, distance from me 10 miles bearing 90°, steering course to the N.W.

1533.—Enemy's course is South.

1545.—Three enemy Cruisers and 10 Destroyers steering South.

1548.—Four enemy Cruisers and 10 Destroyers steering South.
The last signal was not received in the Ship, which I think was due to Seaplane descending at the time and the amount of other W/T going on. Attempts were made to pass these signals on to *Lion* by searchlight but this could not now be done as apparently she had already opened fire on the enemy. An attempt was also made to pass them through *Barham* but this failed also for the same reason.

Whilst Trewin was attempting to send the last message, the fuel pipe to the left front carburettor (the Sunbeam 225 hp V-12 Mohawk had four carburettors) fractured and the engine power fell significantly. Rutland had to make an emergency landing, with Trewin desperately winding in his long trailing aerial with one hand whilst continuing to transmit with the other. 'On landing I made good the defect with rubber tube and reported to the Ship that I could go on again.' *Engadine* had come up whilst Rutland was working on the engine, and ordered them to taxy alongside to be hoisted in. The Short was hoisted in at 4.04 p.m.

After being ejected from his Short, Grahame Donald was given:

A kind of consolation prize for missing the main flight, I was put out on the aft deck in my Schneider-Cup machine to chivvy any Zeppelins which were expected to accompany the German Fleet. But as it happened no Zeppelins put in an appearance which was perhaps rather a good thing for me because by the time the sea got up a bit, if I'd tried to take the little Schneider fighter off I'm afraid it would have been one more crash like the Tondern job—only this time I wouldn't have been able to be picked up. Because nobody can stop in the middle of a naval battle to pick people up.

Bad weather had kept the Zeppelins in their sheds on 30 May and the morning of 31 May, those that did get away in the afternoon saw nothing of the battle in the poor visibility. Only on 1 June did the *Marine Luftschiffabteilung* provide any useful information.

Just eight minutes after hoisting in the Short, Lt Cdr Tovey of the escorting destroyer *Onslow*, signalled by semaphore, 'Can you dispense with my services? If so, I will join 5th B.S.' Clearly, hanging around the seaplane carrier was not to any destroyer man's taste. *Engadine* replied, 'Yes, certainly.' The escort departed without further ado and the seaplane carrier followed the movements of the 5th Battle Squadron, new *Queen Elizabeth* class fast battleships, for a number of hours. Beatty by this time was too busy to give a thought to *Engadine* and any further aerial scouting and she disappears into the smoke and mist for a while.   NOT OBVIOUS FROM TIT ABOVE DESCRIP'N.

The Battle of Jutland was not just a single massive clash of dreadnoughts. As the battle developed, weather conditions began to deteriorate, and the smoke from more than two hundred coal-burning ships steaming at maximum speeds began to cloud the North Sea. Squadrons, flotillas and single ships became detached, many fighting their own isolated battles. One such engagement was fought by the 1st Cruiser Squadron, four ageing armoured cruisers *Defence* (flag, Rear Admiral Sir Robert Arbuthnot), *Warrior* (Capt. Vincent Barkly Molteno), *Duke of Edinburgh* and *Black Prince*. The squadron had lost contact with *Black Prince*, but Arbuthnot led the three remaining ships towards the sound of battle, cutting across the bows of Beatty's battle cruisers in the process. They attacked the crippled light cruiser SMS *Wiesbaden*, of the II Scouting Group, which had been previously mauled by the battle cruisers but was still capable of fighting back. Earlier she had hit Tovey's *Onslow* in the engine room slowing the destroyer to a mere ten knots, undeterred Tovey lashed back and hit the cruiser with a single torpedo. Tovey sailed on and launched his final two torpedoes at the High Seas Fleet before turning away for home. *Onslow* was lucky to escape with just five casualties.

Whilst Arbuthnot concentrated on the crippled *Wiesbaden*, his own doom was fast approaching in the form of battle cruisers SMS *Lützow* and SMS *Derfflinger*. A few quick salvos and *Defence* blew up, there were no survivors from the 900 men aboard. Next in line *Warrior* now received the undivided attention of the two battle cruisers, hit fifteen times she survived and staggered off into the smoke of battle. Coming up behind, *Duke of Edinburgh* bore a charmed life, not seriously damaged, she was able to escape under a self-generated smoke screen, but almost collided with the Grand Fleet in this most confused of sea battles. *Black Prince*, separated from her squadron, met her private doom under the guns of the High Seas Fleet, taking her crew of 857 to their deaths. *Duke of Edinburgh* survived to reach Scapa Flow.

Wiesbaden, crippled and sinking, continued to fight a lonely and epic battle. Never giving in, her crew fought to save their ship and every British warship that came within range. Finally, alone, she rolled over and sank. There was a single survivor, plucked out of the sea by a passing Norwegian steamer.

Warrior on fire aft, one engine room flooded the other flooding, unable to control the remaining engine, over eighty dead or wounded, was limping off to the west. At 6.40 p.m. she was seen by *Engadine* who came to her assistance, keeping company whilst *Warrior* fought for her life. Finally, at 8.00 p.m. *Warrior* semaphored, 'We are nearly stopped. Come and take me in tow.' With considerable difficulty, *Engadine* took the much larger cruiser in tow. At 8.37 p.m. *Engadine* signalled the C in C (Jellicoe) that she had the cruiser in tow. Although she had had revolutions for 19 knots they were only making 8 knots through the water. At dawn it was evident that *Warrior* could not last much longer. At 7.20 a.m. Captain Molteno ordered *Engadine* to drop the tow, and come alongside to take off *Warrior*'s crew.

Grahame Donald later recalled the events of the next hour. The cruiser was many times the tonnage of the seaplane carrier and over 150 feet longer, but:

> Our captain was a marvellous seaman. He and old Handcock, ex of the South Eastern and Chatham Railway, handling her like bringing her alongside the pier, but there was quite a sea running and the *Warrior* was half under water, and she did punch one hole in our stoke hold with one of her casemate guns. One of our firemen saved the situation by stuffing his cap in the hole and shouting to the other chaps "Come on, give us a hand" and they packed it up.

The two ships were tied together, with men on *Engadine* standing by with axes should *Warrior* take a sudden plunge, rising and falling alongside each other with the passing waves. *Warrior*'s men were lined up in divisions ready to transfer, the able bodied men first to make room to transfer the wounded, when she gave a shudder as if she were about to sink.

> It was unmistakable. Apart from pulling us with her, just for a moment there was that look on all those chaps' faces—and keep in mind they'd had an awful hammering. I mean the scuppers were running with blood and casualties. There might have been a panic. The Captain just signalled the bugler. He blew the 'Still'—just one toot. Every man jack stood to attention—and then they carried on in a very orderly manner.

Assisted by the officers and men lining *Engadine*'s side all those who could jumped or scrambled aboard and were hustled below out of the way. Then the walking wounded and stretcher cases were brought aboard, as gently and carefully as conditions permitted.

One fell from his stretcher into the maelstrom between the two ships. Instantly, men from *Warrior* moved to attempt a rescue and had to be ordered to stop by their Captain, anyone caught in the gap between the ships would be crushed. But Flt Lt Rutland could see that the man was resting on the remains of a fender and being carried forward into clearer water where the hull curved towards the bow. Coolly, he went down a rope, swam over to the man and pulled him back to the rope to be hoisted aboard. Rutland was awarded a well-deserved Albert Medal for this act.

Last to leave *Warrior* was her Captain. As *Engadine* cast off, Ganderton remembered the battered cruiser as being 'a truly forlorn spectacle, derelict, battered and battle scarred, forsaken at the last, and yet, with the White Ensign proudly flying at the masthead.' The seaplane carrier set course for Rosyth with 35 officers, 681 men and 27 wounded aboard. She arrived at 1.35 a.m. 2 June. *Warrior* was not seen again and probably foundered shortly afterwards.

Beatty, in his reports, praised the work of *Engadine* as well as Rutland and Trewin.

> The work of *Engadine* appears to have been most praiseworthy throughout, and of great value. Lieutenant Commander C. G. Robinson deserves great credit for the skilful and seamanlike manner in which he handled his ship. He actually towed *Warrior* for 75 miles between 8.40 p.m., May 31st, and 7.15 a.m., June 1st, and was instrumental in saving the lives of her ship's company.

Comments that Jellicoe fully endorsed. Beatty then turned his attention to the flight.

> [My] order was carried out very quickly, and by 3.8 p.m. a seaplane, with Flight Lieutenant F. J. Rutland, R.N., as pilot, and Assistant Paymaster G. S. Trewin, R.N., as observer, was well underway; her first reports of the enemy were received in *Engadine* about 3.30 p.m. Owing to clouds it was necessary to fly very low, and in order to identify four enemy light cruisers the seaplane had to fly at a height of 900 ft. within 3,000 yards of them, the light cruisers opening fire on her with every gun that would bear. This in no way interfered with the clarity of their reports, and both Flight Lieutenant Rutland and Assistant Paymaster Trewin are to be congratulated on their achievement, which indicates that seaplanes under such circumstances are of distinct value.

The Admiralty also agreed. Rutland was awarded the DSC, 'For his gallantry and persistence in flying within close range of four enemy light cruisers, in order to enable accurate information to be obtained and transmitted concerning them. Conditions at the time made low flying necessary.' Trewin was Mentioned in Despatches for his role. Lt Cdr Robinson promoted Commander, 'Was prompt in sending up a seaplane to scout. Handled his ship in a skilful and seamanlike manner, and towed *Warrior* for 75 miles, subsequently succeeding in taking off her crew, thus saving their lives.'

Repeat as p 102

Could *Campania* Have Made A Difference?

On 1 June, as the battle fleet was returning, *Campania* was out in the Pentland Firth exercising her machines. It is hard not to imagine the thoughts of her airmen as they must have passed over those battle-worn ships. But could they have made a difference?

If no accidents or breakdowns had occurred, she could have joined up by about 1.30 p.m., an hour or so before the Grand Fleet was committed to battle. As she carried ten seaplanes, three two-seater Short 184s and seven single-seat Sopwiths, she could have made useful reconnaissance flights at the beginning of the battle. However, the Shorts had not yet been flown from the deck and would have to be launched over the side as were Rutland and Trewin from *Engadine*. That is not to say that an attempt to launch a Short from the deck could not have been made if necessary. The first such flight was made on 6 June, so it is not unreasonable to assume that the required trolley was available. The Sopwiths could have taken off but, without W/T sets, were not suitable for reconnaissance. They were really intended to be used against airships, which Jellicoe and his staff expected would appear.

Could the Shorts have taken off from the sea? *Campania* would have been at the rear of the fleet if she had caught up, in an area disturbed by the passage of more than hundred vessels. As *Engadine* did, she would have had to search for a relatively smooth area of sea. The technique of using the ship to form a slick of relatively smooth water was not unknown, *Empress* was using it in 1917 in the Eastern Mediterranean, but does not appear to have been widely practised at this time. The Shorts were relatively seaworthy and a successful take-off could probably have been made. Weather conditions were similar to those experienced by Rutland and Trewin. The problem is whether their W/T reports would have been received.

Wing Commander Richard Bell Davies, who took commanded of *Campania*'s flight detachment some months after Jutland, recalled several fleet exercises in the spring of 1917.

In each, the first enemy sighting was made by a seaplane, a report being passed by wireless. In none of the exercises did the seaplane's report reach the C in C until after surface contact had been made. The trouble was that we were still using spark wireless sets. For some technical reason the fleet flagship could not keep watch on the seaplane wave length. A battleship in the flagship's division was therefore detailed as aircraft guardship to relay the aircraft's signals to the flagship. There was always a time lag.

All the indications are that at Jutland there was no similar arrangement, perhaps the problem had not been identified, so it was dependent on the initiative of the seaplane carrier to pass on all messages received. Which Robinson did but, even if received, quickly moving events had already made them out of date.

For the RNAS, Jutland was undoubtedly a lost opportunity but also a learning experience.

10

After Jutland Beatty and Aviation for the Grand Fleet

After the battle *Campania* remained at Scapa Flow, attached to the Grand Fleet. Jutland was the first and only opportunity she had to use her machines in a fleet action.

The first Short 184 take-off, by 8058, but the pilot is unknown, was made from her flight deck on 3 June 1916, the floatplane was mounted on a wheeled trolley similar to that used by Walsh almost a year ago. The big Shorts, once raised from the hangar to the aft end of the flight deck, had to be pushed through the gap between the funnels before their wings could be spread. Once that was completed they could be moved back until their wings were just clear of the funnels, from there the flight deck extended almost 200 feet to the bow. Wing Commander Richard Bell Davies, commanding *Campania*'s flight detachment, recalled the Shorts being:

> . . . lowered on to a wheeled axle, held in place by guides on the floats and by a wire span attached to a quick-release gear in the pilot's cockpit. The tail float had a fitting which slid into a split-tube guide set at a height which kept the machine in her flying attitude. After take-off, the pilot released the wheels and axle, which fell into the sea and could be recovered by the attendant destroyers.

We've seen all this before

Machines still could not land back aboard of course, and had to land alongside and the ship stopped to pick them up.

For a time machines from *Campania* re-established a seaplane base at Pierowall Harbour for anti-submarine patrols over the Fair Isle Channel. The great advantage of this establishment, which comprised a single Short 184 and a drifter for communications, was an apparently unlimited supply of fresh eggs, an unheard of luxury. When the Houton Bay seaplane base was established it took over the patrol, expanding and establishing a permanent base in the sheltered Pierowall Harbour. *Oh! Yippee*

Campania was only of limited use however, her great effort before Jutland had been too much for her ageing engines; they became less and less reliable and eventually could only drive her at eighteen knots or less. She took part in a number of fleet exercises, anti-submarine and anti-Zeppelin sweeps but, other than occasional anti-submarine patrols, her aircraft were never used operationally. During one of the fleet exercises Wing Cdr Davies flew a Short on reconnaissance:

> Near the end of the exercise, as the Grand Fleet started deployment, my engine gave out and I had to make a forced landing. Not having had much experience with seaplanes in a heavy sea I tried to put her down too slowly, with the result that I hit the top of a big wave, bounced off it and dropped heavily into the succeeding hollow. Some of the landing struts buckled. The observer put out the sea anchor to which the plane rode, head to wind; but it was a most ignominious situation. Columns of battleships were surging towards us, then wheeling majestically into line and passing a few hundred yards away. I had the most unpleasant conviction that every pair of binoculars in the Grand Fleet was trained on us, broken down and wallowing, helpless and lopsided, in their wash. When the procession had passed, *Campania* came and picked us up.

Campania was probably the only aircraft carrier to have an aircraft designed specifically for its use, the Fairey Campania. In 1915 the Admiralty issued a specification for a floatplane to operate from her flight deck. Not entering service until early 1918, the resulting aircraft was a little smaller than the Short 184 but fitted with a larger engine, either a 275 hp Sunbeam Maori or 335 hp Rolls Royce Eagle. The performance advantage, however, was marginal and only about sixty were completed. They served aboard *Campania, Nairana* and *Pegasus*. However, the Fairey Campania was the first of the company's long line of designs which served with the Fleet Air Arm into the 1970s.

In 1918, *Campania* was based at Rosyth as a base and training ship. Here she met her end. During a gale on 5 November 1918 she dragged her anchor and ran down on the battleship *Royal Oak* then the light battle cruiser *Glorious*, neither of which suffered significant damage. But it was too much for *Campania*'s old hull and she slowly settled by the stern and sank, without loss of life.

After Jutland *Engadine* resumed her duties at Rosyth, mainly training and exercises. However, on 18 August she sailed with the Battle Cruiser Fleet out into the North Sea to rendezvous with the Grand Fleet coming down from Scapa Flow. *Engadine* with two escorting destroyers, *Pasley* and *Archeron*, was detailed to sail at 5.45 p.m. following the 3rd Light Cruiser Squadron. Once at sea she took her place, as before, at the head of the fleet as part of the scouting force.

At 8.29 a.m. an airship was sighted out to starboard and *Engadine* was instructed by Beatty to send off a seaplane if opportunity offered. The airship disappeared soon afterwards, but at 2 p.m. another was sighted to the north. *Engadine* now slowed to a stop and quickly launched a Sopwith Baby. It was a repeat of the all too familiar story, the sea was choppy and whilst attempting to get off the propeller shattered. The seaplane carrier circled round and stopped again to pick up the seaplane she had launched just fifteen minutes earlier. She was now well astern of the light cruisers and the Battle Cruiser Fleet and in danger of being run down by the Grand Fleet. After watching the Grand Fleet steam by, *Engadine* put on speed and was soon steaming at 23 knots and catching up with Beatty. Shortly after rejoining the scouting force, *Falmouth* on her port quarter was torpedoed and sunk. Then *Engadine* was narrowly missed by a torpedo passing under her stern.

During the night the fleets were under constant observation by an airship, which used a searchlight to try to determine the course and position of the ships. It was obvious that any hope of catching part of the High Seas Fleet by surprise had passed, and the fleets turned back to Rosyth and Scapa Flow. *Engadine* returned to training and exercises. She, and the other early seaplane carriers, would be sent to the Mediterranean in 1918. Before that she would be joined at Rosyth by some new seaplane carriers.

Vindex having been a successful conversion, three similar mixed carriers followed through 1916 and 1917. First, to complete the triumvirate of Manx steamers, *Manxman* was requisitioned and sent to Chatham for conversion early in 1916, she proved far from satisfactory. Given a forward hangar capable of housing four assembled aeroplanes, and a larger flight deck, she should have been an improvement on *Vindex*. But, she was smaller, just 334 feet overall, and her engines were tired. When new she was capable of over 22 knots but, after eight years of hard service, she now struggled to maintain just 18 knots. Attached to the Battle Cruiser Fleet at Rosyth between December 1916 and July 1917, *Manxman* went out with the fleet on a number of occasions but was unable to keep up. On 30 January 1917, Signalman Ganderton recalled:

> [*Engadine*] went out at 1500, following *Sydney* and *Manxman*—the latter parted company at 1600 with two destroyers and went on her own as she could not keep up. Her speed is officially seventeen and a half knots. We proceeded at 20 knots, with the B.C.F. 5 miles on our starb'd quarter.

Consequently, *Manxman* was largely limited to training and experimental work before being transferred to the Mediterranean as a base ship in October 1917. Before that, she had one moment in the spotlight.

We have already encountered Flight Lieutenant F. J. Rutland aboard *Engadine* at Jutland. In December 1916 newly promoted Flight Commander Rutland was posted to *Manxman*, then commissioning at Chatham, in command of her RNAS contingent and senior pilot. He had earned his place in the RNAS the hard way, having enlisted in the Royal Navy in 1902, qualified as a diver and had tried service in submarines before being bitten by the flying bug. Still an enlisted man he realised that he would have to gain a commission if he were to have a chance of transferring to the RNAS and learning to fly. By dint of honest hard work he passed all the necessary exams and in 1913 won his commission as a Sub-Lieutenant. Although older than most junior officers he was experienced in the ways of the Navy and was able to get on. His request for a transfer for flight training was approved and in October 1914 he began training at Eastchurch. Training was quick and minimal at that time; the demand for pilots far outweighing the supply, and he gained RAeC Certificate on 26 January 1915 (Rutland recalled his RAeC Certificate as No. 1085, but Royal Aero Club record cards show No. 1053 against his name.). From Eastchurch he was posted to Calshot for seaplane training, and from there to *Engadine*.

Returning to *Manxman*; she left Rosyth on the morning of 28 April 1917, escorted by *Galatea*, the First Light Cruiser Squadron and destroyers. They were to proceed across the North Sea and attempt to catch the airship morning patrol off the Horn Reef. If found, Flt Cdr F. J. Rutland was to fly off and destroy it. The following morning a Sopwith Pup was sitting armed and ready at the top of her flight deck, with another Pup ready to follow. Rutland was sent off at 6.20 a.m., to 'patrol a line North-East and South-West from Horn's Reef to locate hostile aircraft.' Clouds were between 1,000 feet and 4,000 feet, the wind was about fifteen knots out of the west. According to his report he was flying Pup 9920, which rose easily after a short run. The second machine, probably 9918, also took off safely but had to return with engine trouble, unable to land back on *Manxman*, the pilot had to ditch alongside a destroyer, *Patrician*, and was recovered safely although the machine was lost. Rutland meanwhile had set course towards Horn's Reef, about ten miles off the Danish coast.

'About 15 mins. after leaving the ship one cylinder commenced missing and caused a fair amount of vibration; this tended to make the compass very unsteady.' After patrolling for half an hour, without sighting an airship, Rutland turned back towards the ships. At this point, shaken by the rough running engine, the compass began leaking and soon ran dry. He attempted to hold a steady course, but on arriving at the expected rendezvous no ships were in sight. Visibility was no more than one and a half miles as he searched in various directions until, at 8.30 a.m., there was just sufficient fuel remaining to reach the Danish coast. Without a compass he set off downwind in the assumption that the wind direction had not changed since take-off. Twenty minutes later he sighted land and turned north along the coast to ensure he was over Denmark. Sighting a small village, he later learned that this was Agger, some ninety miles north of Esbjerg, he flew over it to attract the villagers' attention then glided down to land about one and a half miles from the shore.

I considered that the natives would accept my statement that I was 3 miles out, but had I landed this distance out I doubt if I could have got ashore. There was a high sea running.

The machine had 4 air-bags in the fuselage, and by kneeling on the tailplane, I was able to keep the machine horizontal for about 10 mins; after about 20 min. to half an hour the machine sank.

A boat was launched, manned by five men, which came out towards the machine. When the boat was about half a mile from the machine, the machine sank, and I swam towards the boat and the crew picked me up.

The fishermen were of the opinion that the machine would never be washed up. These men ran a great risk in launching the boat in the heavy sea then running, they having to go through surf, and they informed me that an hour later no boat could have been sent out.

Rutland was well cared for, given dry clothes, and taken to the local inn. He was shortly examined by the local magistrate, Mr Fugl, who decided that Rutland had indeed landed at least three miles from the shore and could thus be considered a shipwrecked mariner. Rutland was able to contact the British Legation at Copenhagen who arranged for him to travel to Aarhus and then on to Copenhagen where he arrived at midnight on 1 May. From there he was quickly sent on to Helsingborg, Sweden, and then to the British Legation at Kristiania (present day Oslo), Norway, on 3 May. From there he was able to return to Britain a few days later. The five Danish fishermen were subsequently rewarded for their life-saving efforts by the British Minister at Copenhagen.

The two remaining mixed carriers were more than just conversions, both were hulls under construction when the war commenced and work was stopped. The first, *Nairana*, was being built by William Denny Bros, at Dumbarton, for Huddart Parker Limited to be used on mail and passenger services across the Bass Strait between Australia and Tasmania. The hull was well advanced and machinery being installed when work was stopped. Taken over in 1917 she was completed with aft hangar and a forward flight deck. Her most obvious feature was a large fore and aft gantry crane fixed on top of the hangar and arranged to carry a floatplane over the stern of the ship before lowering it on to the sea. This was an improvement on a similar arrangement fitted to *Manxman* where the gantry was installed between two towers located on the quarterdeck. *Nairana* commissioned in September 1917, and was used mainly for training pilots and as an aircraft ferry at Rosyth. She served in North Russia during 1918 and 1919.

The final seaplane carrier was *Pegasus*, ordered as a passenger and cargo steamer the *Stockholm* for the Great Eastern Railway. When work was stopped the hull was fairly well advanced but in such a condition that little reconstruction was required in the conversion. Her engines were converted from coal to oil burning, and bunkerage arranged for three days at full speed. As with all the mixed carriers she had an aft hangar, for four large floatplanes, and a forward flight deck and hangar under the bridge. Instead of gantry, she had two 3 ton capacity cranes fitted aft. The forward flight deck provided a run of eighty-five feet for the five single-seaters that could be accommodated in the forward hangar. *Pegasus* commissioned in September 1917, a few days after *Nairana* she too spent the rest of the war at Rosyth training pilots and as an aircraft ferry taking aeroplanes out to ships of the fleet. On several occasions she accompanied *Furious* to sea during exercises to pick up her seaplanes. In 1919 she also spent some time in North Russia.

Whilst none of the new mixed carriers saw much operational use their contribution, training pilots to take-off from their small decks, was important and invaluable. In general the seaplane carriers were proving to be too small and too slow for service with the big ships of the Grand Fleet and Battle Cruiser Fleet. Other solutions would be sought to provide aeroplanes to accompany the fleets, including larger flight decks on faster ships and the possibility of landing back aboard. But first some big changes took place in the command structure of the Grand Fleet.

Grand Fleet Committee on Air Requirements

After Jutland, Jellicoe was criticised for his perceived defensive attitude towards sea warfare. It was thought that a new broom might change attitudes, and bring about the defeat of the High Seas Fleet. In December 1916, Sir John Jellicoe took over the reins at the Admiralty as First Sea Lord and Sir David Beatty was promoted to command of the Grand Fleet, over the heads of more senior admirals. But Beatty was too wise to change what was working and continued to follow a similar policy to that of his predecessor, maintenance of a numerical superiority over the High Seas Fleet. He clearly saw the need for aircraft with the fleet for scouting, bombing and anti-Zeppelin work, to which end in January 1917 he formed the Grand Fleet Committee on Air Requirements with Rear Admiral Hugh Evan-Thomas, commander of the 5th Battle Squadron, in the chair and Captain C. M. de Bartolomé (*Warspite*) and Flag Commander W. A. Egerton, as members. Whilst none of the members were airmen, the Committee's report, released on 5 February 1917, set the course of naval aviation for the remainder of the war.

The report on Grand Fleet Air Requirements for 1917 was in three sections.

Section 1. Air requirements of the Grand Fleet.

1A. Reconnaissance over the North Sea.
1B. Screening of the Fleet by aircraft whilst on passage.
1C. Heavier than air machines for duty with the Fleet.
1D. Seaplane carriers.
1E. Use of balloons and seaplanes as aids to gunnery.

Section 2. Air requirements for coast defence.

Section 3. Training and organisation of personnel. (? .

Not all Sections concerned or affected the development of naval aviation at sea. Sections 1A and 1B for example are concerned mainly with the provision of coastal seaplane and aeroplane stations and the work of the non-rigid airships. The three remaining parts from Section 1, however, are important to the future of naval aviation, and also provide a snapshot of the state of aviation with the fleet at the time. Section 2 briefly, in just two paragraphs, defines a role that in the next war would become the purview of Coastal Command of the Royal Air Force. Section 3 discusses the state of training in the RNAS with regard to shipboard aviation, but does not advance the cause of naval aviation as such.

(1C). HEAVIER THAN AIR MACHINES FOR DUTY WITH THE FLEET.

8. There are two distinct duties to be performed by heavier-than-air machines carried with the Fleet which cannot be performed by airships, viz:- Close reconnaissance and attack on enemy Zeppelins.

9. The machines for these two duties are necessarily of totally different design, and after consideration and consultation with technical experts the Committee are definitely of the opinion that any attempt at the present time to combine the two duties would only result in impairing their efficiency for either duty, whilst for the purposes of this war it is useless to consider a new design.

10. These two types of machine are known as Reconnaissance and Anti-Zeppelin machines respectively and will be dealt with separately.

11. ANTI-ZEPPELIN MACHINES. The Baby Sopwith seaplane at present supplied to the Carriers is admirably suited for this work, but it is recommended that it should be replaced by Sopwith Pup Aeroplanes in the *Campania* and *Manxman* as this will greatly increase the number of occasions when the Anti-Zeppelin type can be flown from the decks of these ships. It is recommended, however, that this change should be carried out gradually lest the present state of moderate efficiency be impaired.

12. In coming to the conclusion that the number of these machines necessary to meet the requirements of the Grand Fleet is 20, it has been assumed that 6 Zeppelins may be found in company with the enemy's Fleet, that two Anti-Zeppelin machines are required to attack each of them, whereas the evidence of Captain Swann, RN, based on experience, is that two failures out of every five flights must be anticipated, so that with a total of 20 carried, twelve successful flights may be depended upon.

13. It will be shown that the position with regard to reconnaissance machines is bad, and in the view of the fact that it will often happen that Anti-Zeppelin machines can be flown from the decks of carriers when the heavier reconnaissance machine cannot get off the deck, occasions may arise when only the Anti-Zeppelin type are in the air although it may be of far greater importance to report the presence of the enemy than to attack Zeppelins.

The Committee therefore strongly recommend the Anti-Zeppelin machines carried by the Fleet should be fitted with a small W.T. apparatus for transmission at a distance of 5 miles only, which will enable them to return to the extended cruiser line and communicate such important intelligence.

14. At the same time the Committee wish to make it clear that these machines cannot be expected to carry out any thorough reconnaissance work as they are single-seaters, difficult to control and to observe from.

15. RECONNAISSANCE MACHINES. The 240 [hp] Short two-seater machine at present supplied to carriers is in every way suitable for close reconnaissance duties and the number required to meet Fleet requirements is 20, determined on the following basis:-

    It is desirable that two machines should be in the air while the opposing Fleets are gaining touch with each other and that one should be kept in the air subsequently throughout the action with, if possible, a small reserve for use on the morning following the action. This absorbs 12 machines, and, therefore on the basis of 2 failures in every flight of 5 machines, an initial supply of 20 machines is required.

16. To meet these requirements there are at the present time 12 reconnaissance machines carried in seaplane carriers attached to the Grand Fleet, and it is unlikely that they can all be sent up.

17. These machines are intended for reconnaissance duties and should be regarded as being solely for this duty, and since it is essential that they should be as light as possible to facilitate getting off the sea (or deck in the case of *Campania*) all fittings in connection with bomb dropping or torpedo firing should be removed from them. The 14″ torpedoes which are of no military value should also be removed from all seaplane carriers, the duties of aircraft for anti-submarine work being considered the proper function of the shore stations; it is understood that experiments with 18 inch torpedoes are now proceeding independently.

The evidence used by the Committee to assume two from every five flights would be failures was provided by Captain Swann was based on his experience operating seaplanes from *Campania*. He suggested that W/T failures could be expected once in every twelve flights, engine failure every fifth flight, one in eight machines would fail to take-off.

The recommendation to replace the Sopwith Babys with Pups was acted upon quickly. Sopwith Pups were already entering service, some of the first machines being issued to *Manxman*, *Vindex* and *Campania* in the early months of 1917. Flights were made from all three ships' decks before the end of April. The average take-off run being between 35 feet and 45 feet.

The requirement of twenty of each type of machine to serve with the fleet could not be met by the existing seaplane carriers, as is clearly shown in the next section of the Report. The members of the Committee showed by their recommendations that they examined many different solutions to this shortfall.

(1D). SEAPLANE CARRIERS.

18.   The present seaplane carriers attached to the Grand Fleet are as follows:-

Ship	Speed	Reconnaissance machines.		Anti-Zeppelin machines.	
		Number carried.	How sent up.	Number carried.	How sent up.
Campania.	18	6	Deck.	6	Deck.
Engadine.	18	2	Hoisted out.	2	Hoisted out.
Manxman.	16*	4	Hoisted out.	4	Deck.
Furious.		Nil.	-----------	2	Deck.

(* Falls to 14 knots when cleaning fires.)

> It is evident from this that the Air Service so far as it is connected with the Grand Fleet suffers under grave disabilities owing to entire lack of efficient carriers, observing that:-

(a). The reconnaissance machines can, except on a calm day, only be flown from *Campania.*

(b). The probability of the *Manxman being able to be present with the Fleet is small, owing to her lack of speed.*

(c). The Engadine has no launching platform.

> Moreover, as previously mentioned, the total number of machines carried does not come up to requirements.

The inclusion of *Furious* in the above table is one of the earliest mentions of this ship, in the official record, as a potential aircraft carrier. At the time the Report was being written *Furious* was lying in an incomplete state, her future under discussion, along the dockside of her builders Armstrong Whitworth on the Tyne.

19. The Committee have considered various suggestions for improving this situation, including the following:-

(a). The alterations necessary to adapt a ship of the Donegal class.

(b). The alterations necessary to adapt a ship of the Leviathan class.

(c). Improvements to Manxman (reboiling, etc.).

(d). The provision of certain ships which have been suggested , such as the Dublin Mail Packet S.S. Munster.

> Of these (a) and (b) are considered impracticable, (c) would alleviate the situation with regard to the small machines but would not meet requirements with regard to reconnaissance machines and moreover would probably take a long time. With regard to (d) the ships suggested are too small to carry a launching platform for reconnaissance machines.

20. The Committee understands that the *Argus* (late *Conte Rosso*) is unlikely to be ready for sea before November 1917 [*Argus* was not ready for trials until September 1918.], and it therefore becomes necessary to consider other expedients. The Committee are however reluctant to recommend that taking of any other Mercantile Vessel of large size in view of the urgent demands for Mercantile tonnage for other National purposes, but it seems *Furious* would be of greater use to the Grand Fleet as a plane carrier than as a heavy gun platform.

The next five paragraphs of the Report discuss possible modifications to *Furious* and caused much debate when the Report was circulated at the Admiralty. However, they will be looked at in a later chapter which discusses *Furious*.

26. There still remains a deficiency of 6 ANTI-ZEPPELIN machines to be met and it is recommended that they should be carried in certain light cruisers, and that the selected ships should be fitted as soon as possible, observing that the machine to be carried is a very small one (viz., Sopwith Pup Aeroplane).
27. Although some loss of gun power may result from this it appears to the committee essential that the Grand Fleet should be in a position to attack Zeppelins. Machines are now available of a type which has proved successful on shore for this purpose and it only remains to arrange to carry them in the Fleet.

(1E). AIRCRAFT AS AIDS TO GUNNERY.
28. The Committee are of the opinion that the use of Kite Balloons for gunnery purposes has not yet emerged from the experimental stage and that the large provision which has been made in this direction is ample to meet present requirements, […].

The Committee goes on to declare that the retention of balloon ships such as *Menelaus*, *Canning* and *City of Oxford* was wasteful and the ships should be paid off into mercantile service as soon as possible, adding that 'there are 52 officers and 350 men employed in these ships practically doing nothing.' *Menelaus* was paid off in June 1917, becoming an ammunition carrier under the red ensign. *Canning* remained with the Grand Fleet until the end of the war, proving the most efficient of all the converted balloon ships. *City of Oxford* was deactivated as a balloon ship in June 1917, but converted to a seaplane carrier and sent out to reinforce the East Indies and Egypt Seaplane Squadron at Port Said.

32. Meanwhile experimental work should continue with the three balloons carried by *Campania*, any additional ones required being obtained from the

shore stations. It is suggested that these experiments should include the use of balloons for giving warning of approaching torpedoes.

33. The use of heavier than air machines for gunnery purposes is very doubtful, except in so far as the reconnaissance machines may be able to give information of a general character and especially as to the course of the enemy, whilst carrying out their reconnaissance duties during action. It is however considered that further experiments in this direction are required but that all attempts to utilise them for spotting for individual ships should be discontinued as it tends to impair their efficiency for reconnaissance work to which the Committee attach the highest importance.

Whilst balloons and aeroplanes were actively employed spotting for artillery on the Western Front conditions there were very different from those experienced at sea. Both targets and batteries were static, and guns could be ranged individually or in whole batteries. Balloon ships were used successfully at Gallipoli, but under unique conditions. At sea both the guns and targets were in constant motion, and there was no time to range individual guns or even ships. It is difficult to fault the Committee's decision not to employ aeroplanes or balloons to spot for naval gunfire of the fleet whilst operating in the North Sea.

Beatty forwarded the Report to the Admiralty on 7 February 1917. In his covering letter he 'concur[ed] generally with the report, and most of the recommendations would be to the advantage of the service.' Emphasising that 'The provision of efficient ANTI-ZEPPELIN machines and suitable ships to carry them I regard as most important: these machines give promise of an effective reply to the German Zeppelins employed on naval scouting duties and should largely reduce the latter's usefulness.'

He did have a reservation, 'I am not prepared to sacrifice the gun armament of light cruisers in order to use them as seaplane carriers; the Grand Fleet is by no means over strong in this class of ship when the recent additions to the enemy's fleet are taken into account.' Beatty was being a little obtuse here, the Committee was proposing to add a single small aeroplane on a small platform or deck, not a seaplane with all the launching and recovery problems that entailed. Time and experiment would show that a single-seat scout could be carried by a light cruiser with little or no effect on its gun armament.

Beatty's next important innovation, the Grand Fleet Flying Squadron, must wait for a later chapter. The next two chapters will look at some of the results of the Committee on Air Requirements, namely the provision of aircraft on light cruisers and the development of the aircraft carrier.

11

Flying from Small Platforms

Shortly after his return from Denmark Flt Cdr F. J. Rutland was promoted Squadron Commander, and on 29 September 1917 he was awarded a bar to his DSC. He also became involved in flying from a small platform installed on the light cruiser *Yarmouth*. With his experience in taking off from *Manxman*'s short flight deck he had been co-opted to be Technical Advisor to the Aircraft Committee of the 1st Battle Cruiser Squadron at Rosyth. One of the matters coming up for discussion was a proposal by Lt Cdr C. H. B. Gowan, *Yarmouth*'s gunnery officer, to install a 'deck or platform forty-five feet long. Although the forward gun would be masked when actually flying off, it could be unmasked in a few minutes.' When asked if he would be prepared to fly off this deck, Rutland claimed to only require fifteen feet. He proceeded to prove this claim on *Manxman*. Into a wind of only twenty knots he took off in the claimed fifteen feet. The dockyard at Rosyth were ordered to build a flying platform, based on Gowan's design, but providing a maximum run of less than twenty feet.

Immediately ahead of *Yarmouth*'s bridge was an armoured conning tower, ahead of that was the forward 6 inch gun mounting. The platform began just forward of the bridge, and was installed over the conning tower and gun. As originally constructed the deck was quite narrow and had two troughs to guide the wheels of the machine during take-off. Rutland believed this arrangement to be potentially more dangerous than a plain deck, contending that any slight variation in the wind direction would force the machine's wheels against the walls of the trough and impede take-off or upset the machine. After some discussion and argument they were removed and the deck widened by about three feet on each side. The Pup was supported in flying position using a tail guide trestle seven and a half feet in length, and restrained by a quick release cable. Despite the claims of Rutland's biographer, none of these fittings were new, having been employed aboard the seaplane carriers fitted with flight decks for over a year.

Rutland made another trial flight from *Manxman* on 27 June 1917 from a section of deck 'built up 15′ 6″ long and 1 foot high from the Flying Deck proper. After leaving the short deck, I touched the Flying Deck about 20 feet further on with my left wheel very lightly, so lightly that I did not feel it in the machine.' The wind over the deck was 19 knots.

The following day, the Pup was installed on *Yarmouth*'s flying platform. The forward support pillars of the platform restricted the arc of fire of the gun to a narrow angle forward. However before flight the forward pillars, which were temporary supports for the deck whilst at sea, were removed and the gun trained to port, just in case the Pup fell off the end of the platform. Rutland requested *Yarmouth*'s captain, Captain Thomas Drummond Pratt, to maintain 25 knots air speed over the deck. Rutland's report reads as follows.

> The wind fluctuated slightly so that at the moment of flying off an air-speed of 26 knots was showing on the air-speed Indicators (two were used).
>
> The machine left the deck at an angle of about 4 degrees, and went straight up at this angle.
>
> The wheels were chalked, and from observation and chalk marks on the deck, it was found that the machine actually left the deck 4′ 6″ from the end, making a total run of 14′ 9″.
>
> I consider that for the last 3 or 4 feet, the tyres only were touching the deck, and that they bore practically no weight.

Rutland used the same machine, probably 9901, for both the *Manxman* and *Yarmouth* flights. It was fitted with a Lewis gun, two 97 round ammunition trays, a Very pistol and twelve cartridges. Rutland does not mention fuel, but says it was 'fully loaded as for Zeppelin attacks', which suggests a full fuel load.

A few days later another pilot from *Manxman* (they drew lots to see who would fly) successfully flew off the platform. On his return to Turnhouse the pilot believed that the machine had dropped off the end of the deck and he had almost crashed into the cruiser's foredeck. Rutland asked Lt Cdr Gowan what had gone wrong the flight, 'Nothing. He made a damned sight better take-off than you did! When released, he ran about two feet and then climbed fairly steeply. I thought he wobbled a bit at about 200 feet but that was nothing and the last I saw of him he was heading for Turnhouse.'

Rutland's success had opened the doors for aircraft to be carried aboard light cruisers. His next experimental flights would do likewise for larger ships, as Lt Cdr Gowan had not finished with his suggestions. At the next meeting of the Committee he proposed that flying decks be placed on top of the turrets of the big ships. Furthermore he considered that the turrets, or specially built platforms installed on light cruisers, could be trained into the resultant wind from the ship's speed and the true wind. At first even Rutland was doubtful of this, but after some thought decided that it should be possible.

So, a platform was constructed on the roof of *Repulse*'s B Turret. It was narrow at the rear, just wide enough for the tail guide trestle and access to the cockpit.

Forward of the aircraft it widened fan-wise to port and starboard, and sloped at a shallow angle down towards the guns. On 1 October 1917, Rutland successfully took off from this platform in Sopwith Pup N6453. The turret was trained 42 degrees to starboard, the guns were at their lowest possible elevation. With *Repulse* making 24 knots the felt wind along the platform was a little over 27 knots. Photographs of the take-off suggest that once again he used very little of the platform, showing the machine at least ten feet above the end of the platform. The platform was now moved aft to X Turret where it was installed, almost level, with the take-off direction over the back of the turret.

On 9 October the weather was squally, with snow showers, and wind speed varying between ten and twenty-five knots. Rutland recalled:

> I climbed into the plane, ran up my engines and raised my hand. I felt two jerks as I was released but paid no attention at the time. I did, however, realize that I had misjudged the wind, for a lull came at this moment and the speed of the wind on the turret was measured at twelve knots only as I took off. I ran the full length of the turret and dropped slightly on leaving it.

The two jerks he had felt were due to the release cable being rigged too tight and failing just as he ran the engine up. The machine then jumped forward a few feet before the safety rope released. Rutland was very lucky to get off at all.

Again, following on Rutland's flights from *Repulse*, the installation of turret platforms on capital ships proceeded apace. By early 1918 most battle cruisers had been fitted to carry a single-seat machine. Fitting of platforms on battleships was not as rapid as the desire here was for two-seater reconnaissance machines to be carried. An attempt on 5 March 1918 by Flt Cdr D. G. Donald to take off from *Repulse* nearly ended in disaster. The fault may have been due to the nature of the extended flight deck, it was apparently constructed of flexible wire rope. His logbook detailed the attempt.

> [A]n experimental flight from a 'spring mattress' on B turret. Rather a failure as my prop hit the 'mattress' and broke. I just managed to clear the forecastle and dived into the ditch. Picked up five minutes later by *Rival*. Really had a lucky escape, only slightly bruised.

Sopwith Ship Strutter 9744 was lost and the 'spring mattress' removed, never to be used again.

HMAS *Australia* was fitted with a platform of more conventional construction. The turret roof platform was extended by installing portable pieces which rested on light metal frames welded to the tops of the gun barrels. When not required the extensions were stowed on the fixed platform. Using this on 8 March a solo flight was made by Flt S/Lt Simonson in Sopwith Ship Strutter N5644. There is a photograph of this take-off showing the Strutter just leaving the forward end of the extended platform. A month later, on 4 April, Flt Cdr (Captain, RAF) F. J. Fox in another Ship Strutter, carrying an observer and full wireless equipment, made a successful flight from Q Turret of *Australia*.

Operational use of the turret platforms was limited, much more use being made of the smaller platforms installed on light cruisers.

Development of Light Cruiser Flight Platforms.

Yarmouth's fixed platform was only one of several designs installed on light cruisers. It was the simplest, and far from being the most impractical. That award must go to the foredeck troughs installed on *Cassandra*.

Cassandra was a Caledon class light cruiser built by Vickers at Barrow in Furness, she commission at Barrow on 19 June 1917. She was modified whilst building to have a small, a very small, hangar on the starboard side of the bridge structure. This tiny space was just big enough to house a folded Beardmore WB.III, and protect it from damage whilst at sea. The troughs were ahead of the forward gun, raised about four feet above the foredeck in order to clear the windlass and anchor chains. To fly off the machine it was necessary to extract it from the hangar, manoeuvre it around the forward gun and up on to the raised launching troughs and, once there, unfold and lock the wings. It was practically impossible to do this whilst at sea, and if the assembled machine were left in the troughs it was little better than a breakwater for the forward gun. Appointed to her as pilot was Flt Lt M. J. G. Day.

Miles Jeffery Game Day joined the RNAS immediately on leaving school, reporting to Eastchurch on 20 September 1915 to learn to fly. Mainly flying the Caudron G.III, he took his ticket in just of 12 days, receiving RAeC Certificate No. 1949 on 2 October 1915. He was recommended for single-seaters, and posted to *Vindex*, joining her at Harwich on 8 November 1915. However, during the 18 months he was with *Vindex* the ship sailed on only a handful of operations. Whilst at Harwich he had easy access to the air station at Felixstowe. Here he was able to keep his hand in and gain experience on both the Bristol Scout and Sopwith Pup. His immediate superior Flt Cdr B. D. Kilner thought him to be one of the finest pilot's he had ever known:

> A light scout machine, like a horse, needs the right sort of hands, and he has the best hands in the world. A great test—he can do things at slow speed that other people venture on with a rush only; and, of course, he is absolutely all out.

Having quickly made a name for himself as a daring and skillful pilot, it was almost natural that he should get involved in a risky experiment.

In the ongoing search for a solution to the Zeppelin Problem, it was suggested that a large flying boat could serve as an aircraft carrier, transporting a single-seat scout which would 'take-off' to attack the Zeppelin. Presumably, it would also be able to pick up the scout pilot when he came down in the sea. A new flying boat the Porte Baby was available and selected for the trials. The Porte Baby, 9800, was an impressively large flying boat. It had a wing span of 124 feet (Twelve feet more than a Second World War Short Sunderland flying boat.), with three uncowled 250 hp Rolls Royce engines between the two planes. Two engines were tractors the third central engine a pusher. The assembled aircraft must have looked magnificent with its varnished, diagonally planked, mahogany plywood fuselage and unfinished, doped linen surfaces. Then, sitting incongruously on its upper wing leading edge, was a tiny Bristol Scout, 3028. Its wheels rested in short troughs, just eighteen inches in length, which were braced to the engine bearers of the centre engine. The tailskid was supported by a light tubular structure, which held the machine in flying position. The trial took place on 17 May 1916. The flying boat took off as usual, with Day just blipping the engine of the Bristol on and off. At a suitable height, accounts vary from forty feet to 1,000 feet, the Bristol was released. The wheels dropped a few inches after leaving the end of the troughs, hovered for a few seconds, then Day was able to coax the machine into a gentle climb. He climbed away from the Porte Baby and headed for Felixstowe. The experiment with the Royal Navy's most unusual aircraft carrier was not repeated.

At Barrow on 29 June 1917 a Beardmore WB.III, N6100, was delivered to *Cassandra* for trials moving it from the hangar to the troughs. It was returned ashore the same evening. After sea trials, *Cassandra* sailed to join the Grand Fleet at Scapa Flow arriving there, apparently without an aeroplane, on 5 July. On 14 July a WB.III was delivered onboard, this was either N6100 or N6104, and stowed in the hangar. Two days later the aircraft was placed in the troughs and *Cassandra* sailed for exercises. At 5.31 p.m. Jeffery Day flew off and returned to shore. He made no more flights from the troughs. On the morning of 18 August *Cassandra* ran aground on some rocks off Malcolm's Head, Fair Isle. After temporary repairs at Lerwick Harbour, Shetland, she was towed down to South Shields and was dry docked between 21 and 31 August for repairs. Jeffery Day left the ship here and spent some time at the Isle of Grain on test work, before being posted to 13 (Naval) Squadron at Dunkirk on 17 December. He was lost in combat off Ostend on 27 February 1918, by which time he had been credited with five enemy aircraft destroyed. His award of the DSC was announced in the *London Gazette* for 16 March 1918. From surviving letters it is clear that he knew of the award before his death.

Flight Sub-Lieutenant S. D. Culley became *Cassandra*'s pilot in January 1918, he too was able to manage only a single flight from the forecastle. Like Day before him, Culley, 'became gradually less qualified as a pilot and more qualified as a Naval Officer, being required to keep my "day on" as Officer of the Watch, whilst the ship was in harbour, and the "morning" watch, when at sea, besides acting as an assistant to the Navigation Officer at other times.' Culley was posted to Great Yarmouth on 25 March, and it is possibly around this date that the forecastle flying platform was removed and she was fitted with a revolving platform, for a Sopwith Camel, aft of her funnels and mid-ship gun.

Following the success of *Yarmouth*'s platform a number of light cruisers were fitted with similar fixed platforms. This flight deck was not suitable for all light cruisers and had the disadvantage that the ship had to turn into wind before launching the machine.

This drawback was serious, but in view of the success of the experiment in flying from a turret into the relative wind, it was suggested by Captain [John Saumarez] Dumaresq, HMAS *Sydney*, as an alternative to fit the aeroplane on a revolving platform on the forecastle, so that only the platform need be turned around into the wind. Under the guidance of the Grand Fleet Committee a scheme for this purpose was prepared for HMAS *Sydney* and fitted up by Chatham Yard in November 1917. This proved a great success and similar platforms on the forecastle were subsequently fitted in [HMAS] *Melbourne*, [HMS] *Birkenhead*, *Southampton* and *Chatham*. The advantages of this type were so great that it was decided to fit similar revolving platforms, where possible, in place of the fixed platforms already installed in other Light Cruisers. The *Yarmouth* was so modified in June 1918 and the *Dublin* in August 1918, shortly after the fixed platforms had been installed.

Originally intended for the light and handy Sopwith Pup the light cruiser platforms were soon exclusively equipped with the heavier Sopwith 2F.1 Camel, as this Australian account shows:

But Dumaresq was still at loose ends for he had a specially equipped warship for operating aircraft, but no aircraft. This ludicrous situation was unacceptable to the impatient Dumaresq and, on arrival at Scapa Flow, he made arrangements to borrow the Sopwith Pup [9931] which was operating from a fixed platform on the light cruiser HMS *Dublin*. A trial flight was made from *Sydney* on 8 December 1917 when the Pup was launched from the platform in the fixed position; this was the first time on record that an aircraft had actually taken off from an Australian warship. Another 'first' occurred nine days later when the Pup flew off the platform turned into wind—the very first time any aircraft had been launched from such a platform in the revolved position. These two experimental launchings were the only occasions that a Sopwith Pup operated from an Australian light cruiser.

After the first flight of a Sopwith Pup from *Sydney* on 8 December 1917, Captain Dumaresq was anxious to test the cruiser's revolving platform with a more modern aircraft. On 14 December a signal was despatched from *Sydney* to the Scapa Flow aerodrome at Smoogro: 'As *Dublin*'s pilot has to return shortly … requested that *Campania* may be asked to supply a pilot and Camel, complete with 2 mechanics, to *Sydney*.' Two days later, presumably after much worried thought, a perplexed query came back, 'Does Camel refer to part of equipment or to a particular type of aeroplane?' *Sydney* promptly and patiently spelt out the answer, 'The machine referred to is a Sopwith Camel aeroplane. It is the latest standard fighter and has succeeded the Pup.' Perhaps in all fairness to the Navy shore staff they could not be blamed for querying why an Australian cruiser, anchored in the middle of Scapa Flow, was asking for a camel to be delivered to the ship—they probably thought it was some kind of delicacy the wild colonials served for breakfast. Undeterred, Dumaresq persisted in his endeavours and, after an invitation to the captain of the carrier *Campania* to be his dinner guest, eventually got his Camel.

By March 1918, *Melbourne* had been fitted with a revolving platform, similar to that installed in *Sydney*. She rejoined her sister at Rosyth, where both cruisers were part of the Second Light Cruiser Squadron *(Birmingham* [flag], *Dublin* and the two Australians) as part of the screen for the Battle Cruiser Fleet. *Melbourne* took on board her machine in mid-April, but does not appear to made a flight until 10 May. They were to make good use of their Camels a few weeks later as will be described in a later chapter.

Not all light cruisers were able to fit the revolving platform between the bridge and fore gun, for these a modified design capable of being installed aft of the funnels was designed. Whilst training was limited to either beam only, in practice this proved satisfactory with machines able to fly off even if the wind was not directly along the axis of the platform. 'A standard design of revolving platform was prepared, and was of such a nature that these platforms could be made in the absence of the ship and fitted on board in a few hours when the vessel came into port.'

Whether on a light cruiser or battleship the machines were exposed to the worst the North Sea can offer. Attempts to provide shelters were largely limited to light frameworks, built up from 3 inch by 3 inch angle iron, and covered in canvas. The shelters were satisfactory in keeping spray and light winds from the machines, but could not withstand the assaults by waves or strong winds. A variation of *Cassandra*'s hangar was installed on the cruisers *Dragon* and *Dauntless*, two new vessels fitted with superimposed forward guns. The bridge was raised up on two side towers, between these was the flight deck over B gun. The forward end of the flight deck could be raised to protect the machine and free up the training of the gun. By the time the two cruisers were completed the war was over and the flight decks were never used.

Rutland's flights had made it possible for the fleet to go to sea with far more than the few reconnaissance and anti-Zeppelin machines the seaplane carriers could house. Within a year flying off platforms of various designs had been fitted to at least twenty two light cruisers. Also, battleships and battle cruisers were fitted with turret ramps, usually one forward for a Sopwith Ship Strutter and one midships or aft for a Sopwith 2F.1 Camel, for the Camel soon supplanted the Pup as the anti-Zeppelin machine with the fleet.

Whilst all these platforms greatly added to the number of aircraft accompanying the fleet to sea, it would be very wrong to picture swarms of single-seat fighters taking off to attack any airship which was unwise to appear over the fleet. The machines were strictly single use, once launched they could not be recovered aboard ship, so they had to husbanded for the right moment. One has to marvel at their pilots, and observers. When they took off they knew that there could be no return. At best they faced a landing in the sea, close to an escorting destroyer, and hope to be picked up from a frigid sea. Yet they kept going out and trying.

The platform on *Yarmouth* which Rutland had used for his trials remained in place and a permanent pilot, Lt P. G. Williams, appointed. However, on 20 August 1917 he was on leave and Flt S/Lt B. A. Smart transferred from *Manxman* as the cruiser prepared to sail with the rest of the Third Light Cruiser Squadron on a North Sea patrol. The squadron sailed to be off the Danish coast by dawn.

Bernard Arthur Smart had enlisted on 10 November 1914 and after initial training served with No. 3 Armoured Car Squadron, RNAS, at the Dardanelles. He rose to the rank of Petty Officer before transferring to the RNAS on 16 April 1916. Despite his earlier naval service Smart still went through the initial course at Crystal Palace before being posted to Chingford on 10 June 1916. Then on to Calshot for seaplane training, where he was rated a 'V G Pilot.' Smart had flown just thirteen hours and forty minutes when posted for initial service flying at Westgate at the end of November. Westgate seems to have functioned as a First World War equivalent of an Operational Training Unit. He was posted to *Manxman* on 5 January 1917, where he progressed rapidly from Sopwith Schneider floatplanes to deck flying in Pups.

Zeppelin L23, *Oberleutnant zur See* Bernhard Dinter, left Tondern for a routine patrol at 3.50 a.m. on 21 August 1917. At 5.40 a.m. she transmitted a sighting of four *Aurora* class light cruisers and fifteen destroyers, thirty miles west of Bovbjerg Lighthouse sixty miles north of Esbjerg, Denmark.

Smart was called early that morning. A Zeppelin had been sighted in the distance. He set about preparing his machine for flight:

> ...then the plainness of those great big red, white and blue circles and colourings strike me very forcibly. 'Go get me some grey paint and brushes at the double,' I call to one of the seamen looking on and in a few minutes the distinguishing marks are toned down and although still discernable at short distance did not talk quite so loudly as before.

The details are given in his official report:

> At about 6.40 a.m. when in position 54° 47′ N., 7° 55′ E. I received orders to proceed to attack the Zeppelin. I immediately left on Sopwith Pup No. [N]6430. Bearing of the Zeppelin being S.S.W. distance 10 to 15 miles. I climbed steadily at 55 knots until 9,000 feet, keeping the enemy in sight except when occasionally obscured by clouds. Then proceeded in slightly downward course as Zeppelin was far below me, air speed then 100 knots.

His official report continues to give the bare bones of the story, but he is more forthcoming in a letter to his mother.

> I had been slowly descending with full engine and my height was now 8,000; I kept the same speed and was obviously able to out manoeuvre the Zepp to a standstill— each time she made the slightest turn I swerved round to keep absolutely end on, in which position the men in the gondola underneath were unable to either see or attack me. I could see the head of a man and an object unpleasantly like a machine gun on the top of the envelope and now realised that the time had come. I pushed forward the control stick and dived. The speed indicator went with a rush up to 150 mph and I was aiming to cut under the Zepp a few yards astern of her. The roar of the engine had increased to a shrill scream while the wires were whistling and screeching in an awful manner. I completely lost my head—the earth vanished, the sky vanished, the sea was no more, my universe consisted of that great round silvery object, myself and space. Everything then happened automatically: 250 yards astern and the same height as the Zepp I flattened out slightly and pulled the lever which works the fixed machine gun. I had misjudged the angle at which this was mounted on the plane and saw the white stream of my incendiary bullets going too high. In a flash I had nosed down again, flattened out and pressed down the machine gun operating lever again and held it there. The gun spat out and although the machine was wobbling on account of the extreme sensitiveness of my controls due to the enormous speed, I had just time to see about half a dozen [bullets] enter the blunt end of the Zepp and a spurt of flame, before my very soul froze with the thought that in my eagerness to aim [the] gun, I had waited too long and couldn't avoid a collision. Spasmodically I jammed the joystick hard forward and my heart seemed to come into my mouth in the absolute vertical nose dive that followed.

Smart was able to pull out of his dive some 2,000 feet below the Zeppelin.

The stern of the airship was now well on fire, the flames reaching rapidly forward, the whole descending towards the sea at an angle of 45 degrees, tail first.

> It is extraordinary the tricks nature plays on one's impressions at a time like this: I know what struck me more than anything was that the engines were still

turning away merrily with the Zepp enveloped in flames and pointing up at that ridiculous angle. It struck me as the funniest thing I had seen in my life and I laughed like an idiot.

Smart saw what he believed to be a man in a parachute floating down from the wreck. Turning towards the ships he looked back and saw the wreck hit the sea, continuing to burn for several minutes.

The Zeppelin had managed to send out a final brief message, 'Am pursued by enemy forces.' After that last message nothing more was heard. Several seaplanes were sent to search for the airship, but not until the evening was anything found. Twenty five miles south-west of Bovbjerg, a seaplane sighted a patch of oil on the water and landed alongside. The observer was able to pick up a few charred wooden fragments and the tip of a propeller. If anyone had escaped by parachute no trace was found. The Germans were unaware that the Zeppelin had been shot down by an aeroplane, assuming that it fell victim to gunfire from the ships. Smart's success was kept secret until after the war.

Smart himself was now in difficulties. The ships had lost sight of him and the Zeppelin, when they saw the smoke from the burning airship they mistook it for German warships and turned away. Smart was very lucky to literally stumble across them. After searching for some time he had decided to make for the Danish coast, when turning he caught sight of them seven or eight miles away and joyfully turned towards them.

I was now over the squadron and selecting two destroyers near enough together turned off my engine and planed down so as to be a couple of hundred yards ahead. This was my first attempt at coming down on the sea in a land machine, but instinct told me that at all costs I must hit with practically no forward way on whatever to avoid turning head over heels and possibly getting pinned underneath. I undid my strap and put a plug in the tube which acts as a valve to the air bags in tail and when within about 15 feet of the surface pulled back the stick gradually, keeping at that height while the machine was getting slower and slower until I had finally got the stick back as far as possible, the machine lost all flying speed and I dropped like a stone, hitting the water with a nasty jerk which would probably have meant broken bones had it been on mother earth. The destroyers' boats were alongside in a short time but not before the nose of the machine had sunk and left me just hanging on to the tail.

Smart was picked up by boats from *Prince* which also salvaged the Pup's engine and Lewis gun. The remains of the machine were abandoned.

Commodore, *Caledon* to Flight Sub-Lieutenant Smart, *Prince*. You have done splendidly and I am sure your reward will be prompt.

Smart was promoted Flight Lieutenant on 1 October 1917, and made a Companion of the Distinguished Service Order. The award was announced in the *London Gazette* 2 November 1917. In keeping with the secrecy surrounding his success there was no citation accompanying the award. He received his medal from the King at Buckingham Palace on 7 November 1917. A few days later the French Government announced the award of the *Croix de Guerre* (Bronze palm) to Smart. The medal was sent in the mail to his parent's home in Luton.

12

Seaplane Carrier to Aircraft Carrier

Of all the suggestions and recommendations in the Report of the Grand Fleet Committee on Air Requirements none created more discussion than the future of *Furious*.

Furious was the last of three ships of the *Courageous* Class of Light Battle Cruisers or Large Light Cruisers, either term has been used indiscriminately. These ships, *Courageous*, *Glorious* and *Furious*, were the product of Admiral of the Fleet J. A. 'Jacky' Fisher's active mind when he was First Sea Lord. He had them built with the intention that they could spearhead an attack into the Baltic Sea. Known within the fleet as 'Outrageous, Curious and Spurious', they served the Royal Navy well for many years. The first two were completed as designed with two twin 15 inch turrets, *Furious* was to be finished with two monstrous 18 inch guns in single turrets fore and aft. *Courageous* and *Glorious* were completed in 1917 and served with the Grand Fleet and Battle Cruiser Force throughout the war. The future held something different for *Furious*.

When the Report was released *Furious* was lying, incomplete and still known in the yard as Job 896, against the dockside of her builders Armstrong Whitworth at Elswick on the Tyne. Her aft turret and gun had been installed, but the forward gun lay under guard on the dockside. The design intent was to install the turret and gun and to provide a hangar for a Sopwith Baby, under the shelter deck each side of the bridge structure. A 'portable flying deck' would be provided for the two machines. Portable, because it was anticipated that firing the forward gun would wreck any lightly built structure. The Committee recommended that *Furious*:

> . . . should have her forecastle gun removed and a deck built horizontal in her altered trim, which the Committee believe would provide accommodation for a number of reconnaissance machines between the raised platform deck referred to above and her forecastle deck. This would provide sufficient accommodation and leave a flying deck of some 200 feet on which, if desired, more planes could be housed.

Beatty started the ensuing discussion, and argument, with a comment in his covering letter to the Admiralty on 7 February 1917:

> As regards the proposal to remove the forward armament of the *Furious*, I am not aware of what this consists; the latest return in my possession (dated October, 1916) shows that ship as having <u>two</u> 15 inch guns in all, i.e., one forward and one aft. If this is the case I consider that one 15 inch, or possibly 18 inch, gun by itself of little value; but if the armament is similar to that of *Courageous*, then I cannot recommend the removal of two 15 inch guns, which undoubtedly are of great offensive value.
>
> Every effort should be made, however, to render the *Furious* an effective seaplane carrier as, although I am of opinion that the right policy is to employ non-fighting ships for this purpose, I am informed that the *Argus* cannot be expected to join the fleet until the end of the year, and it is most desirable that more seaplanes should be available for operations in the near future.

The Report was circulated through the Sea Lords and was in general received with approval. Jellicoe, however, minuted that, 'I entirely disagree with the recommendations and opinions expressed in Paras. 22 to 25 [which discussed *Furious*] of the Grand Fleet Committee's report, and most strongly deprecate any alteration to *Furious* which would interfere with her fighting value as regards armament and speed as originally designed.' There were also concerns regarding Armstrong Whitworth's ability to carry out the conversion in a timely manner. The Director of Naval Construction, Sir Eustace Henry William Tennyson d'Eyncourt, was asked to comment on the three proposals for the conversion.

Scheme A was the most comprehensive, and would permit the carrying of six reconnaissance and four anti-Zeppelin machines.

> This modification involves the removal of 'A' barbette mounting and the top ring of the armour of this barbette, a slight reduction in the effective arc of training of the two foremost 5.5 inch guns, and removal of torpedo net defence fittings. The weight of the installation including ammunition, fuel, additional stores, workshops, men and effects is 810 tons, but this is more than balanced by the removal of the forward barbette and top ring of armour. Space for the stores and workshops could be found in the magazine, shell rooms etc., which would be left empty by the change. The resulting trim by the stern in the deep condition, that is with mines on the Quarter Deck aft, would be about 58 inches. There is no objection to this scheme on the score of weight, strength or stability.

Armstrong Whitworth estimated a minimum of fourteen weeks would be required for the work, once approved and once all required drawings and materials were provided.

'S.38' rising from ship

Commander C. R. Samson, piloting Short S.38, taking off from the ramp built over HMS *Hibernia*'s forecastle, 2 May 1912. (*Author's Collection*) All of the following illustrations are from the Author's Collection unless identified otherwise.

A popular postcard from the 1912 Royal Naval Review at Weymouth showing a flight by Short S.38 from HMS *Hibernia*. The ship is not under way so this cannot be Samson's flight. Therefore, the date is probably 12 May 1912, but the pilot is unknown.

Another postcard showing Short S.41 at Weymouth in May 1912.

Piloted by Lt R. P. Ross, Caudron G.II, 55, takes off from HMS *Hermes*' forecastle ramp on 28 July 1913. (*Courtesy John Dixon*)

HMS *Riviera* around the time of the Cuxhaven Raid. Minimal work was done to make her into a seaplane carrier, just simple canvas shelters for the floatplanes and two lifting booms on the fore and main masts.

HMS.HERMES WITH HYDROPLANES ON BOARD, AT SCAPA. T.KENT

Following the Naval Manoeuvres of 1913 HMS *Hermes* spent a few days at Scapa Flow, where local photographer Mr T. Kent captured this fine view of her. Caudron G.II, 55, is on the bow ramp and Short Type 74 Folder, 81, is aft. Both machines were in the air during *Hermes'* time at Scapa Flow. (*Orkney Library and Archives, tk208*)

Short Type 81, 120, on the beach at Westgate prior to the war. Flown by Flt Lt Arnold J. Miley during the Cuxhaven Raid, running low on fuel after the raid he landed alongside submarine *E.11* and was taken aboard. The Short was lost at sea.

HMS *Engadine* fully converted to a seaplane carrier, with a large slab-sided hanger aft. A Short 184 stands outside the hangar showing the limited space available to handle machines.

Three early production Sopwith Schneiders outside the Sopwith Company hangar at Woolston, Southampton in early 1915. The large floatplane in the hangar is a Sopwith 860, a two-seater that saw limited service with the RNAS. (*Courtesy Chas Schaedel*)

Opposite above: Deck flying training. A Beardmore WB.III takes off from HMS *Nairana* sometime in 1918. HMS *Furious* lies to port. The Beardmore is fitted with a Lewis Gun on the upper centre section.

Opposite below: Deck landing training. Sopwith Pup, N6176, on the practice deck at the Isle of Grain early in 1918. The wheels have been removed and a landing skid installed. Note the broken skid strut. Like most of the Pups used for deck landing training at Grain it had previously served with an RNAS squadron in France. (*Courtesy William Casey*)

HMS *Vindex*. The forward flight deck and aft hangar made this conversion into the first of the series of 'mixed carriers.'

Cramped conditions on the aft deck of the seaplane carriers, this is HMS *Vindex*, required careful handling of the machines. Short 184, 8033, is being hoisted in front of a Sopwith Schneider. A Bristol Scout fuselage and another Short are housed in the hangar.

Flight Commander B. F. Fowler just leaving *Vindex*'s flight deck in Bristol Scout C, 1255, on 3 November 1915. The run of 46 feet and slight swing to port are clearly marked by the track made by chalked wheels. The ball end fitting clamped to the side of the tail skid can just be seen, this ran in the slot of the tail guide trestle.

On the hook. Short 184, N1667, hanging from *Vindex*'s crane in 1918. Both pilot and observer are aboard, the latter's Lewis gun has a bag to collect spent shell cases. N1667 was built by Brush Electrical Engineering Co and has a 240 hp Renault engine, it is very similar in appearance to N1232 flown by Flt Lt Hopcroft and PO Garner to search for Flt Cdr B. D. Kilner on 25 September 1917.

Bristol Scout D, 8979, being brought aboard *Vindex*, probably in September 1916. To make use of the full length of the flight deck, substantial wheel stops are fitted on its aft edge. The beam for the tail guide trestle is in the 'Y' frame in the entrance to the hangar.

A Short 166 preparing to hook on and be brought aboard *Vindex*. The observer is keeping a careful eye on the ship's motor launch but will soon have to pay attention to the hook, in the foreground, and attach it to cables on the Short's centre-section.

Beardmore-built Sopwith Pup, 9927, alongside *Vindex*. It is fitted for two Le Prieur rockets, with aluminium heat shields on the wings, and has a support for a fixed vertical Lewis Gun immediately ahead of the cockpit. Flt Cdr Bertram Denison Kilner was flying this machine on 25 September 1917. Transport of aeroplanes to the ship was achieved by placing it on one of the ship's boats with two Short 184 main floats and spare booms as outriggers, this was then towed to the ship by a motor launch.

HMS *Campania* following her first conversion. Floatplanes, there are two Short 184s above the hangar aft of the bridge, were lifted off the ship on to the water to take off. There was a shelter just forward of the bridge, under the almost flat flight deck, for single seat floatplanes.

HMS *Campania* at Cammell, Laird and Company, Birkenhead, nearing completion of her second conversion. The lengthened flight deck, split forward funnel and minimal navigating position are visible. The hatch to the forward hangar below the flight deck is open.

HMS *Campania* at sea following completion of the second conversion. There is a Sopwith Baby at the aft end of the sloping flight deck, and a Short 184 on top of the main hangar. The cleared after deck for a kite balloon is clearly seen.

Short 184, 8058, during one of several take offs from the flight deck of *Campania* in June 1916. The main floats were sat on a light wheeled trolley, which was not retained on the deck but was released after take-off. Barely visible under the tail float is the ball which ran in the tube of the tail guide trestle.

The Fairey Campania was uniquely designed for use on HMS *Campania*. N2362 is seen aboard *Campania* in the summer of 1918. (*Courtesy Chas Schaedel*)

One of a series of photographs showing HMS *Campania* sinking in the Firth of Forth on 5 November 1918. (*Maritime Photo Library*)

Sopwith Baby, 8182, damaged attempting to take off from the North Sea. The forward starboard float strut is broken and the propeller smashed. This particular Baby was aboard *Engadine* during the Battle of Jutland, although this photograph was probably taken on 18 August 1916 some weeks after the battle.

HMS *Nairana* dressed up in artist Norman Wilkinson's dazzle camouflage. There is a Beardmore WB.III, with wings folded, under the aft section of the forward flight deck. The structure mounted on the hangar roof was a fixed gantry used to lift floatplanes over the stern of the ship. (*Maritime Photo Library*)

HMS *Pegasus* also in dazzle camouflage. The aft end of the flight deck was moved forward so that aeroplanes could be lifted from the deck in front of the hangar on to the flight deck. The two booms could be worked independently to lift machines from lighters on to the hangar deck. (*Maritime Photo Library*)

Sopwith Ship Strutter, A6006, on B turret, HMS *Barham*, in August 1918. It is held in a ready to fly position with the tail skid in the tail guide trestle. The light frame work on the gun barrels is to support the removable platform, the panels of which are stacked ahead of the Strutter.

HMS *Renown* with a Sopwith 2F.1 Camel on the B turret platform. A similar platform is installed on Y turret.

A Ship Strutter takes off from the B turret platform on HMS *Renown*.

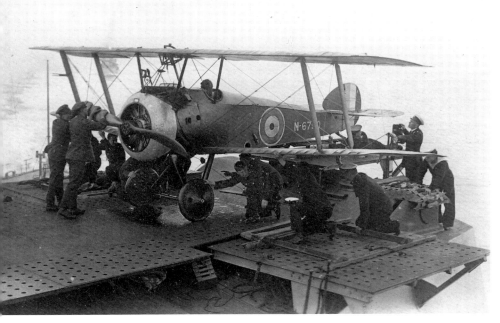

A posed photograph preparing Sopwith 2F.1 Camel, N6750, for flight aboard HMS *Tiger* in January 1919. The rating on the right of the picture appears to have a canvas roll to house all the flight control locks. The wheels are un-chocked and the engine has been primed with fuel, judging by the spillage on the platform. If he is not careful, one of the ratings will lose his cap once the engine is started.

Soon afterward, the Camel in flight. This machine was gifted to the Latvian Air Force in March 1920, where it was renumbered 18, and was still active in 1924.

HMS *Cassandra* at speed during her trials. The aircraft hangar is the boxy structure beside the bridge. The take-off troughs are just visible on the forecastle.

Beardmore WB.III mounted in HMS *Cassandra*'s troughs. The tail skid has an extension to keep the aircraft in flying position whilst in the unusually long tail guide trestle. Note how the forward gun has to be trained to one side when the aircraft is on the forecastle, and how unprotected the Beardmore would be in anything but the smallest seas. (*The Dock Museum, Barrow-in-Furness, 0348*)

When the forecastle troughs were removed, *Cassandra* was fitted with the revolving platform seen here.

HMAS *Melbourne* with a Sopwith 2F.1 Camel on her forward rotating platform. Extensive splinter protection has been installed around the rotation mechanism. The appearance of HMAS *Sydney* was almost identical. (*Maritime Photo Library*)

HMS *Furious* as first completed with a forward flight deck and single 18 inch gun aft. (*US Naval Historical Center, NH60606*)

HMS *Furious* after her second conversion with forward flight deck and aft landing deck. The 'goal posts' aft of the funnel supported heavy cables to prevent landing aircraft over running the landing deck. Behind the wind screens on the fore deck are two Sopwith Ship Strutters.

A fully armed Sopwith 2F.1 Camel on the forward platform of a light cruiser, probably HMS *Royalist*. The small size of these platforms is evident in this view. If the forward guns had to be used the light columns were removed and, it appears that, the forward extension could be retracted under the main platform.

Squadron Commander E. H. Dunning making the first landing on HMS *Furious* on 2 August 1917. Fellow pilots are running out to grab toggles to help pull Sopwith Pup N6453 on to the deck.

Flying off from *Furious'* fore deck was more successful. Here a Short 184 takes off on 15 July 1917 to test the retaining gear for the trolley.

A Sopwith Pup, with landing skids instead of wheels, approaches *Furious'* landing deck. Between 20 March and 26 April 1918 thirteen landing attempts were made, only three were completed successfully with no damage to the machine, six resulted in damage, three were abandoned and one went over the side of the deck. A single attempt by a Ship Strutter, on 8 May, resulted in damage to engine, propeller and undercarriage when it ran into the goal post cables.

An Aircraft Lighter at Great Yarmouth. The Camel is aft supported by the tail guide trestle. The forward side extensions to the flight deck are folded back or retracted, they will only be spread if the aircraft is to be launched.

HMS *Argus* 'The Flatiron' at Rosyth late in 1918. The first fully decked aircraft carrier, *Argus* served the Royal Navy until 1946. A Royal Sovereign class battleship lies beyond her. (*USN Historical Center, NH42235*)

The seven Sopwith 2F.1 Camels on *Furious'* fore deck before the Tondern Raid, 19 July 1918. All of the national markings have been dulled down, probably with pusser's grey paint, but at least four have a fuselage band. The lead aircraft, belonging to Capt. W. D. Jackson, appears to have a white cowling with one or two coloured horizontal bands. (*USN Historical Center, NH42238*)

At sea the Aircraft Lighter was kept on a short tow, in this case behind HMS *Springbok*, usually with just the two lightermen aboard. If required to launch, the flight crew would be transferred to the lighter and a longer tow let out.

HMS *Vindictive* running at speed during her trials at Scapa Flow late in 1918. She had a single hangar under the forward flight deck, the aft landing deck was supported by a light framework. (*Maritime Photo Library*)

Short 184 with 14 inch torpedo. The torpedo was almost completely submerged when the floats were in the water. The Short had to be flown solo, with reduced fuel, to even take off.

Sopwith Cuckoo dropping a dummy torpedo during training at Spithead in 1919 or 1920. The dark lump at the aft end of the torpedo is the wooden drogue used to keep the torpedo level immediately after entering the water. (*Charlie Attrill Collection*)

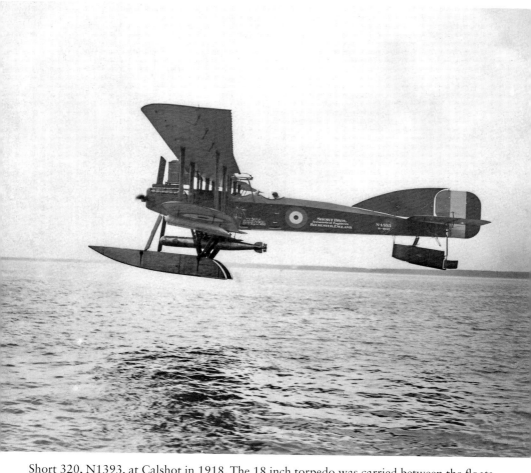

Short 320, N1393, at Calshot in 1918. The 18 inch torpedo was carried between the floats and fuselage and was not submerged when the machine was on the water. Despite having a 320 hp engine it still had to be flown solo when carrying a torpedo. (*Charlie Attrill Collection*)

Sopwith 2F.1 Camel taking-off from HMS *Vindex* in 1918 shortly before she sailed for the Mediterranean. The centre-section has permanent lifting slings and a Lewis gun is installed on the Admiralty pattern mounting. Note how much aileron is being applied to counteract the torque of the engine and, with only a few feet of deck remaining, how much weight is still on the wheels. Clamped to the side of the tail skid is a ball end fitting which slides in the slot of the tail guide trestle just visible at the bottom of the picture.

Scheme B retained the forward gun but added a small hangar, strongly built to withstand the firing of the forward gun, and flight deck forward of the turret for three reconnaissance machines. The two side hangars for anti-Zeppelin machines were also retained. D'Eyncourt foresaw considerable structural problems with this design, owing to the increase of weight forward causing considerable stresses amidships, and he could not recommend this scheme. Scheme C involved the addition of 'portable hangars containing folding aeroplanes on the forecastle, which would have to be removed when the ship was required to fight the barbette [i.e., fire the forward gun].' This scheme was seen as being the only one which would not delay completion of *Furious*. A variation of this scheme saw seaplanes being carried on lighters amidships which would have to be hoisted out, on the lighters, for use.

Not surprisingly, Scheme A was decided on as being the only one that would provide a good seaplane carrier. Approval was sent to Armstrong Whitworth to commence work on 17 March 1917. The flight deck as designed was 228 feet long by maximum 50 feet wide, below the flight deck was a hangar 64 feet long by 36 feet wide. Access to the hangar was through a hatch approximately 48 feet by 18 feet. Machines had to be hoisted through the opening using electric derricks installed on the port and starboard sides of the flight deck. *Furious* commissioned on 26 June 1917, with Captain Wilmot S. Nicholson in command, and Squadron Commander E. H. Dunning as Senior Flying Officer. She joined the Grand Fleet at Scapa Flow on 4 July carrying three Short 184s and five Sopwith Pups.

In her first configuration *Furious* had a large forward flying deck and a single 18 inch gun aft, both had to be exercised. Flt Cdr W. G. Moore was Dunning's second in command, his cabin was immediately below the 18 inch gun:

> . . . and the *Furious* was built in a very light way, certainly not strong enough to carry a gun like that. Every time she fired it was like a snowstorm in my cabin, only instead of snowflakes sheared rivet heads would come down from the deck head and partition.

Flying trials were only slightly less exciting. Taking off from the flight deck was straight forward for the Sopwith Pups, but a little more involved for the Short floatplanes, which required a trolley attached to the main floats. Initially these were dropped after take-off, as in *Campania*. A slot was later installed along the centre line of the deck, in this ran an arm which was attached to the axle of the trolley. The aircraft separated from the trolley as soon as flying speed was attained and the trolley remained on board, available to be reused immediately. The trials were flown by Flt Lt Arthur Noel Gallehawk with Warrant Officer Dan Flemming as observer. Flemming later recalled the first trial:

> When we made the first flight the aircraft was not properly balanced on the trolley and instead of flying off before we reached the end of the run the floats

were punctured by the buffer set up to retain the trolley on board. After the flight we were hooked up by topping lift and left hanging there to drain before being lowered into the hangar.

The second attempt was successful.

The Pups, once they had taken off, had to return to land at Smoogro and be lightered back to the ship. On operations, they would have to ditch alongside a destroyer and wait to be rescued.

Geoffrey Moore described the method required to land back aboard:

What we had to do for the deck-landing experiment was to fly alongside the ship and then slip in sideways, centre ourselves over the fo'c'sle and alight. Well, that sounds easy enough but it wasn't really very easy.

The pilots were keen to give it a go, and on 2 August 1917 Sqn Cdr Dunning made the first attempt. *Furious* was steaming within Scapa Flow at 26 knots into a 21 knot wind:

This gave us an air speed of 47 knots. That was about our landing speed, so we could almost hover over the deck and then alight. But of course, it did mean we were alighting in a gale of wind, and we had no arrester gear other than the hands and arms of our brother officers. Toggles were fixed to the wing tips and tail of the aircraft for the purpose of pulling it down on to the deck.

We were weighed down with brass hats and gold braid that day, as there were many Admirals and even Generals on board to see these experiments.

He took off, and after a circuit of the ship made his approach along the port side, side slipping in and centering up over the deck in the right position. We dashed out and grabbed our appointed toggles. He then cut his engine. We had some difficulty hauling the aircraft down squarely on to the deck and holding it in the wind, but we did so and the aircraft was secured without damage and Dunning stepped out.

Dunning wanted to carry out one more landing before allowing Moore and the other pilots to attempt a landing. Five days later the wind was a little stronger and gusty, Dunning was flying Pup N6453, the same machine he had used for the first landing. His approach was as before, the pilots ran out to grab the toggles to pull him down as before but this time with too much enthusiasm. A gust of wind together with the efforts of the pilots brought the Pup back to the coaming around the hatch down to the hangar, smashing the elevator and a tyre. Moore recounts what happened next:

I was sitting in the second machine, Sopwith Pup No. N.6452, with my engine running, most anxious to show all the assembled top brass what a clever fellow

I was, and how much better I could do it, when Dunning came up to me, tapped me on the shoulder and said, 'Come out of that, Moore. I'm not satisfied with that run and I'm going again.' I was very disappointed. My secret thoughts were, 'You old so-and-so. I wanted to show everybody how much better I could do it.' But, of course, I just got out and he got in. Well, he came in a second time and he didn't like it very much, so he waved us away and opened up his engine to take another run round for a second approach. Most unfortunately he choked his engine, stalled and was blown over the side.

Furious was steaming alone in Scapa Flow, with no accompanying vessel to act as a safety boat. She hoisted out her cutter and reversed engines, but slowing a ship her size takes time and it was almost thirty minutes before they returned to the crash. The Pup was still afloat, supported by the air bags in the fuselage, but badly damaged. Dunning was still strapped in the cockpit, he had probably hit his head and drowned.

Flying continued, but no more attempts to land on were made. Although two approaches were attempted on 11 October by Flt Sub-Lt W. D. Jackson and Flt Lt F. M. Fox. The wind over the deck ranged between 24 and 31 knots. Both pilots reported that once clear of the superstructure the air was smooth. It was suggested that if the felt wind were slightly off the centre line the approach would be simpler, an idea which holds the kernel of the idea which led to the modern angled flight deck.

Moore was made temporary Senior Flying Officer but, lacking seniority, shortly had to hand over command to Sqn Cdr F. J. Rutland. Rutland was not popular with his peers:

Maybe we were a lot of little snobs; anyhow we did not like being bossed by an ex-lower deck, however valiant. Moreover he was very greedy with the limelight. When important experiments were going on we were not even allowed to speak to senior visiting officers interested in what was afoot.

This lack of rapport was evident to Captain Nicholson, Rutland would eventually be replaced by a more supportive officer. Shortly after taking over command Rutland made an attempt to land on the forward deck.

I came within about four feet above the deck and my wing tip was within two feet of the conning tower. Blipping my engine, I landed only a couple of fuselage lengths from it. The airspeed of the ship was approximately twenty five knots; I sat there for perhaps ten seconds, with the tail up, literally flying the plane with my wheels on the deck. Then I flew off, landing at the aerodrome. Next day I issued probably the shortest report ever rendered. 'I beg to submit,' I wrote, 'that, with training, any good pilot can land on the *Furious* flying off deck. But I estimate that the life of a pilot will be approximately ten flights. I shall need tests under sea conditions to determine whether this average would be appreciably less.'

There were no more tests. Shortly afterwards the decision was taken to send *Furious* back to her builders for further modifications.

As first completed *Furious* was effectively just a large seaplane carrier, she could send off floatplanes on trolleys, or land machines from her flight deck, but they could not return back on board. She was too valuable to be permitted to stop to pick up her machines, a prime target for a submarine, so usually one of the smaller seaplane carriers, usually *Nairana* or *Pegasus*, sailed in company to stop and pick up her machines. Very soon there were discussions at the Admiralty about adding a landing deck aft of the superstructure and funnel:

> The deck would be of light structure and placed very high, practically on a level with the existing forward flying deck. The [aft] turret gun and midship 5.5 inch would be sacrificed but it is probable that the remainder of the secondary armament could be retained. It is estimated that the alterations could be carried out in approximately three months.

Furious returned to her builders on 14 November 1917, and recommissioned on 15 March 1918. During this four month period armament and structures above the main deck aft of the funnel were removed and replaced with an aft hangar and landing deck, 284 feet by 70 feet. At the forward end of the landing deck was a large goal-post-like structure from which were hung a heavy rope net, later replaced by a series of vertical cables, to stop aircraft running off the forward end of the deck. The sides of the flight deck were built up about two feet by a box coaming. The hangar was located at the aft end of the deck and measured 70 feet by 38 feet, it was served by an electrically powered lift 48 feet by 18 feet. The forward flight deck hatch was also replaced by a similarly sized electrically powered lift. Port and starboard gangways, for transporting machines, linked the two flying decks. She could carry up to sixteen machines, initially fourteen Ship Strutters and two Pups.

On her return to the fleet in March 1918 *Furious* embarked on a series of flights to test out the new landing deck. When they viewed the deck the pilots were, to say the least, concerned. As early as 12 September 1917 her Commander, Captain Wilmot Nicholson, had pointed out to the Admiralty that an aft deck would be subject to eddying and buffeting air currents flowing around the superstructure and funnel, making landings extremely hazardous. In reply the Admiralty claimed that:

> . . . a landing deck of over 400 feet in length would be obtained while the only structures above it liable to cause air disturbances are the fore bridge, fore mast and funnel, which lend themselves to streamlining.

The vessel as completed had a landing deck only 284 feet long and no attempt had been made to streamline the structures ahead if it.

A series of wind tunnel tests were performed by the Advisory Committee for Aeronautics to determine whether streamlining would actually be effective. The model retained the existing mast and bridge structures, and had a 286 foot long deck, but tested a number of variations of funnel streamlining. Streamlining the funnel alone had no appreciable effect on the air flow over the landing deck. The report also predicted many of the problems experienced and lessons learnt by the pilots attempting to land on the deck. This was not lost on Captain Nicholson and those pilots, apparently including Rutland and Moore, who read the report.

Geoffrey Moore commented that:

> The Naval constructors seemed to have overlooked the fact that when the ship is steaming at thirty knots into a wind, the air currents behind all the super structure lying amidships created a backwash. There were eddies of air there, following along with the ship, and the hot gases from the funnel did not help either. The trouble was that directly we got over the stern of the ship our air speed, on which we depended for keeping us airborne, diminished because the air was going with us, and we just dropped on the deck like shot partridges.

In a talk given after the war Squadron Leader Wilfred Reginald Dyke Acland, who was one of *Furious'* pilots during the war, expanded on Moore's description:

> Further, halfway down the deck the natural wind was so blanketed by the superstructure that it ceased to have any effect on the aircraft, which was thus deprived of a very large proportion of the relative wind. For instance, assume the aircraft in landing into a relative wind of 30 knots composed of the ship's speed 15 and natural wind 15. Halfway up the deck the natural wind was almost completely blanketed by the funnel, mast and bridge, so that the relative wind at this point suddenly dropped by as much as 10–15 knots, a serious matter when the aircraft had to be brought in rather fast because of the bumps caused by the superstructure. Fortunately for the pilots a strong rope net was fixed to the forward end of the landing deck so that no one hit the funnel, although many made determined attempts to break through the net.

Landing experiments had been made using a 200 foot long dummy deck constructed on the airfield at RNAS Grain. Various configurations of ropes, fore and aft or transverse, with aircraft fitted with horns on the undercarriage to catch fore and aft ropes or a hook for the transverse ropes. Trials also took place with skids replacing wheels on the undercarriages. From the results of these trials, *Furious'* landing deck was fitted with a series of raised fore and aft wire cables with a ramp at the forward end of the deck. Moore again:

Our Sopwith Pups now had skids in place of wheels and hooks at their sides to catch up the wires and prevent the aircraft blowing over the side. The hawsers were raised about one foot above the deck by loose wooden pegs in order to enable the hooks to pass below them and so engage if the machines rose again for any reason after landing, as could well be with a gust of wind.

Flt S/Lt Jack McCleery, a junior pilot on *Furious*, kept an illegal diary throughout the war in which he noted down his impressions of the landing attempts. On 20 March:

> Rutland landed on deck at 11.03 a.m.—very bumpy indeed; machine practically out of control. Busteed did it with ship at anchor. Landed much too fast, deleted machine and cut his nose badly. Cheery start off.

Landings were about to get worse. A few days later:

> Jackson landed on deck—horrible sight, but Thyne trying it put the wind up me terribly—and most other people. I didn't feel right for nearly one hour after it. He just missed death by about six inches several times and then was stopped trying it, and flew back. It's by far the most risky job I've come against. It's obvious it's a wash out but I suppose they'll go on till someone's killed before they stop it.

Then on 28 March,

> Rutland landed, and was blown up against the combing [sic] down the deck. The deck party rushed out to catch him, but machine blown over the side about a second too quick for them. I saw the pilot dropping out and the machine going after him. Terrible sight and shook me properly. Luckily machine caught in [torpedo] tubes below—upside down and didn't fall on him. He was in the ditch for about 20 minutes. That washed it out for the day thank heavens. It put the wind properly up a lot of visitors from the carriers.

Rutland was able to reach a life buoy a quick thinking matelot had thrown overboard, and kept afloat until *Furious* had turned a complete circle whilst slowing to be able to drop a cutter. He was hoisted aboard with just two black eyes and a twisted knee for his troubles.

At the end of the series of flights, twelve landing attempts had been made by seven different pilots, only three resulting in landings with no damage to the machine. The experiments ended on 8 May with a landing by Capt. W. D. Jackson, flying a Sopwith Ship Strutter, which resulted in a smashed propeller and undercarriage, and a damaged engine. This was the only attempt by an aircraft other than the Pup. The number of landings was not large but it was evident that only under the most favorable conditions could a successful landing be expected. The Admiralty report summed up, 'In consequence it became apparent that the pilots might not be able to land on the deck after a flight of some hours over the North Sea.' Which appears to be a masterly understatement.

Whilst the aft landing deck experiments were over, it appears that the powers had not completely abandoned hope of using the forward deck to land on. On 4 June, Jack McCleery's diary contains an interesting entry:

> Flew off at about 11.30 and did runs over forward deck with skid 1½ Strutter. Did very well in spite of vertical breeze. Bust skid which took eight inches off prop. Flew back low and slow and turned on my nose in drome: Admiral very bucked. Nice looking waiting ambulance and doctor not needed!

Furious' log book notes that the ship sailed at 9.40 a.m. for 'flying experiments over f'xle', then at 11.34 a.m. two Strutters were flown off. The ship then maintained 'Course & Speed as required for Flying Experiments.' The experiments were carried out to seaward of the Black Rock in the Firth of Forth and *Furious* had returned to its moorings shortly after 1 p.m. Jack made a second series of 'touch and go' approaches the following afternoon. This time with no damage to the aircraft.

With landing experiments over, *Furious* returned to fleet operations which will be detailed in the following chapters. However, the future development of the aircraft carrier was not put on hold. There have already been several mentions of *Argus*, so it is time to take a look at her early history and design.

The origins of, and responsibility for, the final design of *Argus* as a flush deck aircraft carrier, with hangars and workshops beneath the flying deck, is involved. Two names are linked to the idea of a flush decked ship, Flight Commander H. A. Williamson and Lieutenant Gerard Holmes. Of the two Holmes, who had been Assistant Naval Architect for the Cunard line before the war, probably has the stronger case. The genesis for the vessel may lie in a memo from Jellicoe to the Admiralty on 8 May 1916. He enclosed a 'sketch and description of a proposed 27 knot seaplane carrier, which has been sent to me privately.' This was probably a design developed by Holmes with the assistance of Sir John H. Biles a naval architect. The design provided decks for both take-off and landing, although separated by a hangar and superstructure. This was refined following extensive discussions with RNAS officers 'and it was decided to provide the ship with weighted arresting ropes across the landing deck aft; and in conjunction with these a large stop net was to be between two erections, called islands, one on each side of the ship carrying a bridge structure across the top of them.' A design very similar to the Beardmore proposal of 1912. Following the landing trials on *Furious* the side by side islands were dispensed with, *Argus* emerging with an unobstructed flight deck.

Beardmore's had, on the stocks, a large cargo liner *Conte Rosso* being built for Lloyd Sabaudo of Turin, Italy. Work had been suspended on Job No. 519 on the outbreak of war. Lacking a better alternative, the partially completed hull was purchased by the Admiralty on 20 September 1916, launched on 2 December 1917, and commissioned as *Argus* on 16 September 1918.

As completed *Argus*'s flight deck was 549 feet long and maximum width of 68 feet. Her hangar was 330 feet long, maximum 68 feet wide, and 16 feet high. A forward aircraft lift between the hangar and flight deck was installed, measuring 30 feet by 36 feet. A second lift, on the centre line midships, measured 60 feet by 18 feet. The hangar could house around twenty aircraft. The funnels were ducted up the sides of the hull to below the hangar roof and then aft to exit under the flight deck, port and starboard. The lack of a bridge was addressed by a retractable chart house on the centreline which rose out of the flight deck, like a large garden shed, when not operating aircraft. In addition, there were small conning platforms either side of the ship below flight deck level.

Nothing like her had ever been seen before. Squat, box-like and of an unsurpassed ugliness, with no masts and apparently no funnels, one can image the comments on the Clyde as she steamed down river on her maiden voyage.

Argus was quickly nicknamed the *Hat Box* or the *Flatiron* from her appearance.

The first landings were made by Lt Col Richard Bell Davies, the new Senior Flying Officer *Furious*, and Capt. L. H. Cockey on 24 September 1918. No arresting gear was installed during these first landings, the wind was a gusty 22 knots and *Argus* was steaming at 15 knots. Seven landings were made, with the machines taxiing up the deck and flying off over the bow. The ship then slowed to six knots and a further series of six landings were made. Both pilots preferred landing at the lower ship's speed, the faster approach speed giving them more control. Their main concern was the cut outs in the flight deck located in line with the conning platforms. Two days later the flights continued, again without arresting gear installed, with a wind speed of just seven knots the ship making between 15 and 19 knots. The pilots found that the best felt wind speed for landings was 25 knots. *Argus* now went to the dockyard to have arresting gear installed, as described by Davies in his memoirs.

We decided to build two wooden ramps about thirty feet apart, one to be about halfway up the deck. They were to slope upwards from aft [to] forward, the top being about two feet above the deck. Between them, fore and aft wires were to be stretched. The idea was that the aeroplanes would land on the clear deck aft. The pilots should then keep full controllable speed taxiing forward and up the after ramp, when the aircraft would drop off the ramp into the trap and the hooks would engage in the wires. As the aircraft ran up the forward ramp the hooks [on the aircraft's undercarriage] would pull on the taut wires, the resultant friction arresting the aircraft.

The modifications were completed by 1 October, and landing trials recommenced, Davies making three landings. The first two landings were made at felt wind speeds of 26 and 25 knots, in both cases the machine did not really need the arresting gear and had to be taxied up the aft ramp into the trap. The final landing was made with a felt wind of just 12 knots:

> The machine ran on to the first ramp at a good speed and jumped some feet from the top of it before touching the deck again. The wires were caught on touching, and the machine bouncing again was pulled back to the deck by the wires. She ran up and over the top of the fore ramp, coming to rest without any violence or jerk about six feet from the foremost end of the ramp.

Summing up the tests, Davies was of the opinion that:

> Landing on with machines of types similar to 1½ Strutters is a very easy operation in winds felt between 20 and 30 knots, provided sufficient clear deck space is allowed abaft the gear to straighten up the machine and to regulate the speed.

The First World War ended before *Argus* could enter service. Although, had the war continued, she would have had a major role in a proposed operation.

Three further carriers were being constructed as the war ended.

Vindictive was a 'repeat *Furious*' but on a smaller heavy cruiser hull. Just like the larger ship, *Vindictive* had a flying off deck forward, and a landing deck aft of the bridge and funnels. She could carry six to twelve aircraft. *Vindictive*'s main advantage was her speed of nearly 30 knots, well able to keep up with *Furious*. Not commissioned until 1 October 1918, she was still on trials and working up when the war ended.

Hermes, although based on a cruiser design, was the first from the keel up flight deck carrier to be designed. Laid down on 15 January 1918 and launched on 11 September 1919, she was not commissioned until 18 February 1924, fourteen months after the Japanese designed carrier *Hōshō*.

Eagle was built on an uncompleted dreadnought hull, the *Almirante Cochrane* being constructed for Chile. The partially-assembled hull was purchased from Chile on 28 February 1918 to be converted into the carrier. *Eagle* was not commissioned until 20 February 1924.

Both *Hermes* and *Eagle* were originally designed with funnels port and starboard in islands corresponding to the original islands proposed for *Argus*, but the designs were completely reworked to have a starboard island for the funnels and bridge arrangement. On completion of the initial landing trials on *Argus* a mock up island was constructed on the starboard side of the flight deck. Made from canvas over a wooden frame the island included a bridge and funnel. Davies again:

> This narrowed the deck very much. Considering the span of the 1½ Strutter was too great and that I might easily foul the island with a wing tip, I fitted a Sopwith Pup with hooks for the second lot of trials. As these went off satisfactorily it was decided to complete *Eagle* and *Hermes* with islands.

There were other advantages to the island system. The design of the ducting of the funnels was simplified and they did not overheat the hangars, a problem in *Argus*. Finally, the simplified ducting freed up more space for the hangar. By such a simple experiment the future design of the aircraft carrier with an island on the starboard side of the flight deck was settled.

13

The Grand Fleet Flying Squadron

Throughout the remainder of 1917 *Furious* sailed on a small number of exercises and operations with units of the Grand Fleet. Following her second conversion, in 1918 she sailed on numerous operations. All the operations had simple letter and number combinations to identify them. The exercises, often Grand Fleet tactical exercises, appear to have had separate code series, but only three of these have been positively identified. Some operations were uneventful or cancelled due to weather conditions. Although, it should be remembered that any operation in the North Sea took place in areas patrolled by German airships and seaplanes and under the constant threat of submarine attack, chance encounters with mines, with the threat of a sortie by the High Seas Fleet always to be considered. There are frequent mentions in the reports of torpedo tracks being sighted, and attacks by escorting vessels on suspected submarines. Orders often required that all major ships should stream paravanes if mines are suspected, or in specific high risk areas. To detail all of these operations would be repetitious. Therefore, all of *Furious'* known operations are listed in Appendix 2. Only those that resulted in some form of aerial activity are detailed below and in the following chapters.

In her first configuration *Furious* carried Sopwith Pups for anti-Zeppelin work and Short 184 floatplanes for all other purposes. Another seaplane carrier, often *Pegasus*, accompanied *Furious* at sea to stop and pick up her Short floatplanes.

On 11 September 1917, during Operation DN, Flight Commander Geoffrey Moore had what he later recalled as a 'very, very unpleasant experience.' An airship had been sighted about twenty five miles south of the ship, which had to reverse her course to bring the wind down the flight deck. Moore was informed that after take-off *Furious* would turn towards the airship to give him a course to steer. He took off at 7.25 a.m. (GMT) flying Sopwith Pup, N6450.

Off I went and eventually got up amongst the clouds, which were at 10,000 feet. Fortunately, they were broken that day so I could fly in and out amongst them trying to find this Zeppelin. I never got a glimpse of her. Then, after an hour or so, looking down through a hole in the cloud, I saw land beneath me. I hadn't an idea in the world what it was. Holland? Germany? I decided the best thing to do would be to scuttle back to the fleet as fast as I could.

Like many an RNAS pilot before and after him Moore had difficulty finding the ships. Finally, with fuel getting low, he spotted the wake of some ships in the distance, turned towards them and was relieved to find himself over the escorting destroyers.

I flew over the leading one and waved to the people on the bridge. They waved back. I flew on for about a mile and a half, to give them time to pull up, and plonked down in the sea, and was soon in my old familiar position of hanging on to the bracing wire of the tail fin. I had no reason to suspect that I wouldn't be picked up almost immediately.

What in fact happened? The first destroyer came close by me and sent a great wave over my head. I didn't like that very much. And the second did the same thing, and the third, and the fourth, and by that time I was reasoning with myself, and saying, 'Well, of course, I know what it is; there are submarines about, and no ship's captain is going to risk his ship's company just to pick up one silly pilot in a little aeroplane, and I'm going to get left. I can't blame them. Bad luck for me.' But when the fifth destroyer [*Mystic*] came up, she pulled up alongside me— evidently she had been detailed to collect me. Someone threw a handline, and I only just had time to wrap it round my wrist before an enthusiastic sailor yanked me through the water, and up the side of the destroyer and aboard. I was rather like a drowned rat; the water was very cold, but there I was alive and unhurt.

The Pup broke apart behind the pilot's seat and was lost. Dried off, undoubtedly with a tot of Navy Rum inside him, and in a borrowed fresh dry uniform, Moore decided to head up to the bridge to make his thanks. Just as he appeared on deck a great wave washed down the length of the ship and almost carried him off. He retreated down below, got out of his now soaking uniform, and climbed into a bunk, staying there until the destroyer entered the calm waters of the Firth of Forth.

A few days later *Furious* was out again, to conduct Exercises PZ No. 1 and PZ No. 2. She sailed around 2 p.m. of 16 September in company with the Grand Fleet. At 5.45 p.m. the starboard inboard engine broke down and was stopped, but *Furious* was able to continue the exercises on the three remaining shafts. On 17 September Exercise PZ.1 was conducted during the morning and PZ.2 in the early afternoon. At 9.02 a.m. the log noted 'dispatched seaplane,' but failed to record its return. However, Jack McCleery noted that Flt Lt Gallehawk had been sent up to conduct a reconnaissance and landed back alongside *Furious*. He later added an unusual observation, 'Airship broke adrift (engine failure) so [Flt Cdr R. G. D.]

Sibley had to go and look for it. Got going again all right.' From *Furious'* log book we learn that at 3.10 p.m. the carrier had, 'Parted company with Fleet on account of defective engines and proceeded for base, *Pegasus*, *Obdurate* and *Orpheus* in company.' At 5.30 p.m. another seaplane was 'dispatched to search for disabled airship *N.S.3.*' Fifteen minutes later the airship was sighted and Sibley returned to land alongside *Pegasus* to be recovered. The airship eventually returned safely to its base at East Fortune. *Furious'* engine defects must have been repairable by her own engineering staff as there is no mention of dockyard assistance in her log books. She sailed for steam trials on 1 October, which appear to have been satisfactory as she took part in more exercises three days later.

They were at sea again between 16–19 October. What were intended as more exercises turned into a fruitless attempt to intercept a German minelayer and escorting destroyers. On 17 October, the force (*Furious*, 1st Cruiser Squadron (*Courageous* and *Glorious*), 27 light cruisers and 54 destroyers.) missed contact with German minelaying light cruisers SMS *Bremse* and SMS *Brummer*. The German light cruisers attacked a west-bound convoy sailing from Bergen to the UK. The convoy comprised twelve merchantmen with an escort of two destroyers, *Mary Rose* and *Strongbow*, and two armed trawlers. The light cruisers sank both destroyers and nine merchant ships.

Furious' final operation as a seaplane carrier was between 8–10 November. Weather was atrocious and no flying possible. *Furious* left Rosyth for her conversion on the Tyne on 14 November, she maintained 26 knots through the night. Before arriving at the dockyard her three remaining Shorts were flown off to South Shields seaplane station. *Furious*, and her aircraft, missed the last major clash of the big ships, the Second Battle of Heligoland Bight, by just a few days.

A few days later, Beatty wrote to the Admiralty submitting that:

> . . . a Flag Officer may be appointed in command of the Seaplane Carriers of the Grand Fleet, and to undertake the administrative control of all aircraft working with the Fleet and of all arrangements in connection therewith.

Beatty further suggested that *Furious* should be detailed as the Flagship of the Admiral Commanding Aircraft (ACA), at Rosyth. The Admiralty approved and, on 6 January 1918, appointed Rear Admiral Richard Fortescue Phillimore as Admiral Commanding Aircraft.

With *Furious'* return to the fleet, on 15 March 1918, the Grand Fleet Flying Squadron was formed. The squadron comprised *Furious*, *Campania*, *Nairana* and *Pegasus*. Of these only *Furious* was fit to sail and operate with units of the fleet. She would have been joined by *Argus* and *Vindictive* and, eventually *Hermes* and *Eagle*, as their conversions would have proceeded with more urgency had the war continued into 1919. However, throughout 1918 *Furious* alone carried the flag of naval aviation in the North Sea.

On 1 April 1918 a fundamental change came to the Royal Naval Air Service, when it and the Royal Flying Corps were combined into the Royal Air Force. For the remainder of the war, for the men aboard the carriers and ships of the fleet the only visible effect was to change their ranks and, in some cases, their uniforms. The adoption of military ranks further confused the situation, a Flight Sub Lieutenant was now a 2nd Lieutenant, and so on up the ranks until Richard Bell Davies, *Furious'* senior flying officer, became a Lieutenant Colonel. The men of the old RNAS with the Fleet, whatever their rank, whatever their uniform, remained first and foremost naval airmen.

In May 1918, *Furious* began a series of operations, beginning F.1 and continuing through F.13, that would continue until the end of the war. Throughout these operations there was a consistency to the composition of the ships that accompanied *Furious*. She always had three destroyers as immediate escorts, and was normally accompanied by a light cruiser squadron with additional destroyers. The light cruisers were most often from the 1st Light Cruiser Squadron. The composition of the squadron varied but, in July 1918, comprised *Caledon* (Flag, Commodore Walter H. Cowan), *Galatea*, *Inconstant*, *Phaeton* and *Royalist*; all with their own Sopwith Camels; and the destroyers from the 13th Flotilla, comprising mostly modern V and W Class ships. As *Furious* now operated solely landplanes, Ship Strutters and Camels, an accompanying seaplane carrier was no longer required. Whilst pilots had been given permission on return from an operational flight to attempt landing on the aft deck, this was never taken up. Returning pilots were often low on fuel and came down close to the first ships they sighted. Destroyers were detailed to act as recovery vessels for the aircrews and aeroplanes, over time the 13th Flotilla destroyers adapted to this role. In his report for one operation Rear Admiral Phillimore included a request:

> If the exigencies of the Service permit, it is desirable that Destroyers of the XIII Flotilla should be sent for Aircraft Operations. They have drawn extra spars for davits, and fitted extra masthead whips for hoisting in the machines—fittings which the other destroyers have not got.

On most operations a covering force of either a Battle Squadron or a Battle Cruiser Squadron, together with their escorts, would accompany the aircraft carrier squadron.

For the fleet there was no shortage of Camel fighters, they were still in production. But the Ship Strutters were no longer being built. Whilst the remaining stocks of machines were made available to the fleet, most of these had not been converted to Ship Strutters and could only be used for training. Consequently, the available Ship Strutters had to be carefully husbanded until new observation and reconnaissance machines, which were being developed, became ready for service.

Major maintenance and servicing of the aircraft was carried out at East Fortune, Turnhouse or Donibristle. On all operations accurate compasses were essential and, before they were transferred to the ships, all aircraft had their compasses swung and a certificate of variation issued. Transfers were made on lighters or by *Pegasus* and *Nairana*.

Navigation remained a problem to the end of the war. Providing details of the local wind direction and strength before take-off was solved by using the burst of anti-aircraft shrapnel, at a known height, then measuring the drift. A thorough briefing before flight was not always possible, especially for the single-seater pilots, and force of circumstance could require the ships to make big changes in course whilst the aircraft were away. To aid the crews on their return, ships were sometimes stationed close to a known location, often just off the Danish coast.

Improvements in wireless equipment were being made. The early W/T sets available at Jutland were being replaced by new more efficient Sterling light weight transmitters, just 8 inches × 8 inches × 5 inches and weighing less than 10 lb, which permitted observers to communicate directly with *Furious*. However, the set's range was only around ten miles.

Operation F.1, 20–23 May 1918

Furious and three destroyers of the 13th Flotilla with the 1st Light Cruiser Squadron (less *Inconstant*) and four destroyers of the 13th Flotilla, sailed from Rosyth at 3 p.m. on 20 May. Their orders were vaguely framed as, 'To attack enemy aircraft.' They were to proceed to an area of the North Sea that would soon become familiar, the Heligoland Bight north of the Dogger Bank and close to the Danish coast.

On the morning of 21 May the force was in position approximately nineteen miles north of the North Dogger Bank Light Vessel. The patrol line was due east along the 56th parallel to a point some 80 miles off the Danish coast. Here, at 12.20 p.m., a Sopwith Ship Strutter, A5996, was flown off by Lt Melvin H. Rattray with 2nd Lt E. J. Withers as observer. After an uneventful patrol to the north, during which they sighted several (possibly British) submarines, they returned to ditch alongside destroyer *Verulam* around 2.15 p.m. Rattray and his observer were safely recovered together with the remains of their machine.

Overnight the force returned to the light vessel and repeated the patrol the following day. *Furious* and her destroyers were well to the east when the cruisers, following behind, spotted an airship to the south west at 9.35 a.m. Both *Phaeton* (N6644?) and *Royalist* (N6754) sent off their Camels but no contact was made with the airship. Both pilots were picked up and the Camel from *Royalist* was recovered by the destroyer *Vega*. The force was back at Rosyth in the early afternoon of 22 May.

Admiral Phillimore in his summary of the operation suggested that it might be worth 'keeping single Fighter Patrols at 15,000 feet over [the light vessels], watching for the Zeppelins to pass underneath.' This is one of the earliest suggestions for the creation of standing combat air patrols, but would have been extremely wasteful of aeroplanes and, potentially, trained pilots.

Operation F.3, 31 May–2 June 1918

Furious was part of a fleet operation to support the Harwich Force in one of their sweeps against German minesweeping forces in the Heligoland Bight. The Germans usually escorted their minesweepers with a force of light cruisers and destroyers, often with a division of battleships in distant support. Hoping to test this support, and possibly catch a battleship or two, Beatty had sailed a portion of the Battle Cruiser Fleet with a Grand Fleet Battle Squadron in the offing.

On 1 June, *Furious*, the 6th Light Cruiser Squadron and their destroyers were to patrol to the north of the Dogger Bank, approaching within twenty five miles of the Danish coast. The wind was 45 knots out of the north and clouds were at 1,000 feet. Phillimore decided not to send off a reconnaissance machine, noting that it 'would have taken 20 minutes "out" and 1¾ hours "back".' They returned to Rosyth less than forty-eight hours after sailing.

The Harwich Force did not make contact with any German forces, but the destroyer *Shakespeare,* which was towing a high speed lighter with a flying boat aboard, was mined and had to be towed back to Harwich. The flying boat either flew back Felixstowe or the tow was taken over by another destroyer.

The British heavy ships spent the morning of 1 June engaged with German seaplanes. Beatty's main force comprised the First Battle Cruiser Squadron with escorting destroyers, the 1st Cruiser Squadron (light battle cruisers *Courageous* and *Glorious*, with light cruiser *Champion*) and their destroyers. Accompanying these ships was the 2nd Light Cruiser Squadron (*Birmingham* (flag), *Dublin*, *Sydney* and *Melbourne*) with their destroyers. Aboard *Sydney* was Camel N6783 with Flt Lt Albert Cyril Sharwood as pilot, *Melbourne*'s pilot was Flt Lt L. B. Gibson and her Camel was N6785.

At 7.10 a.m. (German times, GMT+1, are converted to GMT for consistency.) four two-seater seaplanes, three Brandenburg W19 (2209, 2212, 2213) and a single Friedrichshafen FF49c (1830), from *Kampfstaffel I* at Borkum, set out to patrol an area approximately one hundred miles west of their base. At 9.20 a.m. they sighted four destroyers, probably part of the Harwich Force, steering south. The seaplanes then turned to the north and quickly discovered Beatty's main force. The German seaplanes later reported having dropped a total of eight 10 kg bombs on the ships, some of which hit the sea close to *Courageous*. No hits were reported.

At 9.55 a.m. Sharwood took off from the flight deck of HMAS *Sydney*, his report noting that he climbed to 2,000 feet and headed off to the south east.

Shortly after I sighted ahead of me two two-seater enemy seaplanes steering approximately South East at an altitude of about 8,000 feet. After about twenty minutes during which time the seaplanes had flown nose down to gain speed, I caught up the rearmost two-seater who was flying at an altitude of about 5,000 feet. I dived and began to open fire on the rear one but suddenly found myself under fire from an enemy single-seater scout, who had dived onto my tail from behind. Previously, this machine has been above me unnoticed. By "cart wheeling" and climbing to the left I found myself able to open fire on his tail. I repeated this manoeuvre twice successfully. In the third dive I noticed my tracer bullets to be entering the scout's fuselage. Soon after this he began to "side slip" and then fell into a spinning nose dive. Not knowing whether he was hit or merely attempting to escape I dived after him. As he disappeared into the haze and clouds below, which were about 2,500 feet, I came under fire of the two-seater seaplanes, then between 4,000 and 5,000 feet. Getting under the tail of one of them I fired one burst, when my Vickers gun jammed with about 100 rounds unfired. As the Lewis gun pan had been emptied during the fight with the scout I had to break off the engagement.

There were no 'enemy single-seater scout' machines over the ships. The combat took place some 120 miles from the nearest land base, well beyond the range of such machines. It is certain that in the adrenalin rush of combat Sharwood mistook one of the two-seaters for a single-seater. It probably dived to get away from him, he was then attacked by at least two of the remaining machines. All four German machines returned safely to Borkum by 11.40 a.m.

Sharwood then adds an intriguing comment:

Communication with British ships by wireless regarding the direction of the escape of seaplanes was impossible owing to my aerial weight having been lost during combat.

A rare confirmation that at least some Camels were fitted with a Sterling transmitting set, as suggested by the Grand Fleet Committee on Air Requirements.

Sharwood searched for the fleet until almost out of fuel, fortunately sighting two light cruisers and several destroyers (part of the Harwich Force) just before having to turn away towards Denmark. As he approached the ships one of them fired on him, he quickly sent off a flare to identify himself and came in for a landing ahead of one of the destroyers, *Sharpshooter*. The Camel dug its nose into the sea, and Sharwood was able to scramble out of the cockpit and cling to the tail until rescued by a boat from the destroyer. The machine was eventually salvaged up by *Canterbury*, but was damaged beyond repair. Sharwood was returned to Harwich.

Two minutes after Sharwood, Gibson on *Melbourne* also took off. Unfortunately he immediately lost sight of the enemy machines, and patrolled over the fleet until, low on fuel, he ditched alongside one of the destroyers. *Courageous* was also preparing to launch her Camel but, observing the two going up from the cruisers, kept it available for another occasion.

The Royal Navy rarely hands out medals just for trying hard, that is expected, so Sharwood had to make do with a Mention in Despatches 'for valuable services rendered—in flying operations against the enemy.' He was also promoted to become commander of the flight of four Camels and designated Senior Naval Flying Officer Second Light Cruiser Squadron.

Operation F.5, 17–20 June 1918

This was to be a second attempt to carry out a reconnaissance of the northern Heligoland Bight. The first attempt, Operation F.4, having been cancelled due to bad weather. The forces employed were the same as Operation F.1. Also at sea were a squadron of minelayers escorted by the First Battle Squadron, cruisers and destroyers. The operation would provoke a number of air attacks which would result in air defence lessons learnt the hard way.

The squadron sailed from Rosyth on the evening of 17 June. The following morning they were off the Norwegian coast, closing to within ten miles of the Lista lighthouse on the south-western tip of Norway. In the evening the squadron set course to the south east to be on the 56th parallel, some 110 miles off the Danish coast by dawn. *Galatea* and two destroyers were detached, at 4.15 a.m. on 19 June, to close the Danish coast to be available to help the reconnaissance machine if necessary.

Furious' aircraft were housed in two hangars, one under the forward flight deck and one under the aft landing deck. Although both decks were linked by gangways the use of these narrow bridges, to transfer fully assembled machines, was probably impractical at sea. As the purpose of this operation was reconnaissance, the forward hangar would have had at least two Sopwith Ship Strutters and, from the course of future events, three Sopwith 2F.1 Camels. Additional Strutters and Camels were in the aft hangar. Typical morning routine, after General Quarters before dawn, was to bring up aircraft from the forward hangar and prepare them for flight. The Strutters would be parked ahead of the Camels, and it is not difficult to imagine the engines being tested and adjusted, ammunition, fuel and oil being checked and topped up, and guns fitted in the observer's cockpit of the Strutters. The reconnaissance flight was due to take-off at 7.00 a.m. At 6.45 a.m. two enemy seaplanes were observed approaching the squadron.

The *Seeflugstation* at List, on the northern tip of the island of Sylt, was responsible for patrolling the North Sea north to Lodbjerg, in northern Denmark at the entrance to the Skagerrak, and as far west as the Dogger Bank Light Vessels. Based at the station were at least fourteen Friedrichshafen FF49c and two Brandenburg W12 two-seater machines. Both types were fitted with a single fixed forward firing Spandau machine gun and a single Parabellum machine gun on a flexible mounting for the observer. At 4.25 a.m. two Friedrichshafen FF49c, 1692 *Flugzeugmaat (FLMt)* Johanny and observer *FLMt* Thaller with 1693 *FLMt* Planert and observer *Leutnant der Reserve der Matrosenartillerie (LtdR(MA))* Hinze, set out to patrol between 55° 20′ N and 56° 0′ N, approximately along longitude 5° E. They located *Furious* just before the reconnaissance Strutter was launched. After dropping two small bombs, which landed close to a destroyer, they circled the squadron at low altitude completely ignoring anti-aircraft fire.

Aboard *Furious*, the Strutters were quickly moved to one side and two Camels were sent off. Captain R. H. Daly was first off at 7.00 a.m. on Camel N6801, followed ten minutes later by Lt M. W. Baseden on Camel N6810. Given that the reconnaissance machine would have to have been moved out of the way before the Camels could take-off, this was commendably fast work. Although comments by senior officers, at the Admiralty, after the event were critical of the time it took to get the fighters off.

The Germans had sent a wireless report of the sighting before attacking with bombs. *Furious*, referred to as a *Flugzeugmutterschiff*, was accurately described, down to the identity letters FU painted on the aft deck. They then noted:

> The carrier turned to the Southwest to get into the wind. From the forecastle when running at high speed three [*sic*] land planes took off. Apart from these another five aeroplanes could be seen arranged on the forecastle. No wakes or wash were seen on the surface of the sea to indicate that any seaplane had taken off. Aeroplanes then lost sight of.

Daly chased and caught one of the seaplanes, 1693. His Vickers gun jammed after a few rounds and a shot from the observers gun damaged the firing mechanism of the Lewis gun. Daly cleared the stoppage in the Vickers, but the gun continued to jam every few rounds, finally becoming impossible to clear. Frustrated, he had to break off and return to the ships, landing alongside destroyer *Valentine* at 8.15 a.m. The German report states:

> At a height of about 1,000 metres an aeroplane was seen circling, identified as an enemy land single-seater. As he saw us he went down in large spirals to 500 metres then turned towards us and performed loops and other aerobatics. He never came nearer than 100 metres and never attacked us.

Presumably the loops and aerobatics took place whilst Daly was trying to clear his jam.

Baseden had a little more luck. He too caught up with one of the raiders, 1692:

> I attacked him from under the tail with my Vickers at a height of 2,000 feet, when he made a flat turn to the right and his Observer opened fire.

Baseden too suffered a series of jams of his Vickers gun, finally resorting to the Lewis gun for a final attack:

> I then climbed and gave a surprise attack from above with my Lewis and observed incendiary and explosive bullets entering his machine close to [the] Observers seat. He dived steeply about 500 feet, turning at the same time. This time I could see no Observer standing up and no answering fire was noticed. I then saw a second hostile seaplane coming towards me and as my Lewis ammunition was expended I returned to the ship, landed, and was picked up by *Wolfhound*.

The crew of 1692 reported, 'The enemy aircraft attacked us only from astern never from the side, they always dived and flew tight turns to escape our fire. During the second attack the observer's gun jammed, in clearing this he was wounded by a shot in the left hand.' Despite the wound Thaller was able to continue returning fire. By the end of the combat he was down to just three remaining rounds. After escaping from Baseden's Camel, the Friedrichshafen headed east, probably intending to join up with 1693 at a rendezvous point, and found *Galatea* loitering close to the Danish coast. Thaller's wound did not prevent him dropping a bomb which landed within 20 yards of *Urchin*, one of the escorting destroyers.

At 7.40 a.m. *Galatea* was about twenty miles from the Danish coast, on a line with Ringkøbing Fjord, steaming at 18.5 knots to the north-west. Her lookouts spotted the approaching seaplane at approximately 5,000 yards. Captain Charles M. Forbes immediately ordered the ship's Camel to be prepared for launching, turning on to a southerly course to head into the wind and increasing speed to 26 knots. After the Camel had taken off, Forbes altered course towards the enemy seaplane, now estimated to be 6,000 yards away, 'in order to give the pilot a guide in case he should lose sight of the enemy whilst flying off.' Whilst engaged in launching the Camel, a signal had been received from *Furious* ordering *Galatea* to rejoin the main force. Course was set to rejoin the squadron, the cruiser was now well to the south of *Furious*, steering to the north-west at 27 knots.

Lieutenant Donald Thornton Simpson flew Camel N6782 off *Galatea*'s platform shortly after 7.40 a.m. He did not immediately sight the FF49c but set course to the south-south-east for fifteen minutes until he estimated he was ten miles from the coast, then altered to the south-east for half an hour by which time he 'judged that I was near the vicinity of Horns Reef.' The clouds were lowering and visibility poor. He was flying below the clouds at 1,300 feet and running into rain storms. At this point Simpson turned to head due north.

> I discovered an enemy seaplane attempting to land on Ringkøbing Fjord and circled round above it to watch the enemy's movements. Instead of landing, however, the seaplane flew out to sea at an altitude of about 500 feet. I then dived on the enemy and opened fire with my Vickers gun at an altitude of 1,000 feet. After firing about

10 rounds the gun jambed badly. I then turned, climbed a little, and dived again, emptying a pan of ammunition from the Lewis gun at the enemy. Several of the shots seemed to enter the seaplane in the vicinity of the pilot's cockpit.

Simpson then lost sight of the seaplane in a rain storm. On their return to List, the crews appear to have combined Daly's and Simpson's attacks into one continuous combat, reporting two machines attacking 1692.

Simpson searched for over 45 minutes for *Galatea*. Steering to the north-west he was forced lower and lower until, to stay beneath the clouds, he was flying at only 800 feet. As his engine began to misfire he turned towards Denmark, then turned north in the hope of finding a vessel outside the three mile limit. With his engine running rougher he finally made for land and made a good landing on the beach about a mile south of the village of Fjaltring, thirty miles north of Ringkøbing. He failed to destroy the Camel as:

the only means that I had of setting fire to the machine was by means of Very's cartridges. Also a large crowd of people had gathered since my landing, and, as I had been unable to clear the jamb in my gun, setting the machine on fire might have caused serious loss of life due to the cartridges still in the machine.

The machine was subsequently taken apart by the Danish Navy and taken to Copenhagen. Simpson failed to qualify as a shipwrecked mariner—the Danish authorities were more punctilious in the observation of the rules—and was sent to an internment camp at the military barracks in Aarhus.

The two FF49c's had returned to List by 9.35 a.m., but had already wirelessed in details of the British squadron. A further search had been sent out at 7.45 a.m., followed by four more. Only the last of these located *Furious*.

After the first contact with enemy seaplanes *Furious* had turned east, *Galatea* and her destroyers rejoined at 8.20 a.m., and the whole force approached to within fifteen miles of the Danish coast. The ships ran into the same bad weather that had made things difficult for Simpson. Not until 9.40 a.m., after it was clear that Simpson was not going to return, did the force alter course to the north-west. They were not rediscovered until almost three hours had passed.

Two Friedrichshafen FF49c, 1817 *Flugmeister* Meyer and *Flugmeister* Dibowski and 1796 *LtdR(MA)* Wenke and *FLMt* Schirra, left List at 10.15 a.m. steering north-west by north, a course that would lead them almost directly to *Furious* and her squadron.

Furious now had a single Camel available on the forward deck, but another was being prepared on the aft deck. At 12.15 p.m. the two Germans found the British ships, dropping several bombs, 'big ones from 3,000 feet and they all lit within 30 yards on our starboard side.' Nicholson was manoeuvring his big ship like a destroyer to avoid the bombs.

The two Camels were sent off immediately. Lt Grahame Heath flew his Camel off the fore deck at 12.35 p.m. without difficulty. Just one minute later, 2nd Lt E. Smith, whilst attempting to take-off from the aft deck, crashed into the sea. The record is silent as to whether he attempted a down-wind take-off over the stern of the ship, or into wind. If the latter, even if starting at the extreme aft end of the deck, he would have to make a rapid turn to avoid flying into the goal posts or fore mast. In his memoirs, Richard Bell Davies mentions Heath's flight but is mute regarding Smith's take-off. It would have been his decision to order the attempt.

Heath, climbing to 4,000 feet, flew towards the German machines:

> I was then above the enemy who was steering away S.E., evidently having exhausted his supply of bombs. He put his nose well down and I eventually caught him at about 2,000 feet, after 20 minutes. I dived on him from the Starboard side, and my Lewis Gun jambed. I zoomed away and cleared the jamb; I then attacked him again, my Lewis Gun jambing. This was repeated four or five times when my Lewis Gun became exhausted of ammunition. I could hear his shots very near, and I could see where some of them had penetrated my fuselage by my seat, one of the bullets hitting my "Very's" lights.
>
> The enemy was turning to avoid me on the way down, and I noticed that he was gliding down, I followed him right down to the water, my Vickers Gun behaving splendidly.
> I saw that he landed tail to wind, and that his engine had stopped. I fired one short burst at him on the water from about 250 feet and then flew back to the ships.

Heath landed by destroyer *Valentine* and was picked up.

Valentine now had Daly and Heath aboard, who were shortly to be joined by Wenke and Schirra from Friedrichshafen FF49c, 1796, which was Heath's prey. Although not formally interrogated it is apparent that the aircrew spent some time in conversation. One of *Valentine*'s officers, Lt Kelsey who spoke German, may have interpreted. Heath discovered that one of the bullets from his Lewis gun had damaged the engine forcing the Friedrichshafen down. Schirra had used up all but fifty rounds in fighting back then, to lighten the machine, had thrown over the gun, remaining ammunition and their camera. The crew were rescued but, despite pleas from the pilots on *Furious*, the Friedrichshafen was destroyed by gunfire from *Valentine*.

The second seaplane returned safely to List at 3.30 p.m.

Furious' squadron returned to Rosyth before dawn on 20 June.

In the same *London Gazette* as Sharwood before him, Grahame Heath received a Mention in Despatches 'for valuable services rendered—in flying operations against the enemy.'

One of the handwritten memos attached to the reports, unfortunately the signature is indecipherable, pin pointed the cause of the problems experienced during Operation F.5.

The reports demonstrate the effect of the lack of experience in active air operations.

The *Furious* and her aircraft failed to make the most of their opportunity by:-

(1) Slowness in getting fighting machines away.

(2) Ineffective A.A. fire from Furious.

(3) Lewis and Vickers guns jambing.

The experience will have been a very valuable one.

The first criticism seems to be a little harsh. Regarding the anti-aircraft fire, it must be admitted that the only thing *Furious'* gunners hit was the ship's galley funnel.

The jamming of the machine guns was not an unusual occurrence, and could have been avoided, or reduced, through careful examination and checking of the ammunition. The Handbook of Aircraft Armament recommended, for both Vickers and Lewis guns, that 'Every round should be carefully looked over for dents, deep-set caps, defective bullets, split cases, etc., before it is placed in the magazine.' After landing in Denmark, Simpson examined his Vickers gun, 'I discovered that two of the cartridges had come out of the links and had caught against the piece of wire which bridges the channel through which the cartridges pass to the feed block.' This problem had been recognised and during 1918 special ammunition, manufactured to tighter tolerances, was being made for the RAF. It was known as 'Red Label' or 'Special'. Whether this had been supplied to the fleet is not known.

14

Operation F.7—
The Tondern Raid, 19 July 1918

The first attempts to raid the airship sheds at Tondern were made by *Vindex* with the Harwich Force in March and May 1916. They could hardly be considered a success. With new ships and new aeroplanes it was time for another attempt. Sir David Beatty submitted to the Admiralty an initial proposal for the bombing raid on Tondern on 15 June 1918. A copy of the Draft Orders for Operation 'F.T.', incorporating requested changes, was returned to the Admiralty on 21 June.

Operation F.6, between 27–29 June 1918, was the first attempt to carry out the Tondern operation. According to Jack McCleery before sailing on 27 June, 'About eight more pilots came aboard for the stunt.' As the original intention was that eight pilots, led by Geoffrey Moore, would raid the Tondern base it may be taken as a clear indication that the raid was to be attempted. Strangely, Moore does not mention this in his memoir. However, Richard Bell Davies does write of this earlier attempt:

> On the day set for the attack *Furious* and her escort of destroyers set out to reach a point off the Danish coast just before dawn. Soon after midnight the weather deteriorated, coming on to rain and blow. The operation had to be abandoned and it was about a week before we were able to try again.

It was in fact almost three weeks before the second attempt.

After Operation F.6, *Furious* went to sea on several occasions, but only to conduct exercises. Then, between 8 and 13 July, lighters and service vessels brought out aeroplanes to the carrier. It is a reasonable assumption that some of these visits delivered the Camels for Operation F.7.

The machines chosen for the raid were all Sopwith 2F.1 Camels with 150 hp Bentley BR1 rotary engines. In addition to the standard armament of a single, synchronised Vickers machine gun and a Lewis gun mounted over the top wing, racks for two 50 lb bombs were installed under the centre fuselage. Other than the bomb racks the Camels were standard machines. The only known photographs of them before the raid are taken from above, these show the national markings painted over, probably at Bernard Smart's suggestion. Several of the machines have identity bands around the rear fuselage, and the lead machine seems to have a painted cowling, white with at least one or two horizontal dark bands. Serial numbers of all the machines used on the raid have not been positively identified and, lacking confirmation, will not be used in this account.

Moore assembled a group of eight pilots, including himself, from those available at Turnhouse and East Fortune and embarked on a hurried training programme. The airship sheds were marked out on the airfield at Turnhouse and they practised low level attacks using dummy bombs, progressing to using live bombs on the foreshore of the Firth of Forth. Richard Bell Davies recalled that the:

> . . . training at Turnhouse had to be a rush job. The six more experienced pilots (Moore had been posted to command station at Turnhouse before the raid.) soon became proficient, but the latest to join, Yeulett, needed longer. I had to tell Yeulett that he was out of the team; a bitter disappointment to him.

He was writing of Operation F.6, but as Jack McCleery noted eight pilots coming aboard *Furious* on 27 June this must have included both Moore and Yeulett. After the cancellation of Operation F.6, as training resumed 'Yeulett improved rapidly and I agreed to put him back in the team.'

Their targets, the airship sheds at Tondern (Tønder, Denmark), were located a little over twenty miles east of the seaplane base at List, about nine miles from the mainland coast and a mile or so north of the town itself. Construction on the airship base had commenced in September 1914, by March the following year the first two sheds, *Tobias* and *Toni*, were complete. Work then began on an enormous double hangar, *Toska*. When finished in January 1916 it measured 240 m × 60 m × 35 m. All three sheds were oriented along an east to west axis. In addition to the airship sheds the base had tanks holding 40,000 litres of petrol, a gas works capable of producing 8,000 m³ of hydrogen per day with storage tanks for 56,000 m³, sufficient to fill one airship. The base was manned by 600 officers and men, excluding the airship crews. There was also a hangar for five Albatros D.III fighters of the defence flight, but they had been withdrawn by 6 March 1918 owing to the poor state of the landing ground. It is not known whether this information was available to *Furious*' pilots as at least one of the pilots was expecting to see hostile aircraft during the raid. Surviving pilot's reports all mention anti-aircraft batteries close to the base.

On the date of the raid *Tobias* only held a captive balloon and *Toni* was being dismantled. Within *Toska* were two Zeppelins, L54 and L60. Both were 196.5 m long and 30 m in diameter, and held 56,000 m³ of highly inflammable hydrogen. L54, commanded by *Kapitänleutnant* von Buttlar Brandenfels, had made 43 flights. L60, a new 'height climber' with special high altitude engines, was commanded by *Kapitänleutnant* Hans Kurt Flemming and had made 17 flights.

The orders for Operation F.7 were issued by Sir David Beatty to senior officers, to be distributed to commanding officers of ships involved, on 16 July 1918, the object being 'To attack the Zeppelin sheds at Tondern with bombs and to attack any enemy airships sighted.' The forces employed were in two squadrons.

Force A, the strike force, was made up of *Furious* and the First Light Cruiser Squadron (*Caledon* (Flag), *Inconstant, Galatea, Royalist* and *Phaeton*) with eight destroyers of the 13th Flotilla. Force A was commanded by Rear Admiral Phillimore.

Force B, the covering force, had the 1st Division of the First Battle Squadron, the Seventh Light Cruiser Squadron, and eight destroyers.

The First Battle Squadron at this time composed ten dreadnought battleships, five older ships (including Jellicoe's old flagship *Iron Duke*) and five new *Royal Sovereign* class ships. Sir Charles E. Madden, commanding the First Battle Squadron, flew his flag in *Revenge*, and the 1st Division comprised the remainder of the class, *Ramilies, Resolution, Royal Oak* and *Royal Sovereign*. Sir Charles' Madden's Second in Command was Rear Admiral Sir William C. M. Nicholson, flying his flag in *Emperor of India*. Beatty's orders that the 1st Division should be commanded by the Second-in-Command during the operation was viewed with a Nelsonian blind eye by Madden who sailed in his flagship. The 7th Light Cruiser Squadron, commanded by Rear Admiral George H. Borrett, comprised *Carysfort* (Flag), *Aurora, Penelope* and *Undaunted*.

Beatty ordered that:

Force A is to leave Rosyth on the night 16th/17th July, and proceed to position A - 237° 14 miles from Lodbjerg Light, and thence to position C–56.03 N., 7.35 E., arriving about 0300 on 18th July. Machines for attacking Tondern are to be flown from position C and force is then to cruise as ordered by Admiral Commanding Aircraft.

Force B is to leave Rosyth after Force A, keeping within supporting distance, proceeding to position 56.45 N., 6.00 E., thence to cruise in the vicinity of the Little Fisher Bank. If no intelligence has been received by 0800 on 18th July, force is to return to Rosyth.

Admiral Commanding Aircraft is requested to give detailed orders to Force A. The Admiral Commanding Aircraft, and Senior Officer, Force B, are to confer prior to sailing with regard to all movements so as to ensure cooperation and support.

If weather does not permit of machines being flown from position C, the Admiral Commanding Aircraft has discretion to postpone the operation for a period of 24 hours, or to abandon the operation and return to Rosyth. If the decision is made to postpone the operation for 24 hours, Force A is to retire to the Northward, cruising as necessary to arrive in position C 24 hours later. A Light Cruiser should be detached to inform the Senior Officer, Force B, of the decision taken.

All in all an admirable set of orders, setting out the requirements but not tying down the commanders on the spot with impossibly detailed instructions.

The ACA, Rear Admiral Phillimore, also provided a set of instructions for the pilots involved.

OPERATION F.7.
ORDERS FOR *FURIOUS* AIRCRAFT.

(1) The two flights for attacking Tondern will leave at as short intervals as possible after 0300, or as soon after that time as light permits of formation being picked up and kept. On account of limited fuel endurance, it is important that time should not be wasted picking up formation.

(2) The attack should be made at low altitude, after which machines of each flight should endeavour to meet at a pre-arranged rendezvous before returning, but only a few minutes can be allowed for this.

(3) Aeroplanes should pass to seaward of Blaavand Huk, and neutral territory should not be infringed.

(4) If a Zeppelin is encountered on the outward journey, it should be attacked, bombs being dropped beforehand. If encountered on homeward journey it should be attacked irrespective of fuel remaining, machines landing in Denmark or Germany afterwards if necessary.

(5) Fighting with enemy aircraft other than Zeppelins should be avoided.

(6) If visibility on return is so low that inshore destroyer cannot be sighted, pilots should endeavour to pick up Fleet by taking their departure and steering N. 45° W. Mag. from Lyngvig Lighthouse.

(7) Pilots are to be instructed in the position and movement of ships between the hours 0300 and 0630.

On return of machines, destroyers when ready to pick up aeroplanes will hoist an affirmative flag. [Flag C in the International Code of Signals.]

Pilots should land about two cables ahead of a destroyer, selecting the one nearest *Furious* which has this flag flying.

The inshore destroyer will not be used for picking up.

(8) If, on return, ships are seen to be steaming away from coast and destroyers are not flying affirmative flag, pilots should close *Furious* and read deck signals on her alighting deck before alighting in sea.

(9) Pilots should be guided by the amount of fuel remaining when deciding to carry out orders in para. (6) and (8).

The two forces sailed shortly after midnight 17 June 1918. On arrival at the launch position the weather was deteriorating and Rear Admiral Phillimore took the decision to delay the attack until the following morning. *Furious*, and her followers, set course to join up with the battleships. The two forces remained in company until 2.00 p.m. when the attack force turned back towards the coast to return to the launch point by 3.00 a.m. on 19 July. Position C was some twenty five miles west of Lyngvig Lighthouse located on the sea coast of Ringkøbing Fjord.

There was a west-south-west wind at 16 knots, limited cloud coverage and fair visibility. Phillimore sent for Bell Davies, 'It's for you to decide and I shan't influence you. But I expect you know what I hope.' Davies promised a decision by 3.00 a.m. (He says 4 o'clock in his memoir, but that would be British Summer Time. All times in the following account are GMT.) 'With the wind as it was, it seemed doubtful if the Camels could get back to the ship after the attack. However as the latest met. report did not suggest any worsening, they would certainly have enough petrol to cross the Danish frontier.' The decision was taken to launch the attack.

> The first "Bombers" (Camel Aeroplanes, each carrying two 50 lb Bombs) left the deck at 0314, and this flight of three machines was in the air, in formation, by 0318.
> The second flight of four machines of the same type was off the forecastle by 0322, and proceeded in formation by 0326.
> First Flight: Capt. W. D. Jackson, Capt. W. F. Dickson and Lt N. E. Williams.
> Second Flight: Capt. B. A. Smart, DSO, Capt. T. K. Thyne, Lt S. Dawson and Lt W. A. Yeulett.

Watching them take-off, Jack McCleery saw a wheel come off Yeulett's Camel just as he was leaving the deck. One of the modifications incorporated on the Camels was a method of releasing the wheels and thus reducing the chances of the machines flipping over when landing in the sea. The wheels were held in place by quick release pins and could be dropped by pulling the pins and side slipping the aeroplane. It is probable that one of the pins holding the wheels in place had not been properly secured on Yeulett's Camel and the wheel came off.

After the machines disappeared from view the force turned west to be at the rendezvous for returning machines by 5.00 a.m. A number of destroyers were positioned on a patrol line from just five miles off the coast at the Lyngvig Lighthouse, to the rendezvous position to give returning pilots the course to follow and to assist any in trouble.

Captain Jackson led his three machines towards the Danish coast, flying in a bowl of limited visibility until, after fifteen minutes, they sighted the Ringkøbing Fjord. Staying well offshore, he turned the formation south towards Blaavand Huk.

> We proceeded to climb above the cumulo stratus clouds keeping the coast in sight at about 65 knots. After a short time I found that we were making practically no

progress against the wind which was very strong at that height. I therefore decided to open out and at the same time to gain speed by losing height making an air speed of about 80 knots. When I got to about 4,000 feet I again climbed to prevent detection as much as possible. On sighting Blaavands Huk I altered course slightly to eastwards passing over Blaavands Point about 35 minutes from starting. At this point the layer of clouds below us prevented my distinguishing the coast easily there being only small gaps in the clouds which were at 3–4,000 feet.

The flight continued to the south and shortly after 4.00 a.m. they saw the northern tip of Sylt below them. Jackson now led them inland, passing over a long pier at Hoyer a few minutes later. Here Captain Dickson takes over the story.

The road from Hoyer was very clearly distinguishable as in fact were all the roads in that part, there being very few except the main ones. We followed this road till we came to Tondern itself. Capt. Jackson then pushed his machine down at a steep angle with the engine on and we circled the town losing height all the time. At first we could see no signs of the sheds or gas plant; only the Railway Junction which is at the south of the town. Jackson then went down in a steep dive or he turned sharply, for in looking for the sheds I lost him for a minute or two.

Jackson recalled what happened at this point.

I had arranged that I would show a red flag as soon as I sighted the objective. When I actually sighted the objective I found that the flag was missing. The others thinking I had not seen the sheds dropped away from the formation. It was here that I last saw Captain Dickson.

He continued to work around the base until he could approach with the rising sun behind him.

I saw Lieut Williams machine diving ahead of me he having cut off the corners. I followed him down and saw him pass over the large shed [*Toska*] and drop his bombs. Both bombs took effect and in less than half a minute the flames issued from the whole top of the shed reaching up to over 500 feet. I then turned to the left making for the smaller shed [*Tobias*] which was about 200 yards to the south of the large shed. When about 500 feet over the shed I dropped both bombs. I felt both explode beneath and saw the smoke of one coming from a hole in the roof.

Dickson, meanwhile, had mistaken a large low shed on the eastern outskirts of Tondern for the airship shed and had dropped one of his bombs on it, with no observable result.

Immediately after this I saw Capt. Jackson at about 3,000 feet above me and a good distance to the East of the town, coming down in a dive, with Lieut Williams about half a mile astern of him. [Dickson naturally expected Jackson to be leading.] I climbed a little and joined in with them and then observed two very large sheds, larger by quite a considerable amount to the main shed at East Fortune Air Station, and also a smaller one. The two large sheds were situated to the North the doors opening to the East and West, the smaller one was about 100 yards further South and the Gas Plant another 100 yards to the Southeast of that.

Dickson's 'two large sheds' were probably *Toska* and *Tobias*, the smaller one the partially dismantled *Toni*. It is not clear in his report which shed he attacked, but he saw the shed 'burst into flames and enormous conflagration took place rising to at least 1,000 feet the whole of the shed being completely engulfed.' After the attack the three pilots scattered, one flying straight on, one to the left and Dickson to the right.

One of the advantages of being an airship commander was that one could pull a few strings and find accommodation off the station and spend some nights with your wife. On the evening of 18 July *Kapitänleutnant* von Buttlar Brandenfels, after a drink in the mess, returned to his wife in a rented flat in the town of Tondern.

From the windows of my flat I could see the aerodrome, which was about half a mile away - a mere stone's throw.

The night was very quiet.

While I was still half asleep I seemed to hear the whiz and whirr of a propeller.

I woke up. The day was just beginning to dawn. I looked at my watch. It was six o'clock.

'Flemming must have received flying orders,' observed my wife.

Flemming? The L60 fellow? But that was not L60's note. It was not the note of a Zeppelin at all!

In a flash I understood. I knew the sound I heard could not be that of an airship's engines. It was too shrill. Could it be possible? Damn it all!

I jumped up and rushed to the window, from which I could get a view over the whole aerodrome.

Suddenly a shadow passed over our house, a few yards above the roof, absurdly low. It was an aeroplane with the colours of the Entente in a circle. A British aeroplane!

In a moment the anti-aircraft batteries began to bark.

The Englishman dropped, if anything, a little bit lower, and made straight for the airship shed. He was already there. Then he climbed a bit.

There was more buzzing overhead and something else approached. Over my head another shadow passed, a second aeroplane! By that time the first was over the shed, exactly above it.

My heart was in my mouth. In a terrible straight column, lit up with flames, the smoke rose skyward from the shed.

Gruesomely beautiful it was, this giant flame of sacrifice in which our L54 and L60 perished.

Starting out just a few minutes after the first flight, the second flight led by Captain Smart, followed a similar course arriving at the Ringkøbing Fjord after fifteen minutes. They then followed the coast to Blaavand Huk.

Here Capt. Thyne dived and left formation due to engine trouble. I turned and slowed to see what had happened to him but lost sight of him. Went dead slow for a time to give him opportunity to pick up, but as he was within gliding distance of the coast, did not waste further time searching, but carried on in V formation of 3 in S.E. direction.

Whilst the three remaining Camels pressed on, Thyne was struggling to return to the ships.

Just as Capt. Smart slowed down to obtain a closer formation my engine gave several large reports as if a valve had become stuck. I dropped 4,000 feet with engine going about 400 revs, when I let go both bombs and pointed the nose of my machine up the coast again. The engine picked up a little, giving about 900 revs, but the machine was still sinking very slowly until I threw the Lewis gun tray away. Very shortly the engine started banging again, off and on, and continued doing so until I landed in the water alongside the destroyer *Viceroy* at 5.30.

Thyne was safely hauled aboard but the destroyer drifted over his machine, breaking it in half, only the tail section being retrieved.

Smart continues.

The clouds were now at 4,000 and it was so difficult keeping one's bearings through the holes in the clouds that I dived and came below opposite the Isle of Fane [Fanø]. Shortly after I sighted railway and having taken careful compass course along this, climbed above clouds again to avoid observation. After 15 mins., which I calculated should have brought me to a point some 2 or 3 miles N. of Tondern, I descended below clouds again.

There is a rail line through Tondern running north to south, close to the west coast, across the then Danish–German border to Bramming. Adjacent to Fanø Island it runs just four miles inland from the mainland coast. The wind above the clouds was stronger than Smart had anticipated and the formation was carried a good way off course. It took a few minutes to locate Tondern, over ten miles away to the south-west. Smart headed the three Camels in the direction of Tondern, but had difficulty locating the base.

Smart continued the story in a letter to his mother:

As I neared the N side of Tondern I began to look around for Zepp sheds. Hardly had I formed this idea in my mind when—'boom, boom'—'woof, woof'—went the guns and two black round puffs of smoke appeared in the sky on my left— then a number of other batteries opened out on us and the flashes of three close together attracted my attention—close to these I saw three Zepp sheds, two large double ones and one small. One of the large ones had a large hole in the roof and was literally belching out thick black smoke from every crack and crevice in the building. I gave the signal and dived on the other big shed at full speed, the 150 knots registered on the indicator giving me a sense of security against the wretched archies, which, although not particularly well ranged, were properly 'putting the wind up me!' Down and down I came until only 800 feet at which height I dropped the bombs in succession and swerved away. I had just a glimpse of one falling short and the other landing in the middle of the shed after which my whole attention was taken up in saving my skin.

As the second flight began its attack, *Kapitänleutnant* von Buttlar Brandenfels was on his bicycle peddling as fast as he could towards the base.

In the centre of the aerodrome, in front of their hutments, the seamen were standing with nothing on but their undergarments, or half naked, and firing with their rifles as hard as they could. They might just as well not have been there. The Englishmen continued circling round without climbing an inch higher. The pilots could be seen quite plainly; they were waving in a most friendly manner to our men, although, being equipped for attacking troops, they could easily have opened fire with their machine guns.

If Smart was typical of the friendly English pilots, nothing was further from their minds. In his letter he recalled that:

The aerodrome I now saw to be absolutely thick with men running wildly in all directions and over the roar of the engine I heard the crackle of numerous rifles and several machine guns—it sounded just like a little infantry attack, that irregular crackle which I had learned so well out east. My 'wind up' was now nothing short of 'kollosal' and I nosed the bus down with full engine till the wires simply shrieked. At 50 feet from the ground I flattened out and skimmed over the ground in a zigzag course at a terrific speed which made it an almost impossible target. I had vague impressions of men rushing about and waving, horses tearing around in mad fright and frightened cattle leaping in all directions to escape the unusual noise of my 150 hp—then I felt I was clear of the guns and began to look around for the other members of my flight and incidentally for Hun planes, but nothing was in sight.

Both Dawson and Yeulett followed Smart down and made their attacks. It is believed that of the six bombs dropped, two hit *Tobias*, destroying the captive balloon, and one of the remaining four hit a wagon holding charged flasks of hydrogen. Although the wagon was damaged the flasks did not explode.

Von Buttlar Brandenfels had now arrived at the base. He noticed that one of the attacking machines had lost a wheel, this could only be Toby Yeulett.

Surely his machine must be damaged! He came down quite low. He was landing! We ran like mad to the spot where he was landing, only to see that we were mistaken. Like his colleagues he had quite rightly flown so low to avoid the anti-aircraft batteries that it was quite useless for the latter to fire. The next moment he was flying under the Tondern high tension wires and away.

Then one of the high tension wires snapped. He had evidently struck it with the top centre section; but nevertheless he flew straight toward the anti-aircraft battery which lay to the north-west. Then he vanished in the direction of the Danish frontier.

Meanwhile I stood facing the burnt out wreck of my ship. I had watched many ships perish, but this was the first time I saw my own destroyed.

But for the bravery of a handful of officers and enlisted men the damage could have been much worse. Lying in *Toska*, adjacent to the airships, were a number of heavy bombs intended to England. *Wachoffizier Kapitänleutnant* von Schiller, second in command of L54, ran into the shed followed by several crew members. They were able to remove the bombs, some of which were already overheated, to a place of safety.

The attackers began arriving at the appointed rendezvous, the town of Bredde (Bredebro, Denmark) to the north of Tondern. First to arrive were Jackson and Williams who had rejoined after the attack. Jackson stated that the clouds were around 2,000 feet and, as they were still being fired upon by anti-aircraft guns, he hid in the clouds dropping below them frequently to look for Dickson. Dickson, meanwhile, had arrived at Bredde below the clouds which he said were at 1,000 feet. After just a few minutes he decided to fly off toward the fleet. He flew to the north-west for about an hour when he sighted the Lyngvig Lighthouse and, in the distance, four destroyers. He flew out to the furthermost destroyer, *Violent*, and ditched about 300 yards ahead of the ship. Dickson climbed out of his cockpit and clung to the tail of his machine until rescued. The time now was about 5.55 a.m.

Back over Bredde, Jackson's engine began giving trouble.

At 4.55 my engine spluttered and stopped and I could only get it to go again by turning over to gravity. I then made off steering 330° engine well throttled down and trying to climb as much as possible. Lieut Williams was following. We lost sight of the ground very quickly. When about 8,000 feet up I had to go through a cloud and lost Lieut Williams. I reached 10,000 feet still being unable to see the ground. At 5.25 knowing that my gravity tank could not last much longer I shut off and glided down through the clouds.

He emerged below the clouds at 1,500 feet and, unable to recognise his position, headed towards the coast. Still unable to get fuel from his main tank, the supply in the gravity tank ran out at 5.35 a.m. with the coast just in sight. Jackson came down close to a farm house outside the small town of Goldwater some five miles from Esbjerg. In landing he caught his wheels on a fence and the machine flipped over.

Having extricated myself from the machine I immediately made preparations to burn it. Although, on starting, I had 10 Very's cartridges I now found I only had two, so I determined to make the best use of these. I removed the charts from the cockpit, placed them on the centre section, and fired a Very's Light. The charts immediately caught fire, and the whole centre section began to burn. I fired the remaining Very's Light at the fuselage by the petrol tank; a little petrol was escaping from the tank. The machine did not burn well, the frame work being left charred, and the wing tips and tail not having burnt at all.

Whilst he was setting his machine on fire Jackson saw another Camel pass by within 200 yards. This was probably Williams who flew on a few miles further, coming down at Skallingen, close to Blaavand Huk. Williams was unable to destroy his machine owing to the rapid arrival of the Danish police.

Smart was unable to reconnect with either of his flight. After a slow circuit over Bredde he proceeded to the north-west in search of the ships. Climbing above the clouds he had to descend to fix his position.

My engine failed to open out and I got to 400 feet before getting a single fire. Then two or three cylinders cut in, but I dropped to about 20 feet before getting 1,000 revs. Which was just enough to keep me in the air. I skimmed along at this height until the engine gradually got better, but it was quite 20 min. before she was doing 1,200 again.

Like Dickson before him he crossed the coast at the Lyngvig Lighthouse and made out to sea. After just a few minutes he saw a destroyer, *Violent* which had just finished rescuing Dickson. Smart dumped his wheels and landed ahead of the ship at around 6.30 a.m. Scrambling on to the tail, he reached to grab a heaving line, missed and was thrown off into the sea, fortunately grabbing a rigging wire. *Violent* quickly launched a boat and a few minutes later he was hauled aboard 'like a sack of flour.'

Whilst Smart was being rescued, German seaplanes (Friedrichshafen FF49c, 1773 (*FlMt* Deidock and *ObMtr* Kämmerer) and 1174 (*LtdR(MI)* Heinecke and *FlMt* Widdau) from List.) made their only appearance of the day. The captain of *Valentine* reporting that:

> Two enemy seaplanes were observed approaching from a Sth. East direction, and fire was promptly opened on them at a range of about 2,000 yards with the 3″ H.A. Gun controlled by Petty Officer Gunners Mate F. W. Tickner. Only four shell were fired, but the bursting had been so correctly judged that both Seaplanes hauled off immediately and disappeared. Subsequently strong Aircraft Telefunken was intercepted, but no further hostile aircraft was sighted.

Lt Dawson eventually landed at Holmsland Klit at the north end of Ringkøbing Fjord. It is not known if he was able to destroy his machine. Unfortunately, his report does not appear to have survived.

The last person to have seen Toby Yeulett may have been von Buttlar Brandenfels who recalled him flying through the high tension cables on the edge of Tondern aerodrome. Von Buttlar Brandenfels mentions the 'top centre section,' perhaps his Lewis gun and mounting cut the cable. The exact details will never be known but if he did fly through the cable some damage must have resulted to his machine. What is clear is that he was still able to control the Camel and was attempting to return to the ships, but crashed into the sea. Yeulett's aircraft was washed ashore near Norre Havrvig, a few miles south of the Lyngvig Lighthouse, on 24 July and his body was found on the 28 July on the shore near Argab, a mile further north. He is buried in Havrvig Kirke churchyard.

Jackson and Williams were taken to Esbjerg where they were questioned by the local Chief Magistrate. Later that day Dawson was brought in to join them, he had been arrested in civilian clothes at a train station whilst attempting to catch a train for Kolding. The three pilots spent a comfortable night at the local Hotellet. The following morning the British Consul, Mr Cross, came to visit them, advising them how to escape. Lieutenant Dawson, the only one wearing civilian clothes, immediately decided to escape with assistance from the Consul. Dawson made his way to Sweden and Norway, returning to *Furious* on 18 August.

Jackson and Williams, after being permitted to buy civilian clothes, were interned and taken to the camp at Aarhus. Here they were greeted by Lt William Garriock (of the submarine *E.13*) and Lt Simpson, presumably late of *Galatea*. Again assisted by Mr Cross, Jackson and Simpson were able to escape from Aarhus on 5 August. After a few adventures they crossed to Sweden and then reached Bergen, Norway, on 11 August. They sailed aboard the SS

Prince Arthur the following day, landing at Aberdeen on the morning of 13 August. Williams managed his escape a few months later, reaching the UK on 10 November.

The *London Gazette* for 20 September 1918 contained details of the awards to the pilots.

Dickson was awarded the DSO, for having:

> Displayed great skill and gallantry on the occasion of a long distance bombing raid. He succeeded in dropping bombs on an airship station from a low altitude with destructive effect, and although subjected to severe fire from the enemy obtained valuable information.

Smart received a bar to his DSO for having:

> Led his flight for 160 miles over sea and land, and destroyed by bombs an important enemy airship shed. This service was carried out under exceptionally difficult circumstances, requiring great skill, and was most creditably performed.

Both Smart and Dickson had already received their medals from the King on 23 July, at an award ceremony on the deck of *Queen Elizabeth* during the Royal annual inspection of the Fleet.

> Dickson and I were saved till last when the battery of cameras and cinematographs made us absolutely quake! As the senior I went up first and to my surprise did everything correctly, coming to a halt three paces from him, smartly saluting and advancing without falling over the steps to the dais!
>
> The King seemed awfully pleased and knew practically every detail. He talked to me for nearly ten minutes and wanted to know all about the show. His questions were really very sensible and to the point. Having given me the bar he shook hands, after which I saluted and walked off when Dickson had to go through the mill!

Jackson was awarded the DFC for having:

> Led his flight in a long distance bombing raid on an enemy aircraft station under very difficult circumstances, and carried out a successful attack from a low height, in the face of severe enemy fire.

Dawson, Williams and Yeulett (posthumously) were awarded the DFC. Each 'Was engaged in a long distance bombing raid on an enemy aircraft station under very difficult circumstances, and, carried out a successful attack from a low height in the face of severe enemy fire.'

Yeulett's posthumous award is most unusual. Until recently the only British awards for valour that could be awarded posthumously were the Victoria Cross and a Mention in Dispatches. It is probable that the awards were rushed through to accommodate the King's visit to the fleet and whilst hope still existed for Yeulett's survival.

Poor Thyne, for returning with a faulty engine, received no recognition.

The raid had cost the life of Toby Yeulett and the loss of seven Camel aircraft. What had been achieved?

The two Zeppelins inside *Toska* had burnt out and been totally destroyed. But, as they did not explode, the shed itself was only slightly damaged. The captive balloon inside *Tobias* was lost and shed slightly damaged. One man of the ground troop was slightly wounded by a splinter. An L54 crewman was slightly injured and another burned. A crewman from L60 was severely wounded in the abdomen by a bomb splinter. Fear of a repeat attack meant that the station itself was only used as an emergency landing ground for the remainder of the war.

The last word is best left to *Kapitänleutnant* von Buttlar Brandenfels:

The attack had been carried out extremely smartly, and had been an entire success. Two airships had been completely destroyed, and the airship base had been rendered harmless for some considerable time.

The fact that during their attack they had refrained from firing on our men with their machine guns, but had shown an obvious readiness to be friendly with them and spare them, and had executed their orders without shedding blood, made us particularly sympathetic to these brave airmen.

15

Such a Light Affliction

After the Tondern Raid the routine patrols and reconnaissances must have seemed a little anti-climactic. But they were important as part of the ongoing process by the Royal Navy to dominate the North Sea. At this time the morale ascendancy of the Royal Navy over the High Seas Fleet was overwhelming. Although unknown to the Grand Fleet, the big ships of the High Seas Fleet were drifting toward mutiny, largely due to their inactivity. The small ships, U-boats, the *Marine Fleigerabteilung* and the *Marine Luftschiffabteilung*, remained largely untainted until the very end of the war. Certainly, the Royal Navy and its fliers could not afford to relax.

Furious took part in six recorded operations after Tondern. On only the first and last of these were aircraft launched, but all took the ship deep into the Heligoland Bight or close to the naval air stations at Borkum and Norderney. However, before looking at any of these operations, a brief digression into development of high speed aircraft lighters and Coastal Motor Boats is required.

The large twin-engined flying boats arriving in increasing numbers to coastal stations such as Felixstowe and Great Yarmouth had good endurance, between six and seven hours, but it was insufficient to carry a load of bombs to German bases in the Heligoland Bight and return. An idea by Commander John Cyril Porte, designer of the Porte Baby and the series of Felixstowe Flying Boats, to increase their range was to tow the flying boats out into the North Sea on lighters, then launch them and send them on their way. The first lighter was completed by mid-1917 and, after successful trials in the protected waters of the Solent, another fifty were ordered. The aft end of the lighters were cut away to provide a sloped slipway up which the flying boat could be hauled by a winch in the bows. To ease handling, the stern of the lighters could be lowered by flooding tanks which were then blown empty using compressed air. The lighters were designed to be towed behind destroyers at up to 25 knots.

Lieutenant Colonel C. R. Samson, whom we last met in 1913, had had a busy war. In August 1914 he had led a contingent of the RNAS into Belgium. Here he forsook the air to drive around the countryside in home-made armoured cars, seeking out German cavalry patrols. From Belgium he had been sent to the Dardanelles in command of land based 3 Wing, RNAS. Then he had taken over *Ben-my-Chree* and command of the East Indies and Egypt Seaplane Squadron. After having *Ben-my-Chree* sunk under him, the sole seaplane carrier lost to enemy action during the war, he had returned to command the seaplane station at Great Yarmouth. He saw the lighters as ideal launching platforms for Sopwith Camels.

> I decided to construct a runway on the lighter, put a Camel on it, and get a destroyer to tow at full speed. We could thus be taken fairly close to the Zeppelin's patrol, fly off and bag the Zeppelin. Admiral Sir R. Tyrwhitt, who was in command of the famous Harwich Light Cruiser Squadron, was most enthusiastic over the idea.

Samson had a simple track way, similar to that on *Africa* in 1912, constructed over one of the lighters, *H.3*. Having decided that skids would be better than wheels, his first attempt to take-off was nearly disastrous. The Camel dived into the water directly off the port bow of the lighter, the skids having jammed in the troughs. Fortunately Samson managed to extricate himself, struggle to the surface and hang on to the wreckage until rescued. Samson now approached Lt Stuart D. Culley, who is also familiar to the reader. They modified the platform to provide a flat take-off area thirty feet long and twenty feet wide and installed a tail guide trestle, the deck was inclined at rest but level at towing speed. Using Camel N6812 Culley made a successful take-off on 31 July 1918.

Another new weapon we need to briefly consider is the high speed Coastal Motor Boat (CMB). These were the idea of three young officers from Harwich Force destroyers, Lieutenants Hampden, Bremner and Anson. Armed with a single torpedo, launched tail first from a trough in the stern of the boat, a very high speed was necessary to avoid being 'Hoist with his own petard.' Designed and built by John I. Thornycroft & Company Limited, the first boats were forty feet long and powered by a single petrol engine of 250 hp or 275 hp. The boats were capable of over 30 knots. Crew was just three, a commanding officer who also conned the boat, a second officer as navigator and torpedo officer and a motor mechanic. Defensive armament was limited to one or two Lewis guns. The boats were organized into a Flotilla based at Queenborough on the Medway, but often operated with the Harwich Force which transported CMBs on the motor boat davits of light cruisers.

When Tyrwhitt submitted ideas for operational employment of the CMBs to Sir David Beatty, The latter suggested that he would like to synchronise operations with *Furious* in the northern part of the Heligoland Bight with the CMB operations. However, as *Furious* was to operate as usual off the Danish coast well to the north of the proposed operational area of the CMBs, the Borkum to Wangeroog area, any support would have been distant at best.

Operation F.8 and Operation CMB4, 1–3 August 1918

The first operation by *Furious* that came close to fulfilling these wishes was Operation F.8 between 1 and 3 August; Harwich Force Operation CMB4 was scheduled for 1 August. However, F.8 was intended primarily as a reconnaissance of the northern Heligoland Bight. Force 'A', *Furious* and the 1st LCS, with their escorting destroyers from the 13th Flotilla, did not sail from Rosyth until 10.02 p.m. on 1 August. They were followed out by Force 'B', the 2nd Battle Squadron, 7th LCS and destroyers.

Meanwhile the Harwich Force had sailed the previous evening and was off the Dutch coast at dawn on 1 August. Operation CMB4 was intended to search out and torpedo any German minesweepers found operating off the Friesian Islands. The intention was that flying boats, being towed on lighters by the force, would take-off and escort the CMBs. The weather was poor and the flying boats were unable to take-off. Then the force was located and bombed by a Zeppelin. No CMBs were launched, and the Harwich Force had returned to base before the Rosyth units sailed.

The weather was no better off Bovbjerg Light on the morning of 2 August and *Furious* withdrew from the coast to return the following morning. Although not ideal, the wind was 18 knots from the East, a Sopwith Ship Strutter, A6985, was sent off shortly after 5.00 a.m. on 3 August. The pilot was Capt. Wilfred R. D. Acland and observer 2nd Lt A. F. Adams. Jack McCleery recalled that he had been 'told I was to fly off at 5.30. Bolted my breakfast and got on deck; Acland already there; then washed out as wind was getting up. Other machine got back about 8.15 with 1¼ gallons of petrol left!' Rear Admiral Phillimore, in his report, noted that after Acland took off the wind increased to 25 knots at the surface and 40 knots at 1,000 feet. So, it is not surprising that McCleery was 'washed out.'

Acland and Adams headed towards the Danish coast hoping to make landfall close to Blaavand Huk. After seventy minutes they were close to the coast but initially unable to identify their location, then realised they had been blown well to the north and were approaching Lyngvig lighthouse. Acland decided to turn down the coast toward their intended landfall, effectively reversing the direction of the intended reconnaissance. Other than two sailing ships nothing was seen during their flight. At 7.18 a.m., with just an hours' fuel left, Acland altered course to look for *Furious*. The ship was sighted in the distance after half an hour. Now their difficulties really began.

Acland mentioned that all ammunition, 300 rounds for the Lewis Gun only as the Vickers was not installed to save weight for the W/T equipment, was fired off before landing.

After closing *Furious*, I prepared to land ahead of *Westcott*. On trying to inflate the [flotation] bags, Air Bottle appeared to have very little air in it, hardly enough to inflate the bags at all. I therefore proceeded to try to pump them up by hand. This proved impossible as I had also to keep the petrol pressure up by hand, the Rotheram [sic] Pump having given out after first hours flight.

The Rotherham Air Pump was driven by a small propeller and was often attached to the right hand aft cabane strut, just behind the pilot's head.

I therefore decided to land without the bags. Machine landed alright, but Pilot's seat immediately became submerged and also Observers seat. We were unable to detach the wings, but managed to get the machine alongside *Westcott*, when she turned turtle and sank about 2 feet under the water. Lewis Gun, bearing plates, Verys Pistol, Watch, One ammunition tray, Aldis Lamp and battery lost when machine turned turtle.
All W/T gear that was left in the machine was recovered—Code Book safe.

After recovering the airmen Force A headed towards the north east, making visual contact with one of Force B's scouting light cruisers shortly after noon. They then turned eastward to search for a 'derelict barque with a cargo of pit props', a valuable cargo at that time. Later, as the weather and visibility deteriorated, the search was abandoned and the Force turned towards Rosyth, arriving at 8.30 a.m. 4 August in 'thick weather.'

The next operation, F.9 between 7–9 August, was hindered by poor visibility. After spending a day cruising along the east side of Dogger Bank, and sighting nothing, the force returned to Rosyth.

Operation F.10 and Operation CMB5, 10–11 August 1918

This is the only time *Furious* and the CMBs operated in anything approaching conjunction.
Furious' orders were 'To attack enemy aircraft in the vicinity of South Dogger Bank Light Ship.' This time only the carrier and her usual consorts, the 1st LCS and 13th Destroyer Flotilla, were involved. They were informed that:

[I]t is possible an operation will be carried out by units of the Harwich Force a.m. tomorrow, Saturday [11 August] but date has not been definitely fixed. The starting point for this operation will be Lat. 53° 29′ N., Long. 4.22° E., units being in position by 0600. Coastal motor boats will proceed from there on course 95° until the three mile limit is reached, then along the coast eastward as far as radius of action will permit with the object of attacking enemy minesweepers and surface craft.

The Rosyth force sailed on the evening of 9 August and spent the following day from 6.00 a.m. to 9.00 p.m., 'when it was too dark to fly or see flag signals,' on patrol in the vicinity of the light vessel. No enemy airships of aircraft were seen, only a large number of Dutch fishing vessels, some of which were boarded. One suspects that fish for the galley was more important than intelligence or contraband.

The excitement of the day was provided by the light cruiser *Inconstant*. At 6.45 p.m. an aircraft was seen flying toward the squadron, out of the east and at low level. Very suspicious, although the squadron had been warned before sailing that Large America flying boats from Great Yarmouth might be patrolling in the area. *Inconstant*, on the principle better safe than sorry:

> . . . opened a prompt and accurate shrapnel fire on her and also flew her aeroplane [Camel, N6834, pilot unknown.]. [Commodore Walter Cowan] was able to signal 'cease fire' before any harm was done and the America after exchanging recognition signals proceeded West.

The pilot and Camel were later collected from the sea by either *Viscount* or *Vivacious*, the reports name both destroyers. However, Commodore Cowan noted, 'Though *Inconstant*'s proceedings were misguided it was a very great pleasure to observe the promptness of her aeroplane's action.' Shortly after the recovery the force set course back to Rosyth.

What of the Harwich Force? Well, just as *Furious* and her squadron were turning back towards Rosyth, Rear Admiral Tyrwhitt was leading his ships out of harbour. Rosyth and Harwich clearly had to work on their coordination. Tyrwhitt's force consisted of four light cruisers, *Curacao* (Flag), *Coventry*, *Concord* and *Danae*, with eight escorting destroyers. The last three cruisers each carried two 40 Foot CMBs on their motor boat davits, *CMB.41, CMB.42* (carrying the Flotilla Commander, Lt Cdr Anthony L. H. D. Coke), *CMB.44, CMB.46, CMB.47* and *CMB.48*. Four destroyers, these were probably additional to the eight escorting the cruisers, were towing lighters. *Teazer, Thisbe* and *Retriever*, each had a Felixstowe F.2A flying boat on their lighters, *Redoubt* was towing lighter *H.3* with Sopwith 2F.1 Camel, N6812, aboard. The lighter crew comprised Lt Stuart D. Culley, pilot, Lt-Col. C. R. Samson, second pilot in charge of operations, five airmen and two lighter men. The Camel's armament had been changed to two light Lewis Guns, fixed above the upper wing centre section, each with a single 97 round ammunition tray. The heavy Vickers machine gun and its ammunition supply system were removed to save weight.

The ships were to transport the CMBs close to the German coast and send them on their way to attack targets of opportunity. It was intended that the three flying boats would take-off at the same time as the CMBs left the squadron, to provide air cover. Additional patrols were flown by more flying boats from Great

Yarmouth. The Camel was intended to attack any patrolling airships that came within view.

At 5.30 a.m. the Harwich Force squadron was approximately 25 miles north-west of the Dutch island of Vlieland. The CMBs were lowered into the water and, half an hour later, set off in an easterly direction towards Ameland. From there, keeping outside the Dutch three mile limits, the intention was that they would follow the line of islands towards German waters. The three flying boats were floated off their lighters but, with a light wind and a long swell, in their overloaded condition were unable to take-off. Tyrwhitt recorded:

> This was a calamity that had never crossed my mind as I considered the conditions ideal. Knowing, however, that the Yarmouth seaplanes were due, I had no misgivings regarding the coastal motor boats which were already beyond recall.

At 6.14 a.m. four German seaplanes were sighted to the east. The squadron opened anti-aircraft fire on them and drove them off towards the north. At 7.10 a.m. the flight of three flying boats from Great Yarmouth arrived overhead.

The report on Coastal Motor Boat Operations continues:

> Admiral Tyrwhitt endeavoured to point out the enemy seaplanes [to the flying boats], but apparently his signal was not understood although acknowledged as the flight proceeded to the northward. At 0816 the three flying boats returned. The following signal was made and acknowledged: 'Meet coastal motor boats which should be returning steering west by north.' Once again it did appear that the signal was [not] understood as the flight remained in the vicinity and was generally in sight of the Squadron until it was necessary for it to return to the base.

The report later clarifies that the signals were understood, but visibility from above was poor, although on the surface it was excellent. The Coastal Motor Boats, however, were left without air cover.

Lt Cdr Coke's terse report was forwarded by the British Naval Attaché at S'gravenhage (The Hague) on 16 August.

> On 11 August at about 5 miles NW of Ameland Tower, flotilla of 6 CMBs steering easterly, number 42 in command was engaged by eight enemy aircraft with machine guns and bombs. Enemy was prevented from getting within effective machine gun range. At 7.55 a.m. course was altered to Westward and four fighting planes reinforced enemy. About 8.10 almost all our guns had jambed or run out of ammunition, so course was altered for Terschelling coast. Two monoplanes then joined enemy. At 8.40 all boats were outside territorial waters seeking shore. Numbers 46 and 42 outside territorial waters had broken

down, guns out of action, so crew took to water after destroying their boats: these crews swam for shore and were picked up by two Dutch TBDs in territorial waters. Number 47 was on fire with two crew badly wounded, so steamed within half mile of shore and was then blown up. Captain swam ashore and crew were rescued by Dutch sailors who swam out from shore. Number 41 steamed ashore but crew were prevented from destroying their boat by Dutch authorities who fired on them. One enemy aircraft attacked her for quarter hour after she was ashore. Number 48 smoke tank was punctured and boat untenable. Number 44 rescued crew and left boat outside territorial waters and apparently sinking. Number 44 then had her engine disabled by gun fire and drifted inside territorial waters. She was approached by Dutch TBs and her Captain asked if he might destroy his boat after crew were taken off, but on getting alongside Dutch Captain forcibly took possession of motor boat and towed it in to shore. Dutch TB then picked up CMB 48 which had drifted inside territorial waters and although damaged was still afloat, pumped her out and also brought her in. Four German destroyers then appeared and patrolled outside territorial waters, eight more enemy aeroplanes appeared. One enemy aeroplane was destroyed during fight and another forced to land. Boats and crews are interned by Dutch but [British] Minister discussing question with Dutch Minister for Foreign Affairs.

All confidential papers were destroyed by the crews. Of the thirteen officers and six mechanics on the six CMBs, none were killed but six were wounded. The CMB crews were interned for the duration of the war. The *London Gazette* for 26 November 1918 announced the award of the DSO to Lt Cdr Coke and the DSC to Lts E. R. Lewis (*CMB.42*) and G. Cockburn (*CMB.47*).

The first seaplanes to attack the boats were from *Kampfstaffel* V, *SFS* Borkum. The flight comprised three Brandenburg W29 monoplanes (2525, 2524, 2529) and a single Freidrichshafen FF49c (1829). They were joined by another four Brandenburg W29 (2249, 2253, 2212, 2260) and a single FF49c (1819) from *Kampfstaffel* I also at Borkum. The final attacks were made by machines from the *Kampfstaffel* of *SFS* Norderney, two Brandenburg W12 biplanes (2051, 2100), two more W29 monoplanes (2296, 2297) and another FF49c (1759). One Brandenburg W29, 2297, and crew (*FlMt* Nagorsnick and *ObMtr* Wohlfeil) was 'lost at sea.'

An account from the German side was provided to C. F. Snowden Gamble, by an anonymous 'German officer', and recounted in his history of Great Yarmouth Air Station:

The Borkum fighting squadron met six coastal motor boats between Terschelling and Ameland going east at full speed.

After dropping bombs under heavy machine gun fire the boats turned round and were now attacked at close quarters with machine gun fire. Meanwhile, the

Norderney fighting squadron arrived also and took part in the fight. Two coastal motor boats were chased by well-directed fire on to Terschelling beach and they then caught fire. A machine of the Norderney fighting squadron set a boat on fire by dropping bombs on her, but came down in flames itself. The three remaining coastal motor boats lay stopped, smoking and burning, two without crews, and the third, with a crew from another boat, waving a white flag.

In an account published after the war Cedric Outhwaite (commanding *CMB.48*), told of his rescue by *CMB.44*, then, after being brought to a halt just half a mile from Dutch territorial waters:

A brilliant idea suddenly struck us: let us see what we can do with the torpedo as a means of propulsion. The torpedo lay in a trough down the centre of the boat, its propellers being towards the stern. We had only to loosen and it would slide stern first into the water. This we did, only leaving a portion of it still in the trough, and rigidly fixed it in this position with chocks. By doing this we had its propellers nearly submerged in the water, and if its engines were started up they would rotate and give the whole boat a slight forward movement. In order to start the torpedo's engine the captain sat astride its stern where the starting device is, and gradually started it up. He stayed like this, keeping the speed regulated, as we did not wish the propeller to race needlessly, and so lose a maximum effort.

With the aid of the torpedo we had got appreciably closer to the shore, and must have reached Dutch waters before it gave out. In all probability the set of the tide and what wind there was helped as much as the torpedo, but it certainly contributed, and one feels that never before has a torpedo been put to such a use. We pushed it out of the trough into the water, its sinking valve having been opened.

They were picked up as noted above by the Dutch navy.

Whilst the CMBs were going through their torments, the *Marine Luftschiffabteilung* suffered the last of a series of losses that had begun at Tondern less than a month ago. It was the end of a period one historian of the Naval Airship Division has called *Götterdämmerung*.

The twilight of the airships began on 5 January 1918 with the loss of five airships at the Ahlhorn airship base. A fire, thought to have started below one of the engine cars of Zeppelin L51 in the double Shed I, *Aladin*, quickly spread to L47. From there the conflagration spread in a series of increasingly violent explosions to three more sheds. Fourteen men, military and civilian, were killed and thirty more wounded. Although stunned by the loss, the airshipmen continued to make scouting flights over the North Sea and raids on England. Then came Tondern, and the loss of two more airships. But it was the events of early August 1918 that crippled the *Marine Luftschiffabteilung*.

Five Zeppelins set out from their bases on the afternoon of 5 August: L53, L65 and L70 from Nordholz, L56 from Wittmundhaven and L63 from Ahlhorn. L70 was carrying *Fregattenkapitän* Peter Strasser, Chief of the Naval Airship Division. In the gathering gloom, as the airships approached the coast, one the aeroplanes rising to attack them was a de Havilland DH4, A8032. Designed as a bomber it had been modified into an airship hunter by the RNAS at Great Yarmouth late the previous year. Piloted by Major Egbert Cadbury with Captain Robert Leckie as observer, the DH4 attacked the leading Zeppelin L70, Leckie firing new explosive bullets from the observer's Lewis Gun. The new bullets were horrifyingly effective, L70 quickly caught fire and plunged to the North Sea 16,000 feet below. There were no survivors. The remaining airships turned back towards their bases. The *Marine Luftschiffabteilung* never fully recovered from the loss of their much beloved leader.

To return to the Harwich Force. Shortly after 8 a.m. on 11 August an airship (L53, *Kapitänleutnant* Eduard Prölss) was sighted by the patrolling flying boats. Their leader, newly promoted Major Leckie, recalled:

> . . . a Zeppelin was seen approaching at a height of about 15,000 feet. Now, I was aware that Culley and his Camel were with the flotilla, and I had no intention of spoiling his show by commencing an attack on the Zeppelin which would be certain to prove abortive, and as I could not break W/T silence, I turned back and upon reaching the flagship reported by visual signal as follows—'Zeppelin NE of flotilla, steering W.' Whereupon I received the signal—'Do not interfere, Camel is going off.'

To send the Camel off from a lighter was more complex than sending one off from a cruiser platform. During passage the lighter was usually on a fairly short tow, 36 to 60 feet, with only the two lighter men aboard. At daybreak the destroyer would come to a stop, and transfer the flight crew. The lighter tow was then let out to 600 feet.

The men aboard the lighter now opened out the extensions to each side of the fore part of the flying deck, checked over and prepared the Camel for flight. The Camel was in flying position on the tail guide trestle, with wheel chocks and axle clamps in place, release wire attached and taut. With the controls still locked the engine was started up and tested. If a launch was intended the towing destroyer would send up a white Very light and signal, either by semaphore or Aldis Lamp, the rendezvous position (usually a single letter, from several already marked on the pilot's chart) and the bearing of the airship. Then the flight deck was cleared and all control and wheel locks removed. Meanwhile the destroyer would be working up to 25 to 30 knots and turning into wind. The engine was started and, once the destroyer signalled it was at speed, run up to full speed. Once satisfied with his engine, the pilot would release the hold back cable and fly off. The destroyer now slowed a little, turned in the direction of the airship and made smoke. This would give the pilot his initial course to steer.

Culley was away at 8.58 a.m., according to Samson his take-off run was only five feet, and climbing hard to catch the Zeppelin. At 18,000 feet Culley, who had been advised, almost ordered, to attack from above by Samson, realised he had little chance to climb above the airship and despaired of even catching it. Still climbing slowly, he realised that the airship had turned and was now heading directly towards him. With a closing speed of close to 120 knots Culley decided his one chance was to attack immediately. As the bow of the airship came into view over his wing Culley pulled up the nose of the Camel and fired into the belly of the Zeppelin. The port Lewis jammed after just fifteen rounds, but the full tray of 97 rounds from the starboard gun found their target. The Camel stalled and dropped away. Culley was too busy regaining control to see if his attack had been successful. But on the sea far below the men of the CMBs saw the aftermath of his attack:

> I had been keeping my eye on the Zeppelin, which was getting closer every minute, when suddenly a sheet of flame shot out from the envelope. What had happened? It very soon became a flaming mass, and dense clouds of smoke issued. We saw men jump out in parachutes, bombs were dropped, and shot enormous columns of water into the air as they exploded in the sea. The airship then buckled in the centre. It seemed to drop for ages before reaching the water, throwing it up in sheets as it struck. Later we learnt that one of our small air scouts had brought this Zeppelin down.

Cedric Outhwaite is mistaken in his observations, men may have jumped to their death rather than burn, but parachutes were not carried in order to save weight and enable the airship to climb higher.

The combat was not witnessed by the men aboard the ships of the Harwich Force. Some heard a faint rattle of machine gun fire, then they saw a sheet of flame behind a cloud bank and the airship falling from beneath it. Tyrwhitt's biographer recorded the subsequent events:

> At the suggestion of his flag-lieutenant, Anthony Floyer, and after hastily consulting a hymn book, Tyrwhitt ordered a signal to be made to all ships: 'See Hymns Ancient and Modern, Number 224, verse seven'—which is
> O happy bank of pilgrims,
> Look upward to the skies,
> Where such a light affliction
> Shall win so great a prize

Meanwhile, having regained control, Culley watched the Zeppelin burn and fall. Before it disappeared into the haze below him he noted the German ensign still flying from the unburnt tail of the ship. The haze, that had earlier made observation difficult for the flying boats, now made his return to the ships problematic. Squadron Leader T. D. Hallam, having interviewed Culley and writing immediately after the war, tells what happened next:

> Having finished the Zeppelin, Culley suddenly awoke to the need of looking out for himself. He few straight to the Dutch coast, went south until he arrived at the Texel, and then went out to the rendezvous at Terschelling Bank. Here, at six thousand feet, there were patchy clouds between him and the water, and he could see no destroyers.
>
> His pressure petrol tank ran out.
>
> He switched over to the emergency gravity tank. It contained only enough petrol for twenty minutes, not nearly enough for him to get back safely to the Dutch coast.
>
> Looking down, he saw a providential Dutch fishing boat, and decided to land beside it. As he dived down he saw two destroyers come out from under the edge of a cloud. And then he saw the whole flotilla.
>
> Looping and rolling over the fleet to relieve his pent up feelings, he picked up his destroyer with the lighter, fired a [Very] light as a signal, and landed in front of her. He was picked up, the Camel was hoisted on the lighter, and the flotilla started back for Harwich.

Culley's report was brief and to the point:

> 8.58, flew from lighter to attack Zeppelin in sight to eastward. Rose to 18,700 feet. Attacked Zeppelin from 300 feet below. Fired 7 rounds from No. 1 gun, which jammed, and a double charger from No. 2. Zeppelin burst into flames, and was destroyed. Returned to squadron, and landed on the water with one pint of petrol in tank.

P 175 says he was too busy to see the result.

However, the Harwich Force did not immediately start back for base. Culley had returned and been picked up at 11.40 a.m. The fate of the CMBs was still unknown, although they were now several hours past their expected return time. Hoping to find out what had happened, Tyrwhitt requested another flight of flying boats from Great Yarmouth. These finally arrived over the squadron at 4.15 p.m., and were asked to sweep eastward to the coast and return over the Terschelling Light Vessel. At 5.30 p.m. the flight returned having found nothing. At this point Tyrwhitt gave orders for the Harwich Force to return home.

Culley was recommended for the award of the Victoria Cross. But the Admiralty, pointing to the precedent of Lt B. A. Smart, approved the award of the DSO instead. The citation for the award appeared in the *London Gazette* for 2 November 1918:

Ascended to a height of 19,000 feet, at which altitude he attacked an enemy airship and brought it down in flames completely destroyed. This was a most difficult undertaking, involving great personal risk, and the highest praise is due to Lieutenant Culley for the gallantry and skill which he displayed.

Perhaps the award Culley most appreciated was an engraved silver cigarette case from Rear Admiral Tyrwhitt. The inscription simply read, 'Hymn 224, v.7.'

16

Final Flights of the Grand Fleet Flying Squadron

For the CMBs the August raid was the last attempt to work with the Harwich Force. Recovery from the loss of six crews and their boats did not happen overnight. Their great moment came after the war, in the Baltic Sea, and will be briefly mentioned later in this chapter.

August had also been disastrous for the *Marine Luftschiffabteilung*, but they kept flying. No more bombing raids on the United Kingdom were attempted, but they still flew scouting missions over the North Sea.

Furious sailed for several operations during the remaining months for the war. The weather became a major factor for these operations and only two of them resulted in any aerial activity. Typical of the weather encountered was during a Fleet Tactical Exercise commenced on 22 August. About this trip Jack McCleery later wrote to his parents:

> I spent the afternoon on top [Jack stood watches in the ship's foretop, high up on *Furious*' tripod mast.]. You have an idea of the height of our top hamper, well from there you could see destroyers and light cruisers disappearing from view altogether in the trough of the waves. How any human being can stand a TBD for several days in a sea like this I don't know. Out of the wardroom scuttles, which were mostly under water, you could not see any other ships at all for the waves.

Towards the end of September there was an operation which Jack McCleery refers to as a PZ, but *Furious*' log book records as Operation FC.4. This was another Fleet Tactical Exercise as the fleet was manoeuvring in the middle of the North Sea between Scapa Flow and Norway. *Furious*' log book for 24 September notes '8.21 Despatched two "1½ Strutters" for Reconnaissance.' According to Jack's diary entry he:

> Flew off with [2nd Lt] Paddy Hayes and did a 3½ hour reconnaissance. Did the job very well I believe. Awful visibility—nil. Landed in ditch beside the *Umpire*

and was picked up; sea getting up considerably. Was sick after lunch and in the evening. Next TBD had her bridge carried away in the storm.

The weather when the Strutters were sent off was good with a wind speed of less than ten knots, but was clouded over, on their return the wind had increased to fifteen knots and by mid-afternoon to over thirty knots. The pilot and observer of the second machine are unknown.

Operation F.13, 21–23 October 1918

Rear Admiral Phillimore was increasingly confident in the growing abilities of his aircrews. Weather conditions that just a few months ago would have led to cancellation of any operations were now looked upon as acceptable. This operation would test his confidence and the skill of his aircrews.

Although unknown to the participants this would be the final operation of the First World War for *Furious* and her airmen. On the day they sailed Jack McCleery received his appointment as Captain, RAF, 'dated back to 8th August!! Not so bad, if it's not a mistake.' With the promotion came added responsibilities, Jack was now flight commander of *Furious*' F Flight, the two-seaters.

Operation F.13 was an attempt to complete the previous Operation F.12 (15–17 October), which had been cancelled due to poor weather conditions, to make a reconnaissance of the northern area of the Heligoland Bight. *Furious* in company with light cruisers *Caledon, Galatea, Phaeton, Royalist* and *Inconstant,* of the 1st Light Cruiser Squadron, and destroyers from the 13th Flotilla, *Woolston, Wessex, Winchelsea, Westcott* and *Walpole,* constituted Force A. The covering force, Force B, comprised the 1st Battle Cruiser Squadron, *Lion, Tiger, Repulse* and *Renown,* escorted by light cruiser *Champion* and eight more destroyers of the 13th Flotilla, *Vimiera, Vega, Vectis, Vidette, Umpire, Tristram, Tower* and *Patrician.* The force began leaving Rosyth at noon on 21 October.

Force A was approximately 100 miles west of Bovbjerg lighthouse at 4 a.m. the following morning. Force B was some 50 miles to the north-west. Rear Admiral Phillimore detached *Phaeton* and three destroyers to close the Danish coast near the light house. They were to stand by, just outside territorial waters, to recover the airmen when they returned. Two hours later, as the first flight was due to take-off, the wind was rising with frequent rain squalls. The operation was postponed in the hope of improvement in the weather.

Jack McCleery with Paddy Hayes were the first crew on the flying list, their machine Sopwith Ship Strutter, A6988, had been on deck since dawn. Jack's diary entry noted, 'Stood by to fly off at 6.15 a.m.; washed out till 8.30; weather still very bad, but sent me off.' In his report Phillimore recorded, 'The first aeroplane was flown off at 0837 as, though the wind was S by W on the surface, calculations made from A.A. Shell bursts at 2,000 feet showed a South West wind of 44 knots at that altitude.' The Strutter's cruise speed was barely twice the wind speed, returning to the ships would call for good piloting and navigation. Immediately after Jack took off, the Admiral detached *Inconstant* to join *Phaeton* off the coast, 'in order that that ship should not be left too long unsupported.'

The intention was that a second machine would be sent off an hour after the first. The appearance of storm clouds to windward caused a delay. At this point the remaining light cruisers were sent to join the two already loitering off the coast, *Furious* retaining the remaining two destroyers as escort. The second machine, Strutter A6000, with 2nd Lt Haines (pilot) and 2nd Lt W. A. Thompson (observer) flew off *Furious'* fore deck at 10.12 a.m. *Furious* then set course to join the remainder of Force A off Bovbjerg lighthouse.

Jack's observer Paddy Hayes left a very interesting report. He noted that they took off at 8.35 a.m. then steered a southerly course at 2,500 feet in poor visibility. At 9.25 a.m. they were forced down to 1,500 feet in heavy rain squalls. Once the rain had passed visibility improved but clouds remained low. Then at 9.55 a.m. they:

> Sighted six small steamers—single funnel—probably sweepers. Estimated their course 210° at moment of sighting, in line abreast, three cables apart (approx). Sweeps were not passed. One destroyer—old type—stationed astern 5 cables. Height of machine 1,000 ft. It is probable that this machine was sighted by this flotilla.

This report was subsequently of interest to Beatty's Chief of Staff as Phillimore supported Hayes' observations, adding 'He is sure the sweeps were not out, and, having had two year's experience in Sweepers, he knows.'

At 10.12 a.m., just as the second Strutter was taking off from *Furious*, Jack and Paddy recorded sighting two seaplanes on the surface close alongside a surfaced submarine. The Strutter was seen and the two seaplanes took off and gave chase. A few minutes later Jack was able to evade the German machines by flying into a cloud bank. This was most fortunate as Hayes had earlier experienced jamming problems with his Lewis Gun and, although he had cleared it, must have been concerned that it might jam again if needed.

Half an hour later they saw Blaavand Huk some eight miles distant in improved visibility. From here Jack turned due north following the Danish coast past Lyngvig lighthouse and on to Bovbjerg lighthouse. Almost immediately, at 11.19 a.m., they sighted a destroyer and turned towards it. Jack continues in his diary:

> Landed beside HMS *Wessex*; tail broke up in sea. Our undercarriage stove in the whaler and when we got to ship we had to jump for the life lines as she was just sinking. Had a dry change and lunch; then slept till dinner at 8 o'clock. Stayed on deck till 11 o'clock; not very rough.

The second Strutter also reported encountering two German seaplanes. After leaving the carrier Haines and Thompson was been forced to fly 'at heights ranging from 400 feet to 1,500 feet to obtain view of the sea as weather permitted.' They sighted Blaavand Huk at 11.25 a.m. then flew a patrol to the south-west and then back to the north-east, sighting land once more, ten miles north of Blaavand Huk, at 12.43 p.m., turning then to the north. At 12.50, whilst off Lyngvig lighthouse, they sighted the two German seaplanes 'flying low over the water, steering to the southward. At this time we were at 2,000 feet and were apparently unobserved, no attempt being made to attack.' Fifteen minutes later, off Bovbjerg Lighthouse, they altered course seaward quickly sighting *Furious* and the destroyers. They landed at 1.35 p.m. and were picked up by the destroyer *Woolston*.

Furious and her escorts now turned towards Force B, joining up at 3.20 p.m. With Force A leading the whole squadron turned towards Rosyth, arriving at 10.27 a.m. 23 October.

Checking the German records for 22 October shows that there were no flights made prior to 11 a.m. GMT. The air stations in the area were reporting winds of 45 knots from the WSW and a Sea State of 6 to 8 (Waves from three metres to six or more metres.), completely unsuitable for operating seaplanes from the open sea. The only sighting of a British aeroplane was at 10 a.m. GMT by *Vorpostenboot* (patrol boat) *Admiral von Hipper*. The enemy plane was seen flying at low altitude in a southerly direction. The small patrol boat was probably the 'old type' of destroyer reported by Paddy Hayes, the times concurring reasonably well. However, the submarine and the two seaplanes cannot be explained. Seaplane patrols were sent out by some *Kampfstaffeln* after 11 a.m. GMT, the seaplanes sighted by Haines and Thompson at 12.50 p.m. may have been two of these.

Back at Rosyth the Grand Fleet remained on tenterhooks. Nobody believed the war could last much longer, progress on the Western Front was becoming more and more rapid, but nobody could believe that the High Seas Fleet would give up without another sortie. The fleet remained on high alert, just in case.

Within a few days the news that Turkey and Austria were giving up the fight led to increasing rumours of peace. Jack McCleery recorded on 7 November, 'At 4 o'clock, signal from Vice Admiral Battle Cruiser Fleet "Hostilities ceased at 2 p.m. today (official)." Some noise in the mess!' This was premature, and an hour later the signal was cancelled. The Grand Fleet remained constantly on two-and-half-hours' notice for the next few days. However, on 9 November, 'No special news till the evening when we heard definitely, the Hun delegates had arrived with Foch. Mutiny in the German Fleet. Kaiser and Crown Prince have abdicated.' Then, two days later, 'PEACE.'

We got the peace news, or rather the armistice news this morning and after dinner tonight the fun started. Firstly *all* the searchlights in the Grand Fleet began to give a show, Very lights and all description of rockets went up and burst into coloured lights, and the sirens were blowing till it was perfectly impossible to even hear each other yelling. After a while different ships began to paint their searchlights with fine effect.

Then suddenly a burst of cheering was heard from far up the line of battle cruisers and battleships; the cheering grew and finally an American launch, packed with men came past playing 'Tipperary' and 'Pack up your Troubles' etc., and at the bows, held up by some of the sailors were the Stars and Stripes and the White Ensign flying side by side. It was too thrilling for words and I feel it was worth five years' life to see it. The Silent Navy—Ye Gods!

The final act of the naval war was the surrender of the High Seas Fleet on 21 November. The Grand Fleet, five Battle Squadrons (including the 6th Battle Squadron of US battleships), two Battle Cruiser Squadrons, the First Cruiser Squadron (including *Furious*), and several hundred light cruisers and destroyers, sailed from Rosyth and formed up in two lines to await the arrival of the German ships. As the High Seas Fleet was led between the two lines, the British ships turned in succession through 180° to take up positions on each side. Jack McCleery, in a piece published in the *Belfast Telegraph* a few days later, recorded that:

At times they were hard to see owing to the mist and their being at about the limit of visibility. Astern of us we have the *Vindictive* and the *Minotaur*. We kept position about three miles on the last Hun ship's beam for some time, then altered course to round up the light cruisers. We saw seven or eight of these— bigger ships and bigger targets than ours, with three big funnels. Then we met the TBDs—hundreds of them, the Huns being in the middle of ours. I have never seen so many destroyers since I came to sea and as the sun had condescended to show itself, it was a most wonderful sight.

The German ships were escorted into the Firth of Forth, where they anchored. Beatty signalled them, 'The German flag will be hauled down at sunset today and will not be hoisted again without permission.'

Whilst the guns fell silent along the major war fronts, peace proved elusive in many parts of the World. Wars and revolutions spawned by the First World War were to continue for another four years, and more, involving many of the major belligerents often with conflicting aims and in unlikely cooperation. For the Royal Navy in particular, the war was not over.

In December 1918 the Grand Fleet Flying Squadron comprised, *Furious, Argus, Nairana, Pegasus* and *Vindictive*. Six months later three of these were involved in the Russian maelstrom. *Nairana* had already had a taste of Russian affairs, having spent from July to October 1918 in the White Sea, she was to return there between May and October 1919 in company with *Pegasus*. Their operations in the area, where they acted as transports and seaplane tenders, form no part of this story, but those of *Vindictive* in the Baltic might be considered relevant.

Laid down as one of five *Hawkins* class heavy cruisers, *Cavendish* was the only one completed before the end of the war. Built by Harland and Wolff at Belfast she was launched on 17 January 1918, and renamed *Vindictive* on 29 June to commemorate the ship which led the St George's Day Zeebrugge Raid. She commissioned 1 October under the command of Captain Henry Edgar Grace. As noted in an earlier chapter, in appearance, *Vindictive* was a smaller copy of *Furious*. But there were some important differences. As completed, *Vindictive* only had a forward hangar under the flight deck. The aft landing deck was constructed on an open framework of girders. The two were linked by a long, eight foot wide gangway on the port side of the ship. The hangar, 78 feet long and varying from 44 to 48 feet wide, could house up to six machines. The flight deck formed the roof of the hangar and was fitted with a narrow 28 feet long extension over the forward gun. Two derricks were provided to lift machines out of the hangar through a hatch in the flight deck. The aft landing deck was 193 feet long and 57 feet in width. As an aircraft carrier, the ship retained four of the cruiser's 7.5 inch single mountings. *Vindictive* worked up at Scapa Flow, only arriving at Rosyth on 20 November 1918, the day before the surrender of the German Fleet.

Flying trials were conducted at Scapa Flow on 15 November and Rosyth on 29 November. Although, on 1 November, Capt. W. W. Wakefield flew a Sopwith Pup out to the ship and made a safe landing on the aft deck.

At Scapa on 15 November two take-offs were made. The first was by Capt. W. W. Wakefield with Sopwith Pup, 9944, one of the few still in service. The Pup was flown off the aft landing deck. *Vindictive* was steaming at four knots with the stern into a wind of between fourteen and fifteen knots, to give a wind over the deck of just over ten knots. The Pup took off without difficulty, after a run of fifty five feet, and flew on to land back at Smoogro.

On the forward flight deck stood Grain Griffin, N100. The Griffin was one of the rarer types to go to sea, only seven were built and *Vindictive* was the only ship to carry them. The aeroplane was an attempt to navalise the single-seat Sopwith B.1 bomber, and convert it into a two seat reconnaissance machine with folding wings, radio and flotation gear. 'Not surprisingly, the aircraft did not lend itself readily to this kind of metamorphosis, and difficulties were encountered.' Initially powered by a Sunbeam Arab V8 water cooled engine, when this proved unreliable most machines were converted to, or completed with, Bentley BR2 rotary engines. At the time of the flight Griffin, N100, still had the Arab engine, 'Full fuel and oil, new type chassis with hydrovane, wireless gear, and equivalent weight of 2 Lewis Guns and 7 double trays of ammunition.' The pilot was Lt Col L. Tomkinson with observer 2nd Lt L. J. Booth. Wind over the deck was twenty three and a half knots and the Griffin got off after just thirty five feet. The crew, after climbing the Griffin to 3,800 feet, carried out a full calibre shoot for both *Vindictive* and

Minotaur. The machine then circled *Vindictive* to permit the H.A. gun crews to practise laying their guns.

After completing the gunnery exercises, *Vindictive* turned to bring the felt wind fifteen degrees on the port bow. The Griffin now made some practise approaches to the aft landing deck. 'Machine throttled down extremely well and speed of advance over the ship was not more than 12 miles per hour.' It must be assumed that these were made to test the air flow disturbance over the deck due to the funnels and bridge structure as an into wind landing would be impossible due to both sides of the deck being built up with substantial box like coamings.

At Rosyth on 29 November two Griffins were placed on the forward flight deck. N100 was flown by Lt Donald T. Simpson and his observer was 2nd Lt A. I. Redman, the machine was fully loaded as on its earlier flight. N103 had Lt L. M. Hilton as pilot and 2nd Lt F. C. Jenner as observer, it is not known what load this Griffin carried. Both machines were fitted with Sunbeam Arab engines. The first machine to take-off, N100, 'flew off the deck from position on port side, set at an angle of 24 deg. on starboard bow, ship steaming so that machine was head on to relative wind.' The machine was held in flying position by a Tail Guide Trestle eight feet in length. Into a wind over the deck of twenty knots the Griffin got off in less than thirty feet. The second machine left the deck after just twenty six feet into a twenty three knot wind. 'After the machines had flown off the deck, both proceeded to make practise runs over the Landing-on-Deck; ship steaming with relative wind about 15 deg. on starboard bow.' A number of straight runs at the deck and passes to either side of the deck were carried out. Bad bumps were only encountered when Lt Simpson flew an approach through the funnel smoke. For the final run the ship had turned directly into wind, Lt Hilton made a straight in approach and encountered severe bumps. Returning to Donibristle, N103 made a safe landing, but N100 crashed and was written off, the crew were safe.

Whilst the intent of these flights was to find a safe method of landing back on the ship, no full landings were ever made using the Griffin. The only landing made on *Vindictive* was that by Captain Wakefield on a Sopwith Pup at the beginning of the month.

In July 1919 *Vindictive* sailed from Rosyth to join the British fleet in the Baltic, under the command of Rear Admiral Walter Cowan. Briefly, the intent of this intervention in Russian affairs was to help the Baltic States, Estonia, Latvia and Lithuania, maintain their newly proclaimed independence from Russia. *Vindictive* carried a mix of aircraft, Sopwith 2F.1 Camels, Sopwith Ship Strutters, Short 184s and at least two Griffins. She was based in the Gulf of Finland, between the mainland and Bjorko Island (Beryozovye Island, Russia). The landplanes were sent to a small airstrip at Koivisto (Primorsk, Russia) and the Finns laid out seaplane moorings at Sidinsari, a bay on the sheltered east side of Bjorko Island.

Vindictive's aircraft were involved in the first major bombing raid on Kronstadt, Operation DB. In total three Short 184s, two Ship Strutters, two Griffins and three

Camels were involved in two raids on the morning of 30 July. The floatplanes took off from Sidinsari and Camels from Koivisto, the Strutters and Griffins took off from the ship. This was the only time aircraft flew operationally from her flight deck.

At 11.00 p.m. on 29 July *Vindictive* steamed out into Bjorko Sound heading SSE to the open waters at the end of the island. At 00.17 a.m. speed was increased to 19 knots and five minutes later the first Ship Strutter took off. *Vindictive* then manoeuvred within a swept area preparing to launch two more machines. At 1.10 a.m., whilst steaming at 22 knots, a second Strutter and the first Griffin took off. The ship then returned to Sidinsari, the three machines were seen returning from Kronstadt at 3.00 a.m. Sailing again an hour later *Vindictive* returned to the earlier launch point and sent off the second Griffin at 5.25 a.m. This machine suffered engine trouble and was seen to drop her bombs and turn toward the airfield at Koivisto, where it landed safely

The final flights from *Vindictive*'s deck and, incidentally, from the first generation of aircraft carriers took place during a demonstration for Admiral Cowan on 13 August. One of the Griffins, N105, crashed into the sea. The crew were saved, but Lt Norman Samuel Taylor, RAF, was killed when his 2F.1 Camel, N6825, crashed whilst taking off.

Throughout the remainder of the year frequent bombing raids were made over Kronstadt, mostly by landplanes operating from Koivisto. The bombs carried were small, none larger than 112 lb, and little actual physical damage was done. Nonetheless they were annoying to the Russians, tying up scarce anti-aircraft guns and affecting morale, and kept the Allies informed of the status of ships in the harbour.

Stuart Culley, who had just received a permanent commission in the RAF with the rank of Flying Officer, was one of the pilots based at Koivisto. He flew Sopwith 2F.1 Camels on patrols and bombing raids over Kronstadt, attacking kite balloons on two occasions. In October he flew at least nine missions over Kronstadt, bombing the battleship *Andrei Pervozanny* and twice machine gunning a Bolshevik destroyer. He also bombed a railway station and the fortress of Krasnaya Gorka several times. He was later Mentioned in Despatches for his service in the Baltic.

Vindictive became the base ship for a flotilla of Coastal Motor Boats. There was also a detachment of two CMBs based at Terrioki (Zelenogorsk, Russia), further along the coast towards the Russian border. These were initially used to insert and recover secret agents, a role for which the CMB was not ideal being extremely noisy at speed. Tiring of the secret operations Lt Augustus Agar, commanding the detachment, persuaded Cowan to allow him to attempt to attack ships in Kronstadt, the role for which the CMB was designed. Piloting *CMB4* he succeeded in sinking the Russian Cruiser *Oleg* on 4 June 1919. For this he was awarded what became known as the 'Mystery VC', the British Government not wishing to advertise its involvement in Russia. Later in the campaign, during Operation RK on 18 August 1919, the CMB flotilla attached to *Vindictive* made an attack on the Russian naval base at Kronstadt, damaging the battleships *Petropavlovsk* and *Andrei Pervozanny* and sinking a submarine supply ship, *Pamiat Azova*. The airmen from Koivisto had assisted by making a series of night bombing attacks over the harbour, their bombs did little damage but the aircraft distracted the defenders and the noise of their engines helped conceal the engines of the CMBs.

All was not well on *Vindictive*, and whilst in Copenhagen taking on stores there was a mutiny aboard. Trouble had been brewing throughout the summer, the crews aboard ships in the Baltic were largely 'hostilities only' and their grievances were centred on their still serving under wartime conditions. There had been previous outbreaks on other ships and Captain Grace handled the mutineers on *Vindictive* considerately but firmly. He discussed their grievances and persuaded most back to work. The ring leaders and persistent trouble makers were arrested, court martialed and sent for periods of hard labour in a Naval Prison in the UK. After a few days all the crew were back at work. *A part from there*

As the Baltic began freezing over, bringing an end to the campaigning season, the bases on Finnish territory were closed down. *Vindictive* returned to the United Kingdom in time for Christmas leave. In the New Year she was placed in Reserve, to be partially converted back to cruiser configuration.

As *Vindictive* was in the Baltic the Grand Fleet Flying Squadron was breaking up. *Nairana* and *Pegasus* returned from North Russia in October 1919, the former to be paid off. *Pegasus*, however, was retained in naval service. Her forward flight deck was removed and she served as a seaplane carrier or tender for several more years. *Argus* continued trials and development work, becoming part of the Atlantic Fleet from 1920. In July 1919 the Admiral Commanding Aircraft, Rear Admiral Phillimore, hauled down his flag, the post being reduced to that of a Captain. Captain Wilmot S. Nicholson taking on the role until *Furious* was placed in Reserve on 21 November 1919, effectively ending the brief existence of the Grand Fleet Flying Squadron.

17

Wilhelmshaven 1919
What Might Have Been

If the First World War had continued into 1919 the Royal Navy was making plans to send its growing fleet of aircraft carriers to attack the High Seas Fleet at its home base, Wilhelmshaven. The attack would have been made by a new type of aeroplane, the Torpedo Bomber, the development of which, beginning before the war, was finally coming to fruition. The following brief history keeps to the highlights, with not too many digressions.

Italian Army Captain Alessandro Guidoni had been experimenting with bombs since 1912 using a Farman biplane, but this was incapable of carrying more than 80 kg. When he became interested in torpedoes a more capable machine was required. Enter Raúl Pateras Pescara de Castelluccio, marquis Pateras-Pescara, an engineer and inventor originally from Argentina. Together they developed the Pescara-Guidoni PP, a huge monoplane with a wing span of 19 metres driven by two double 100 hp Gnome rotary engines. The fuselage was in two parts, forward with the pilot in the nose and one engine behind him driving a pusher propeller, and aft with another engine driving a tractor propeller and a seat for the 'engineer' behind the engine. The two propellers were located in a cut out in the middle of the wing. This assemblage was mounted on two equally impressive floats by a veritable forest of struts. Using this machine Guidoni dropped a mock up torpedo, weighing 340 kg, in the lagoon of Venice in February 1914.

On 28 July 1914, Sqn Cdr Arthur Longmore, commanding the Royal Naval Air Station at Calshot, flying Short Type 81, 121, powered by a 160 hp Gnome rotary engine made the first drop of a live torpedo.

I succeeded in getting this machine off the water with the torpedo slung below and in launching it for its run. It all worked well but, of course, it was a 'stunt'. No technical expert could pass the factor of safety of the machine so loaded, petrol was sufficient for about half an hour and there was no passenger carried. To think that large numbers of torpedo carrying seaplanes could be immediately ordered as a result of this was nonsense. However, this preliminary success was very encouraging to the torpedo expert, Flt Lt Hyde Thomson, who had done such excellent work in adapting the torpedo for release from the air and in designing the torpedo carrier which fitted on the seaplane under the fuselage between the two floats.

Longmore's machine was issued to *Engadine* in September 1914. On 21 September, using this machine, Flt Cdr Robert Peel Ross made a practice torpedo attack on the seaplane carrier. Ross struggled to take-off and was unable to rise above fifty feet. He let go the torpedo about 100 yards from the ship, but aimed at one of *Engadine*'s motor boats moored ahead of the ship. The torpedo porpoised on hitting the water but ran close to its target.

The first operational use of the air-dropped torpedo was from *Ben-my-Chree* at Gallipoli in August 1915. The seaplane carrier had arrived at Mytilene on 12 June. Two of her pilots Flt Lt George Bentley Dacre and Flt Cdr Charles Humphrey Kingsman Edmonds were given the task of pioneering the operational employment of the air delivered torpedo. There were two Short 184s aboard the ship, 184 and 841, a third, 842, was delivered soon afterwards. For the attacks Dacre flew 184, the prototype which differed in detail from the production version, and Edmonds 842.

The weapon available was a 14 inch Mark X (1897 model) torpedo. Originally developed for use by steam picket boats, a number had been adapted for aviation use since 1913. It was the same type of torpedo dropped by Longmore and Ross. Whilst it had the advantage of lightness, 762 lb, it only delivered a 77 lb warhead. The torpedo had a range of 800 yards at a maximum speed of 30 knots; its compressed air engine could be adjusted to increase range for a reduction in speed. (For comparison the torpedoes used during the Fleet Air Arm attack on Taranto in 1940 were 18-inch Royal Naval Torpedo Factory Mark IX, which weighed 1,077 lbs and delivered a 250 lb warhead over 2,000 yards at 29 knots.) The torpedo was carried between the floats on arched cross-bars, to which were attached torpedo crutches to hold and support the torpedo. When the Short was at rest on the water the torpedo was almost completely immersed, increasing drag at take-off. Upon release a cable attached to the aircraft fuselage pulled free of the torpedo, starting its engine. Early flights demonstrated that in the high temperatures of an Aegean summer, whilst loaded with a torpedo, the Short had to be flown solo, stripped of all non-essential equipment and even then could carry only half the maximum fuel load.

The two pilots were up daily experimenting with carrying, aiming and dropping torpedoes, trying to determine the best height and speed from which to launch the weapons. Initially, dropping heights of 45 feet were attempted but practice soon showed the best height to be between 10 and 15 feet. Concerning the speed they did not have much choice as the speed envelope of a fully loaded Short 184 was not large. Assisting the two pilots was a very efficient torpedo department headed by CPO Charlie Attrill. Attrill had joined the Royal Navy as a Boy 2nd Class on 11 May 1892, when he was just fifteen years old. He had been attached to the RNAS as a torpedo specialist since early 1915, and on joining *Ben-my-Chree* in May he was a qualified Torpedo Instructor. From this time on he would remain a constant thread in the development of the torpedo for aerial use.

Two separate torpedo attacks were made. On 12 August 1915, with a new machine and engine Edmonds had no difficulty climbing to 1,500 feet before crossing the Peninsula. Once across he turned up the coast, towards the Sea of Marmora, heading for the steamer reported by an earlier reconnaissance flight. Dacre struggled to take-off, without success, until he saw Edmonds returning and had to abandon his attempts. Edmonds reported:

> Approaching Injeh Burnu, I glided down and fired my torpedo at the steamer from a height of about 15 feet and range of some 800 yards, with the sun astern of me. I noticed some flashes from the tug previously mentioned, so presumed she was firing at me and therefore kept on a westerly course, climbing rapidly. Looking back, I observed the track of the torpedo, which struck the ship abreast the mainmast, the starboard side. The explosion sent a column of water and large fragments of the ship almost as high as her masthead. The ship was of about 8,000 tons displacement, painted black, with one funnel and four masts. She was lying close to the land, so cannot sink very far, but the force of the explosion was such that it is impossible for her to be of further use to the enemy. She appeared to have settled down a little by the stern when I ceased watching her.

Five days later both machines were able to get over the Peninsula. Edmonds attacked and hit a steamer in the anchorage at Ak Bashi Liman. Dacre, struggling with a recalcitrant engine, was forced to land on the Straits. Waiting to let a hospital ship sail past, Dacre waved to the patients who all waved back:

> [I] could see two ships in a little bay. One a large old wooden sailing ship which hardly looked sinkable and a large tug alongside a new wooden pier. I taxied up to within 500 yds of it and let go my torpedo, turning round directly after up the Straits. A terrific explosion followed and as I looked over my shoulder I could see spray descending and the tug giving a huge lurch. Then all of a sudden rifle shots pattered in the water beside me and my first idea was to get out of it being in a desperate funk. By a miracle nothing hit me and, inspired by the thought of a bullet in my back, I cranked the engine up slightly and after taxiing 2 or 3 miles got off again, then again a touch and off again to my great joy.

Edmonds first target was an armed transport, *Mahmud Shevket Pasha*, which had been torpedoed a few days earlier by the submarine *E.14*. Despite damage from two torpedoes, and being burnt out, *Mahmud Shevket Pasha* was towed to

Constantinople and repaired. After long years of service, ship was scrapped in 1935. His second victim has been identified as the German steamer *Kios*, or *Chios*, of 3,304 gross tons. Damaged by Edmonds torpedo, the ship was run aground and later salvaged, where it was found at anchor off Ak Bashi Liman and finally sunk by submarine *E.11* on 25 August. The identity of Dacre's target has defied all attempts at identification. It has been suggested that it may have been a 'personnel raft', possibly a self-propelled barge similar to the X-lighters being employed by the British at Gallipoli.

No further torpedo attacks were attempted. Yet the attacks of 12 and 17 August 1915 were seminal events in the development of naval aviation. They may not have been recognised as such at the time, or for some years after, but the successful attacks encouraged continued development of the torpedo as an aero-naval weapon. For, under the pressures of war, experimental work with torpedoes had lapsed overtaken by seemingly more important work. Within a few months Edmonds and CPO Atrill were transferred back to Britain expressly to work on torpedo development. That Attrill, a non-commissioned officer, had been specifically requested is a clear indication of his importance to airborne torpedo development, by January 1917 he had been promoted Warrant Officer, for torpedo duties in the Air Service.

Before looking at the further development of British torpedo aircraft, it should be noted that Britain was not alone in experimenting with aircraft-launched torpedoes. In using the twin-engined floatplane the German Naval Air Service followed a line of development that had been abandoned by the British. Between April and September, 1917, seventeen attacks on shipping in the Dover Strait area were made by Gotha WD.11, WD.14 and Brandenburg GW floatplanes operating from Zeebrugge. These all carried a single 45 cm torpedo with a 350 lb TNT warhead. At least three British ships were sunk before the attacks stopped. Apparently the Germans found the cost in men and machines lost to accident too great for the return.

One of the ships sunk was SS *Gena*, off Aldeburgh south of Lowestoft, on 1 May 1917. All of her crew were rescued. Two German torpedo seaplanes attacked the ship, the first hit the ship and escaped. As the second was coming to attack the naval gunners on *Gena* opened fire with the anti-submarine gun; they hit the attacking seaplane with their second shot, and brought it down on to the sea where it promptly sank. The two crew members, *Leutnant zur See* Richard Freude (pilot) and *Flugmaat* Karl Berghoff (observer), were rescued. Berghoff was uninjured, but Freude suffered from a gash to his forehead, which was treated at Yarmouth General Hospital. Both, when questioned, provided much useful information.

They had taken off from Zeebrugge that morning in company with a second machine. The torpedo seaplanes usually worked in pairs, one acting as escort whilst the other attacked. Freude and Berghoff were flying seaplane 703, a Brandenburg GW floatplane powered by two 160 hp Mercedes engines armed with a single torpedo and a two defensive Parabellum machine guns. The second machine was unidentified.

They had started their 'swoop' (*Anlauf*)—an essential preliminary to torpedo firing from a seaplane—when they suddenly collapsed, and found themselves in the water. The prisoners agreed finally that they must have been hit, but added that the incident occurred so quickly that both had difficulty in taking in the situation. Their consort saw that they were in distress, but could do nothing owing to the presence of the motor patrol boat. When their consort had flown away, and the remains of their seaplane had sunk, they both swam towards the English boats, and were picked up.

The Italian and Austro-Hungarian Navies were experimenting with torpedo aircraft. Details are lacking, but only small numbers of aircraft seem to have been involved, and little use made of them operationally.

At an Admiralty meeting on 4 January 1916 it was recommended that, 'Messrs. Short may be given an order for a 1,000 lb torpedo-carrying seaplane adapted to the present seaplane carriers.' This resulted in the Short 320, capable of carrying the 18-inch, Mark IX, torpedo which weighed 1,000 lb and had a 170 lb TNT warhead. The machine looked like an overgrown Short 184, with a 320 hp Sunbeam Cossack engine. It was designed as a two-seater, but it was still only able to carry the torpedo if flown as a single-seater. Its performance was no better than that of the Short 184. However, it was designed so that the torpedo was carried between the floats and the fuselage, and not partially submerged; which was an improvement.

In April 1917 an RNAS base was established at Otranto in Italy, with twelve Short 320s and two more at a Torpedo Training School at Malta. The Otranto base was commanded by Wing Commander C. H. K. Edmonds, heading up the torpedo section was Warrant Officer Attrill. There were questions about the structural integrity of the Short, two examples having crashed at Malta with loss of life. It was determined that inadequate bracing of the fuselage had led to failure in flight. These accidents probably delayed the operational debut of the Short 320 until 2 September 1917. Six Shorts set off from Otranto under the tow of Motor Launches, the intention being to bring the torpedo machines within range of the Austro-Hungarian base at Cattaro (Kotor, Montenegro). The operation had to be abandoned due to bad weather, one Short was lost and the others damaged whilst on tow. No further operations were attempted.

Edmonds remained in command at Otranto, which became a patrol and observation base for the remainder of the war, but Attrill was soon on his way back to Britain. His experience was required preparing torpedoes for the new Sopwith Cuckoo torpedo bomber. It was becoming clear that the future of naval aviation lay with land planes operating from an aircraft carrier. On 9 October

1916 Commodore Murray Sueter, Superintendent of Aircraft Construction, wrote
to Tom Sopwith requesting:

> Will you please go into the question with as little delay as possible *re-* Torpedo
> carrying aeroplane with 4 hours' fuel and pilot.
>   (1) To carry one 1,000 lb locomotive torpedo.
>   (2) To carry two 1,000 lb locomotive torpedo.
> Torpedo aeroplane will probably be discharged from a catapult, giving the
> machine an acceleration of 90 f.s. in 60 ft.

This request eventually led to the Sopwith T.1 Cuckoo, single-seat torpedo
bomber. The Cuckoo was the first aeroplane capable of taking off from an aircraft
carrier with a torpedo, carrying out a mission, then returning to land back on
board. The mention of it being 'discharged from a catapult' is interesting as one
of the earliest indications of RNAS interest in such a device. Experimental work
was carried on throughout the war eventually, in the late 1920s, leading to the
installation of catapults in cruisers and battleships to replace the platforms.

   The earliest suggestion of a torpedo attack on Wilhelmshaven also came from
Sueter in a self-serving memorandum dated 20 December 1916. Whilst containing
the earliest known exposition of a torpedo attack on the High Seas Fleet, he goes
on to laud his work with Sopwith where he:

> [S]ecretly got out a torpedo carrying aeroplane, and one is being built. This
> machine should be able to get off any 200 ft. deck, and as she will be without
> floats she will be lightly loaded.
>   Her characteristics are:-
> Tractor Biplane. 200 H.P. Hispano Suiza engine.
> 4 hours fuel and oil. Speed of 83 knots.
> Load per sq. ft. 6.4 lbs To carry an 18″ torpedo.
> I feel confident that the torpedo aeroplane has a great future before it, and
> therefore submit that the Operations Division be asked to consider whether this
> weapon could be utilised.

The memorandum did the rounds of the Admiralty receiving some approval
but with many cautious comments. The conclusions by Captain G. P. W. Hope,
Director of Operations Division, were ultimately approved by the First Sea Lord
and First Lord of the Admiralty. Hope considered that, 'Lack of experience and the
difficulties of transporting large machines across the North Sea to within striking
distance of German Fleet render it inadvisable to undertake an enterprise against
Wilhelmshaven for the present.' The proposal was dropped, but not forgotten.

   Whilst still being worked on in the dockyard *Argus* was seen as a possible carrier
of torpedo aeroplanes, although 'her speed of 20 knots makes her incapable of

effective service in the Battle Cruisers' Line, and her position must necessarily be with or to the rear of, the Battleships.' Nonetheless, *Argus* was being prepared to operate a squadron of eighteen or twenty torpedo aircraft:

> Arrangements are provided for stowing 30 Torpedoes in the hangars; overhead runaways are provided for transporting the torpedoes through all the hangars. A special Torpedo Shop is provided, where an additional 28 Torpedoes can be stowed, if required. Steam heating arrangements are fitted for warming the torpedoes when in place on machines on the flying deck.

To keep the torpedo motor warm in flight, extensions of the Cuckoo's exhaust pipes were run alongside the torpedo.

The next serious proposal came from Admiral Beatty, C-in-C Grand Fleet, in a letter to the Admiralty dated 11 September 1917. Most importantly, he provides clear reasoning for the operation:

1. *Object.* All measures of blocking the exits of German harbours to the passage of submarines, whether by means of cruising vessels, mines, blockships or other obstacles are only effective if the enemy is unable to remove them. So long as he has a force in the [Heligoland] Bight superior to any which we can permanently maintain there to prevent the removal of the obstacles, we are unable effectively to limit the operations of his submarines. It is therefore of the highest importance to immobilize the High Seas Fleet, or, if that be not completely effected, to drive it to the East and block its return, so to prevent it from operating against an inshore squadron of the type we desire to maintain for the purpose of preventing the enemy from removing the obstacles in the approaches to the German Harbours in the Bight.

2. It is suggested that the new type of Torpedo plane affords us a weapon with which this can be done, provided it is produced in large numbers and used in masses, and that the full benefit of surprise is obtained by means of complete secrecy of our intentions. It is understood that these planes have a speed of 90 mph, a radius of action of from 3½ to 4 hours, and are capable of carrying a gun in addition to the torpedo if light weight pilots fly them.

3. *General Idea.* As many machines as possible, and *not less than 121* [author's emphasis], to be carried in specially fitted carrier ships to within not more than one hour's fly from Wilhelmshaven. This R.V. to be reached at or before daylight. Planes to be flown from the ships in flights of 40, so as to reach their objective in strong forces in close succession.
   The objectives, in order of importance, should be:-
   (a) Battle Cruisers and Battleships (including old Battleships),

(b) Dock Gates and Floating Docks,

(c) Light Cruisers,

(d) Torpedo craft—surface and submarine.

The audacity of this proposal is breathtaking. The Fleet Air Arm attacked the Italian Fleet at Taranto on 11–12 November 1940 with just 21 Fairey Swordfish. The Japanese attack on Pearl Harbor comprised two waves of 183 and 171 planes, with just 40 torpedo bombers in the first wave only. Given the problems of developing a new weapon system, even in the early days of aviation, his numbers were impractical. Beatty's suggestion that 'ordinary merchant ships could be fitted to carry torpedo planes, and launch them from the deck, by building flying decks to them,' is unlikely to have found favour at the Admiralty. If the attack had taken place, the Sopwith Cuckoos would almost certainly have been limited to those capable of being carried aboard *Argus* (20), *Furious* (perhaps 12) and *Vindictive* (perhaps 8). Speeding up work on *Eagle* and *Hermes* might have provided two more decks, another 40 machines at the most.

The Admiralty had been working along similar lines. A Memorandum dated 6 September 1917 had been drawn up by, recently promoted, Rear Admiral G. P. W. Hope, Director of Operations Division, on the 'Suggested Policy and Necessary Preparations for an Aerial Offensive.' In it Hope considered using *Campania, Furious, Argus* and the light battle cruisers *Courageous* and *Glorious*. The carrying capacity of the first three would be increased where possible and *Courageous* and *Glorious* would have their turrets removed and replaced with flying off decks.

The Admiralty response to Beatty's proposals, following as they did their own ideas, were lukewarm. In response to a further letter from Beatty in October, the Admiralty replied that:

> . . . under existing circumstances, the air presents the greatest facilities for conducting an offensive against the enemy's vessels and bases, and the possibilities of developing such an offensive in the future are being fully considered. My Lords are fully alive to the importance of air attacks against the enemy's North Sea bases and are determined that the possibilities of such attacks from seaward shall be given full consideration and be correlated to the general scheme of operations.

After that rebuff, Beatty turned his attention, for the moment, to other affairs.

Meanwhile, development of the Sopwith Cuckoo was proceeding slowly and it was being built in small numbers, but sufficient for torpedo training to commence at East Fortune. In June 1918 the Fleet and Torpedo Pilot Finishing School was formed, undergoing many name and designation changes until becoming the Torpedo Training School in April 1919. Most pilots chosen to fly the Cuckoo had previous single-seater experience, and must have found the large single-seater rather overwhelming on first experience.

Pilots received their training at East Fortune, where lecture rooms, torpedo-parting rooms, and instructors have been provided. Owing to shortage of Torpedo Officers in the Navy, the Admiralty were not able to land any Torpedo Officers for instruction. It thus became necessary for the RAF to train their own Torpedo Officers.

The RAF sent four officers to the Royal Navy Torpedo School at HMS *Vernon* for special training, a fifth officer, 2nd Lt Charlie Attrill, did not require training. After returning from Otranto he was based at East Fortune and Gosport, also spending time at sea with *Argus*. He transferred to the RAF on 1 April 1918, with the rank of 2nd Lieutenant (later Flying Officer), and continued his long service as Torpedo Officer at Gosport. Whilst serving with 210 Squadron at Gosport in 1921 he was promoted to Flight Lieutenant. He was retired from the RAF on 17 November 1925. Charlie Attrill was appointed MBE in recognition of his wartime services.

The pilots, after completing a short course of lectures and ground torpedo instruction, commenced flying operations with the 'T' machines. Eventually torpedo dropping practice is carried out, using dummy torpedoes. Dummies are necessary, as no damage results owing to drops from great heights, which frequently occur during training. These drops are carried out alongside a motor drifter, the drifter's mast providing a suitable guide to the pilot for height above the water. Running with Mark IX Torpedoes follows after the pilot has done three or four dummy drops. Torpedo running commences with dropping close alongside the drifter, then continues with attacks on the drifter at anchor [and] underway, eventually attacks in formation with dummies, and later with the actual torpedoes on the drifter. Finally attacks in formation with actual torpedoes set to run underneath the destroyer, which is periodically lent the Grand Fleet for this practice.

On qualifying, the pilots were posted to either 185 Squadron at East Fortune (disbanded in April 1919) or 186 Squadron, assigned to *Argus*, later moving to Gosport in February 1919. It was renumbered 210 Squadron on 1 February 1920. As 210 Squadron it remained active, including deck landing training on *Argus*, until disbanding on 1 April 1923.

Ira 'Taffy' Jones, an RFC and RAF pilot with 37 victories during the First World War, was serving with 210 Squadron at Gosport during the summer of 1920. *Argus* was steaming in the Solent ready to receive the fledgling deck landers. She retained the ramp and longitudinal wire arresting gear arrangement from Richard Bell Davies' earlier experiments.

I saw an oblong object, like a coffin, moving slowly through the water. At first the sight conveyed nothing to me, but when I realised that I had to land on it, I said to myself: 'Good Gosh, have I got to land on that?'

I was gliding at sixty miles per hour, but due to the breeze over the carrier my touching down speed would be in the region of thirty-five miles an hour. I had been told that it was important to knock down the first ramp so that the hooks on the undercarriage should bite the wires which ran the length of the deck quickly, their function being to pull up the 'plane and stop its forward motion. I had been warned that I must expect a bump as I passed over the aft portion of the deck where the funnel was located, as the hot fumes caused an air disturbance. I was gliding confidently on to the deck when my machine reared as it passed over the funnel and we went ballooning into the air. For a few seconds I lost sight of the deck. Leaning over the side, and being short in the leg, I altered the position of the rudder so that when we did touch the deck we were drifting. Consequently two wires were caught in one hook; after running a few yards the wires naturally crossed, and the dear old Cuckoo went very gently on to its nose, smashing the propeller. I was down and not dead. Once again the Devil had looked after his own, according to the views of my friends.

He made six more landings, four ending on his nose. Jones was posted shortly afterwards to a squadron based in Iraq, perhaps he was deemed too expensive to retain as a torpedo pilot.

Whilst the end of the First World War brought the end to any ideas regarding attacks on Wilhelmshaven, the development of torpedo aircraft and the method of attack continued. Throughout 1919, 186 Squadron was the Torpedo Development Squadron at Gosport and was working hard to establish a workable method of mass torpedo attack in daylight. They put their ideas to the test on 6 September 1919 in an attack on the Second Battle Squadron of the Atlantic Fleet moored in Portland Harbour. Eleven Sopwith Cuckoos in two flights made the attack, eight carried torpedoes with dummy warheads and the remaining aircraft carried smoke bombs. The first flight of five torpedo aircraft and two smoke bombers attacked from over the land, making hits on the battleships *Barham, Malaya* and *Implacable* (twice). The second flight of three torpedo aircraft and a single smoke bomber, benefiting from the distraction caused by the first flight, made an undetected attack hitting *Queen Elizabeth* with two torpedoes. The shallow water in Portland Harbour was a problem the squadron had prepared for, only two torpedoes diving to the sea bed after release. It had been discovered that, 'The centre of pressure [of the torpedo] can be brought further aft by means of using drogues, which are towed for about 50 yards and then disengage.'

The attack was judged a great success. Admiral Sir Charles Edward Madden, commanding the Atlantic Fleet, believed that even with the time of the attack known enough aircraft would have escaped anti-aircraft fire to make their attacks. The second flight would have been able to attack completely unopposed. He further stated that the torpedo was potentially a more effective form of attack than bombs.

Almost a year to the day (7 September 1920) the squadron, now renumbered 210 Squadron, made an attack on *Queen Elizabeth* underway in the English Channel. Twelve Cuckoos made at least four hits on the battleship. The method of attack is not known, but may have been three or four flights attacking simultaneously from different directions.

Torpedo development continued in the period between the wars, but the attack on *Queen Elizabeth* was the last hurrah for the Sopwith Cuckoo. The last Cuckoos were retired when 210 Squadron disbanded in April 1923. With its retirement departed the first generation of British naval aircraft.

At the end of the First World War, the Royal Navy was the undoubted leader in the practice and employment of naval aviation. At the outbreak of the Second World War it was a poor third to the Imperial Japanese Navy and the US Navy. How the Royal Navy came to be in this sorry condition is a complex and involved story, and the subject of other works.

Between the wars, whether RAF, RN or Royal Marine, the personnel were above politics. Their job was to fly naval aircraft, which they did to the best of their abilities. Many RAF permanent force pilots and maintainers spent several years with the Fleet during the 1920s and 1930s. Some enjoyed the experience, some did not. A small number of RAF officers and enlisted men chose to specialise in naval aviation. On 1 April 1924, the Fleet Air Arm of the Royal Air Force was formed, absorbing all RAF units involved in naval aviation. In June of that year No. 1 Naval Pilots Course commenced at 1 FTS, RAF Netheravon, there were nine Royal Marine and eighteen Royal Navy officers on the course. The Royal Navy had been training Observers since 1921 and Telegraphist Air Gunners since 1922.

When the Fleet Air Arm reverted to Royal Navy control in 1937, it inherited less than 200 front line aircraft, mostly obsolescent, and under 400 aircrew. The Royal Navy possessed six aircraft carriers, all with First World War origins and names familiar to readers of this book, *Argus* (commissioned 1918), *Eagle* (1923), *Hermes* (1924), *Furious* (1925 following a major reconstruction), *Courageous* (1928) and *Glorious* (1930). The last two being *Furious*' sisters, the light battle cruisers of Grand Fleet fame. The original *Ark Royal* was still in service, soon to be renamed *Pegasus*, and continued to serve throughout the Second World War. In 1938 a new *Ark Royal* joined the fleet, with three new armoured fleet carriers under construction.

When the next war came the men of the Fleet Air Arm rose to meet their challenges, as had their predecessors of the Royal Naval Air Service. As have their successors, regardless of political support or lack of it.

Appendix 1
Performance Comparisons of RNAS Aircraft

The following tables present a comparison of the typical performance of all the main two-seater and single-seater machines used in RNAS operations in the North Sea. Performance measurement at this time was in its infancy, and variations exist between published figures. In an attempt at consistency, the tables use data from several official sources originally compiled and published by Jack Bruce in a series of articles on *Historic Military Aircraft* published in *Flight* between 1952 and 1958. These were later revised and updated in other books and articles, but remain the root source of most performance data of British First World War aircraft published today.

PERFORMANCE COMPARISON OF RNAS TWO SEATERS

	Short 830 (Floatplane)	Short 184 (Floatplane)	Sopwith Ship Strutter (Admiralty Type 9700). (Landplane)	
Engine	135 hp Salmson (Canton Unne)	240 hp V-12 Sunbeam Gurkha	110 hp Clerget	130 hp Clerget
Weight Empty	2,622 lb	3,634 lb	1,259 lb	1,305 lb
Weight Loaded	3,324 lb	5,009 lb	2,149 lb	2,150 lb
Max Speed	70 mph	75 mph	100 mph	100 mph
Climb	10 min 25 sec to 2,000 feet.	39 min to 6,500 feet.	20 min 25 sec to 10,000 feet.	17 min 50 sec to 10,000 feet.
Endurance	3½ hrs.	4½ hrs.	4¼ hrs.	3¾ hrs.
Typical Armament†	One Lewis Gun on a free mounting in rear cockpit. Up to three 112 lb bombs.	One Lewis Gun on a free mounting in rear cockpit. One 14 inch torpedo, or up to 520 lb of bombs.	One fixed and synchronised Vickers Gun and one Lewis Gun on Scarff Ring in rear cockpit. Either two 65 lb or up to twelve 20 lb bombs.	
† All machine guns are 0.303 inch calibre.				

PERFORMANCE COMPARISON OF RNAS SINGLE SEATERS

	Sopwith Baby (Floatplane)	Bristol Scout C	Sopwith Pup (Admiralty Type 9901)	Beardmore WB.III (S.B.3D)	Sopwith 2F.I Ship's Camel	Sopwith T.I Cuckoo*
Engine	130 hp Clerget	80 hp Le Rhone	80 hp Clerget	80 hp Le Rhone	150 hp B.R.1	200 hp Sunbeam Arab
Weight Empty	1,297 lb	766 lb	820 lb	849 lb	1,036 lb	2199 lb
Weight Loaded	1,742 lb	1,195 lb	1,114 lb	1230 lb	1,530 lb	3883 lb
Max Speed	90 mph	93 mph	108 mph	90 mph.	124 mph	103.5 mph
Climb to 10,000 feet	35 min.	21 min.	13 min.	20 min.	11½ min.	31 min.
Endurance	2¼ hrs.	2½ hrs.	3 hrs.	2¾ hrs.	2½ hrs.	4 hrs.
Typical Armament†	Two boxes of 24 Ranken Darts, or up to 100 lb of bombs; or One or Two Lewis Guns arranged to fire outside the propeller. Note: Armament added to the Schneider/Baby was limited largely by the operator's ingenuity. The above are the more common arrangements.	Two boxes of 24 Ranken Darts. Later, a single Lewis Gun could be added as in the Sopwith Schneider/Baby.	One Lewis Gun on tripod mounting firing through upper wing centre section, and/or up to 8 Le Prieur rockets.	One Lewis Gun on overwing drop down mounting.	One fixed and synchronised Vickers Gun and one Lewis Gun on upper wing mounting. Tandem Raid: The Vickers and Lewis Guns plus two 50 lb bombs.	Single 18 inch Mark IX Torpedo, fitted with 250 lb TNT warhead. Torpedo weight 1,086 lb.

† All machine guns are 0.303 inch calibre.

* Data from J M Bruce, *Sopwith B.I & T.I Cuckoo, Windsock Datafile 90* (Albatros Productions Ltd, 2001).

Appendix 2
HMS *Furious* Operations, 1917 and 1918

The main sources for this list are ADM 137/876, Grand Fleet, Reports of Proceedings, Oct-Dec 1917 and ADM 137/877, Grand Fleet, Reports of Proceedings, 1918. Additional information has been drawn from *Furious'* log books and other official records.

Operations 1917 – HMS *Furious*, as first completed

Date	Operation*	Object	Comments
5–7 September	MS	Unknown	Appears to have been a typical sortie into the North Sea in the hope of provoking some enemy reaction. Furious with four destroyers, Lion, 1st BCS, Pegasus, Light Cruisers and Destroyers. No aircraft were sent off.
10–12 September	DN	A patrol into the Heligoland Bight north of the Dogger Bank.	Flight Commander Geoffrey Moore flew off in a Pup attempting to intercept a Zeppelin. See Chapter 13.
16–18 September	PZ No.1 and No.2.	Grand Fleet Exercises.	Furious, returning to Rosyth with engine defects, tasked to search for disabled airship N.S.3. See Chapter 13.
16–19 October	---	Exercises.	Exercises terminated and force sent to attempt to intercept two German light cruisers. See Chapter 13.
8–10 November	MB	A patrol into the Heligoland Bight with the intention of attacking German minesweeping forces.	Very rough weather, several destroyers suffering damage. Furious, 1st BCS, 2nd and 6th LCS, destroyers. No flying possible.

* As shown in *Furious'* log book.

Operations 1918—HMS *Furious*, after second conversion

Date	Operation	Object	Comments
16-18 May	A.47*	Escorting minelayers.	Good weather. Minelayers undisturbed. No aircraft were flown off.
20-23 May	F.1	To attack enemy aircraft.	See Chapter 13.
27-29 May	F.2	To attack enemy aircraft in vicinity of North Dogger Bank Light Vessel.	This involved just *Furious* with destroyers *Wessex, Winchelsea* and *Westcott*. No enemy airships or seaplanes were seen. No aircraft were flown off.
31 May—2 June	F.3	To support the Harwich Force	See Chapter 13.
11-13 June	F.4	A reconnaissance of the northern Heligoland Bight.	Cancelled due to bad weather. No aircraft were flown off.
17-20 June	F.5	Repeat of F.4.	See Chapter 13.
27-29 June	F.6	First attempt to raid the airship sheds at Tondern.	Cancelled due to bad weather off the Danish coast. No aircraft were flown off. See Chapter 14.
17-20 July	F.7	Tondern Raid.	See Chapter 14.
1-3 August	F.8	To attack enemy aircraft and carry out a reconnaissance of the northern Heligoland Bight.	See Chapter 15.
7-9 August	F.9	Repeat of F.8.	Cancelled due to poor visibility. No aircraft were flown off.
10-11 August	F.10	To attack enemy aircraft in vicinity of South Dogger Bank Light Vessel.	Operation also in support of Harwich Force operation CMB.5 with Coastal Motor Boats. See Chapter 15.
13-15 August	F.11	To attack enemy aircraft in vicinity of North Dogger Bank Light Vessel.	No enemy airships or seaplanes were seen. No aircraft were flown off.
23-25 September	FC.4*	Fleet Tactical Exercise.	See Chapter 16.
15-17 October	F.12	A reconnaissance of the northern Heligoland Bight.	Cancelled due to fog and poor weather. No aircraft were flown off.
21-23 October	F.13	Repeat of F.12.	See Chapter 16.
21 November	Operation 23	Surrender of the *Hochseeflotte*.	

* As shown in *Furious*' log book.

Sources

Archives

UK. The National Archives

ADM 1/8430/233. Seaplanes flying off ship's deck. Report from HM Carrier *Campania*.

ADM 1/8432/253. Report on Experimental Work Connected With Use and Design of Flying Deck Fitted in HMS *Vindex*, November 1915.

ADM 1/8436/17/122/753. Notes on aircraft and seaplane carriers.

ADM 1/8477/307. Policy to be followed as regards development and use of torpedo carrying seaplanes.

ADM 1/8486. Admiralty letter to Admiral Beatty, 25 September 1917.

ADM 1/8682/124. HMS *Campania*. Movements prior to Battle of Jutland.

ADM 53/21953. HMS *Hibernia*, log book for May 1912.

ADM 53/36857. HMS *Campania*, log book for May 1916.

ADM 53/42235 to 42237. HMS *Furious*, log books September to November 1917.

ADM 53/42242 to 42249. HMS *Furious*, log books April to November 1918.

ADM 137/302/3. HMS *Engadine*. Reports from Battle of Jutland. Containing reports from Lt Cdr Robinson, Flt Lt Rutland, and Assistance Paymaster Trewin.

ADM 137/875 and 876. Grand Fleet, Reports of Proceedings, 1917.

ADM 137/877. Grand Fleet, Reports of Proceedings, 1918.

ADM 137/1956. Paper on the Development of Aircraft Carriers, 13 September 1918, the Director of Naval Construction, Sir Eustace Henry William Tennyson d'Eyncourt.

ADM 137/3617. HMS *Vindex*. Failure of seaplanes to fly, May 1916.

AIR 1/148/15/86 and /88. Proposals and Reports raids on Kiel, Borkum, Emden, etc 1915.

AIR 1/148/15/87. Operation of Schneider Cup seaplanes from Light Cruisers.

AIR 1/279/15/226/129. Training and Status of RNAS Observers

AIR 1/343/15/226/283. Destruction of a Zeppelin by Lieutenant S. D. Cully.

AIR 1/345/15/226/295. Report on Coastal Motor Boat Operations.

AIR 1/436. HMS *Engadine*. Failure of seaplanes to fly, May 1916.

AIR 1/455//15/312/44. Reports and Notes on Bombing of Tondern.

AIR 1/626/17/46. Report on Royal Navy manoeuvres and use of HMS *Hermes* carrying seaplanes.

AIR 1/631/17/122/36. Vessels fitted to carry seaplanes.

AIR 1/636/17/122/132. HMS *Campania* utility to the Royal Navy as seaplane carrier.

AIR 1/648/17/122/380. Description of proposed seaplane carrier.

AIR 1/648/17/122/382. Air Requirements of the Grand Fleet.

AIR 1/648/17/122/383. Air Requirements of the Grand Fleet and alterations to HMS *Furious*.

AIR 1/648/17/122/387. Report on naval operation code number R.62.

AIR 1/657/17/122/564. Attack by Lt Freeman, RN, on Zeppelin and subsequent rescue by Dutch ship.

AIR 1/659/17/122/615. Proposal to attack German Fleet with aerial torpedoes.

AIR 1/663/17/122/680. Training seaplane pilots. HMS *Campania*, 1917.

AIR 1/663/17/122/685. Training in RNAS.

AIR 1/665/17/122/716. Report of seaplane attack with torpedoes.

AIR 1/667/17/122/748. Landing Trials on HMS *Argus*.

AIR 1/667/17/122/753. Notes on aircraft and seaplane carriers.

AIR 1/667/17/122/754. Deck landing experiments.

AIR 1/733/187/4. Aeroplane practice flights from decks of HM ships.

AIR 1/2099/207/23/4. Seaplane Operations against Cuxhaven.

AIR 1/2103. Aircraft Carriers, DNC Department, Admiralty, 1918.

AIR 1/2391/228/11/153. Service Experiences by Flt Lt S. D. Culley. RAF Staff College, Andover, May 1930.

AIR 2/36. Documents/reports about/by Flt Cdr F. J. Rutland.

Canada. Library and Archives of Canada

RG24 Accession 1992-93/169, Box 51.

Department of Naval Service File, 7-4-3 "C" 96. Cully, Stewart [*sic*] D., Flight Sub-Lieut.

Canada. Directorate of History and Heritage, Dept of National Defence

DC 77/661 - Biographical cards for Culley, S. D.

Books

Agar, Capt. Augustus, *Baltic Episode* (Hodder and Stoughton, 1963).

Allen, William J., SS *"Borodino" M.F.A. No 6: A Short Account of the Junior Army and Navy Stores Ltd With H. M. Grand Fleet, December 1914– February 1919* (The Fleetway Press, 1919).

Anon, *AP1344, History of the Development of Torpedo Aircraft* (HMSO, 1919).

Anon, *Battle of Jutland, 30th May to 1st June, 1916.* (HMSO, 1920).

Bartlett, C. P. O., *Bomber Pilot 1916–1918* (Ian Allan, 1974).

Bennett, Geoffrey, *Cowan's War* (Collins, 1964).

Brown, Malcolm, and Patricia Meehan, *Scapa Flow* (Allen Lane, 1968).

Bruce, J. M., *Sopwith B.1 & T.1 Cuckoo, Windsock Datafile 90* (Albatros Productions Ltd, 2001).

Bruce, J. M., Gordon Page and Ray Sturtivant, *The Sopwith Pup* (Air Britain, 2002).

Burns, Ian M., *Ben-my-Chree - Woman of My Heart, Isle of Man Packet Steamer and Seaplane Carrier* (Colin Huston, 2008).

von Buttlar Brandenfels, Horst Freiherr Treusch, *Zeppelins over England* (Harrap, 1931).

Cochrane, Thomas, 10th Earl of Dundonald, *Autobiography of a Seaman, Vol. 1* (R. Bentley, 1860).

Corbett, Sir Julian Stafford, and Sir Henry John Newbolt, *Naval Operations*, 5 Volumes (Longmans, Green & Co, 1920 to 1931).

Cronin, Dick, *Royal Navy Shipboard Aircraft Developments, 1912–1931* (Air Britain, 1990).

Davies, Vice Admiral Richard Bell, *Sailor in the Air* (Peter Davies, 1967).

Day, Jeffery, *Poems and Rhymes* (Sidgwick and Jackson, 1919).

Dodds, Ronald, *The Brave Young Wings* (Canada's Wings, 1980).

Fife, Malcolm, *Scottish Aerodromes of the First World War* (Tempus Publishing, 2007).

'Flight Lieutenant', *Hints for Flight Sub-Lieutenants* (Forster Groom and Co., 1916).

Friedman, Norman, *British Carrier Aviation* (US Naval Institute Press, 1988).

Gamble, C. F. Snowden, *Story of a North Sea Air Station* (Spearman, 1967).

Ganderton, H. Y., *Under The White Ensign. From a Bunting Tosser's Log* (Private, ND, c.1968).

Hallam (PIX), Squadron Leader T. D., *The Spider Web* (William Blackwood, 1919).

Hayward, Victor, *HMS Tiger At Bay, A Sailor's Memoir 1914–18* (William Kimber, 1977).

Herris, Jack, *German Seaplane Fighters of WW1* (Aeronaut Books, 2012).

Jarrett, Philip, *Frank McClean, Godfather to British Naval Aviation* (Seaforth, 2011).

Jellicoe, Admiral Viscount, of Scapa, *The Grand Fleet 1914–1916* (Cassell, 1919).

Jones, Ira, *An Air Fighter's Scrapbook* (Nicholson & Watson, 1938).

Knight, E. F., *The Harwich Naval Forces—Their Part in the Great War* (Hodder & Stoughton, 1919).

Layman, R. D., *Before The Aircraft Carrier—The Development of Aviation Vessels 1849–1922* (US Naval Institute Press, 1989).

Layman, R. D., *The Cuxhaven Raid* (Conway Maritime Press, 1985).

Layman, R. D., *To Ascend from a Floating Base* (Associated University Presses, 1979).

Lee, AVM Arthur Stanley Gould, RAF, *Open Cockpit* (Jarrolds, 1969).

Livock, Group Captain G. E., *To the Ends of the Air* (HMSO, 1973).

Longmore, Air Chief Marshal Sir Arthur, *From Sea to Sky, Memoirs 1910–1945* (Geoffrey Bles, 1946).

Marder, Arthur J, *From Dreadnought To Scapa Flow*, 5 Volumes (Oxford University Press, 1966 to 1970).

Moore, Major W. G., *Early Bird* (Putnam, 1963).

Patterson, Alfred Temple, *Tyrwhitt of the Harwich Force* (Macdonald and Jane's, 1973).

Popham, Hugh, *Into Wind* (Hamish Hamilton, 1969).

Raleigh, Sir Walter, and H. A. Jones, *The War In The Air*, 6 Volumes (Oxford University Press, 1922 to 1937).

Rimell, Raymond Laurence, *Zeppelin!* (Canada's Wings, 1984).

Robinson, Douglas H, *The Zeppelin in Combat, A History of the German Naval Airship Division, 1912–1918* (University of Washington Press, 1980).

Roskill, Capt. S. W. (Editor), *Documents Relating to The Naval Air Service* (Navy Records Society, 1969).

Samson, Air Commodore Charles Rumney, *Fights and Flights* (Ernest Benn, 1930).

Snowie, J. Allan, *Collishaw & Company, Canadians in the Royal Naval Air Service 1914–1918* (Nieuport Publishing, 2010).

Steel, Nigel and Peter Hart, *Jutland 1916* (Cassell, 2003).

Stell, Geoffrey, *Orkney at War: Defending Scapa Flow, Volume 1 World War 1* (The Orcadian, Kirkwall Press, 2010).

Stumpf, Richard, *The Private War of Seaman Stumpf* (Leslie Frewin, 1969).

Sturtivant, Ray and Gordon Page, *Royal Navy Aircraft Serials and Units, 1911–1919* (Air Britain, 1992).

Sueter, Rear Admiral Murray F, *Airmen or Noahs* (Issac Pitman, 1928).

Taylor, John W. R., *CFS Birthplace of Air Power* (Putnam, 1958).

Till, Geoffrey, *Air Power and the Royal Navy, 1914–1945* (Jane's Publishing Company, 1979).

Trimble, William F., *Hero of the Air. Glenn Curtiss and the Birth of Naval Aviation* (US Naval Institute Press, 2010).

Warner, Guy, *World War One Aircraft Carrier Pioneer, The Story and Diaries of Jack McCleery* (Pen and Sword, 2011).

Woodling, Bob and Taras Chayka, *The Curtiss Hydroaeroplane; The U.S. Navy's First Airplane – 1911-1916* (Schiffer Military History, 2011).

Young, Desmond, *Rutland of Jutland* (Cassell, 1963).

Periodicals and Annuals

Acland, DFC, Squadron Leader W. R. D., Deck Flying, *The Journal of the Royal Aeronautical Society*, May 1931.

'An Eye-Witness', The Strafing of L.Z.76, *Blackwoods Magazine*, February 1922.

Bullen, Dr John, The Royal Navy and Air Power: The Projected Torpedo Bomber Attack on the

High Seas Fleet at Wilhelmshaven in 1918, *Imperial War Museum Review*, Number 2, 1987.

Cronin, Dick, Camel Lighters, *Cross and Cockade International*, V26N2, 1995.

Goodall, Michael H., Lighters, *Cross and Cockade Great Britain*, V12N2, 1981.

Harlin, Eric, The Avro Types 501 & 503 Floatplanes and Their German Derivatives, *Cross and Cockade International*, V45N3, 2014.

Hobbs, David, *The First Pearl Harbor,* Warship 2007 (Conway Maritime Press, 2007).

Imrie, Alex, translation of *Mitteilungen aus dem Gabiete des Luftkrieges Nr 38, 29-6-18*, in *Cross and Cockade International*, V23N1, 1992.

Isaacs, Group Captain Keith, Australian Naval Aviation in WW1, Part 3, *Naval Historical Review*, March 1974.

Johns, Sir Arthur W., Aircraft Carriers, *Transactions of the Institution of Naval Architects, Vol LXXVI*, 1934, pp. 1-19.

Layman, R. D., Furious and the Tondern Raid, *Warship International, No.4*, 1973.

Layman, R. D., *Naval Warfare in a New Dimension, 1914–1918*, Warship 1989 (Conway Maritime Press, 1989).

Newman, Grant, Pioneering Torpedo Training at East Fortune 1918, *Cross and Cockade International*, V36N3, 2005.

Newman, Grant, A German Copenhagen, *Cross and Cockade International*, V41N4, 2010.

Outhwaite, Cedric, ,The Sea and The Sky, *Blackwood's Magazine*, November 1927.

'R. L. C.', Argus, 1914–44, *The Naval Review*, Vol. XXXIII, No. 1, February, 1945.

Roskill, Capt. S. W., The Destruction of Zeppelin L.53, *US Naval Institute, Proceedings*, August 1960.

Sandwell, Flt Cdr A. H. Sandwell, War-Time Reminiscences, *Canadian Aviation*, June 1936–February 1937.

Saul, Lt Cdr A. M. Kinnersley, Flying off in '17, *The Navy*, November 1937, p. 348/9.

Miscellaneous

Fleet Air Arm Museum. The Diary of Flt Lt G. B. Dacre.

Imperial War Museum: REC/1 1914–1918. The Private Papers of Lt Cdr R. E. Childers, War Diary, Volume 1.

Imperial War Museum Sound Archive: Captain Grahame Donald interview 27 September 1972.

Mott, Chas. Biographical notes Charlie Attrill.

Nailer, Roger. Research notes on British Seaplane and Aircraft Carriers.

Voices in Flight, the First World War in the Air. Anna Malinskova interview with Gordon Hyams, 3 August 1978. (www.voicesinflight.webs.com)

Index